Population Issues

International Institute for Population Sciences, Mumbai

Vision

To position IIPS as a premier teaching and research institution in population sciences responsive to emerging national and global needs based on values of inclusion, sensitivity and rights protection.

Mission

The Institute will strive to be a centre of excellence on population, health and development issues through high quality education, teaching and research. This will be achieved by (a) creating competent professionals, (b) generating and disseminating scientific knowledge and evidence, (c) collaboration and exchange of knowledge, and (d) advocacy and awareness.

Population Issues

Studies from Uttar Pradesh and Bihar

Edited by

Harihar Sahoo | F. Ram | B. Paswan
H. Lhungdim | Dipti Govil

International Institute for Population Sciences, Mumbai

RAWAT PUBLICATIONS
Jaipur • New Delhi • Bangalore • Guwahati • Kolkata

ISBN 978-81-316-0850-0

Published by
Prem Rawat for **Rawat Publications**
Satyam Apts, Sector 3, Jawahar Nagar, Jaipur 302 004 (India)
Phone: 0141 265 1748 / 7006 Fax: 0141 265 1748
E-mail: info@rawatbooks.com
Website: www.rawatbooks.com

New Delhi Office
4858/24, Ansari Road, Daryaganj, New Delhi 110 002
Phone: 011 2326 3290

Also at *Bangalore, Guwahati* and *Kolkata*

Typeset by Rawat Computers, Jaipur
Printed and bound in India

Contents

Foreword

The International Institute for Population Sciences (IIPS), Mumbai, India has contributed significantly towards the development of the discipline of demography and population sciences primarily through its regular teaching programme. The Institute's involvement in generating valuable pool of demographic data is also well-recognized. Such data, apart from assisting the policy and programme formulation, help to nurture and sustain valuable research, understand the dynamics of a population in as vast and diverse a country as India. Another dimension, less recognized is its organization of an annual seminar on the developmental issues focusing on specific regions of the country – one that also helps immensely in energizing and motivating the younger generation to undertake research.

The present book is a culmination of one such endeavour which importantly focusses on the demographic features of two states, Uttar Pradesh and Bihar. These are the two most populous states in the country that together comprise more than one-fourth of the country's population. They are also recognized to be the most laggard ones, slowing down the country's entry into 'demographic comfort zone' – the threshold where the fertility attains the replacement level that corresponds to around two children per woman.

True, the country has entered a comfortable era in terms of its young age structure that can be a potential boon for its development of economy and prosperity. The younger generation, in the working age, constitutes the productive population. Whereas most other countries, particularly in the developed region are experiencing a fall in their working age population relative to the dependent population, in India it is just the reverse. But realization of the true potential of this surging younger generation requires that they be fruitfully engaged in the process of production. The focus should be on quality education and appropriate skill formation, without deviating from the goal of progression towards the 'demographic comfort zone'.

The key to this lies in the socio-economic development of population – one that helps both the population stabilization and extraction of maximum dividend from the emerging age structure. However, there are instances where the success in fertility reduction has been achieved in spite of sub-par socio-economic development. There is a need to understand how family planning programme in the two states can be geared to achieve improvements in maternal and child health as well as the desired reduction in the level of fertility by eliminating the unwanted births.

These two states are also known for their unfavourable status of women. The presence of strong son preference can be an additional factor retarding the process of population stabilization. Research has shown that a strong preference for a small family size combined with a proclivity for sons, lead to sex selection. Such sex selection is, however, found to be dominant only among the educated group. The chances of having a son in the normal reproductive process, among the lower educated group, has been high since their family size happened to be large. Research is lacking to understand whether son preference among this group will also lead to sex selection when their fertility declines, as has been observed recently.

The present book ably edited by the well-experienced team of faculty members of the institute discusses many of these issues. I am sure, it will provide valuable insights to better understand the population situation in this region.

T. K. Roy
Former Director,
International Institute for Population Sciences,
Mumbai, India

Preface and Acknowledgements

Uttar Pradesh and Bihar together constituted over 303.9 million population in 2011, which accounts for more than one-fourth of the India's population. These states are the poorer states and ranked among the slowest growing regions of the country. High maternal mortality, low life expectancy, high fertility, high unmet need for contraception, low literacy rate, low coverage of child immunization, and high child malnutrition are the main demographic characteristics of these two states. Since 2005, with the launch of the National Rural Health Mission (NRHM) and various other developmental programmes, Uttar Pradesh and Bihar have shown perceptible progress in some of the crucial demographic and health indicators. For instance, compared to 2006 levels, infant mortality rate fell from 61 (per 1,000 live births) to 42 in 2013 in Bihar and similarly, from 97 per 1,000 live births to 50 by 2013 in UP. Similarly, progress is also observed in the proportion of mothers who received medical attention at delivery from 22 per cent in 2006 to 60 per cent by 2013 in Bihar, and in UP from 15 per cent in 2006 to 58 per cent by 2013 (SRS Statistical Report, 2013). However, there remain challenges and areas of concern pertaining to population growth, health outcomes, gender inequality, unmet needs, and nutrition among children. Uttar Pradesh and Bihar together contribute maximum to the total births, under-5 deaths, unmet needs, and people below poverty line in the country. The low rate of contraceptive use and high level of fertility in these states are of considerable concern to the Indian Government, which has launched innovations in family planning services intended to increase contraceptive use in the state. The International Institute for Population Sciences (IIPS), Mumbai, a premier institute in training and research in the field of population felt the urgency to further sensitize the academic community and planners on the vicious nexus between population and development in Uttar Pradesh and Bihar. It is in this spirit, that IIPS organized a three-day national seminar in Lucknow, the capital of Uttar Pradesh, during 11–13 March 2014 in collaboration with the Sanjay Gandhi Post Graduate Institute of Medical Sciences (SGPGIMS), Lucknow, who was the local organizer of this important national seminar.

The seminar offered a platform to researchers, academicians, programme managers and other experts to come together and share their findings; debate and discuss on the population and development issues in the two states, and contribute to programmes and policies concern of the states. Besides, the seminar provided an opportunity to young demographers and other researchers to share their views. Covering a broader perspective on inter-linkages between population and development, the three-day seminar was divided into fourteen technical sessions, two plenary sessions and two poster sessions. Realizing the importance and relevance of the seminar theme in the context of Uttar Pradesh and Bihar, it was thought prudent to publish some of the selected papers in the form of a book. It is in this light, that the present volume *Population Issues: Studies from Uttar Pradesh and Bihar* is brought before the fellow researchers and programme managers.

This volume contains 16 selected papers from the seminar dealing with various issues of fertility, nuptiality, abortion, unmet need for family planning, reproductive and child health, migration, household environment, etc. Most of these papers provide a very detailed analysis at the state and district levels using available data from National Family Health Surveys, District Level Household and Facility Surveys, Sample Registration System, and Census of India, and so on. We hope that the present volume will serve as a ready reference material for those who are interested in population and development issues in Uttar Pradesh and Bihar.

The Ministry of Health and Family Welfare, Government of India financed the seminar. We are grateful to Professor F. Ram, Director, IIPS, for his guidance and moral support in organizing the seminar and bringing out this book. We are also thankful to the Director, Professor R.K. Sharma, SGPGIMS for the wholehearted support and collaboration. Professor C.M. Pandey, Dr. Uttam Singh and Dr. Anupam Kumar, SGPGIMS, Lucknow, for their active support in organizing the seminar. We are thankful to the paper contributors, chairpersons, co-chairs, rapporteurs and media persons for their enthusiastic cooperation. The secretarial assistance was provided by Dr. P. Murugesan. We appreciate the contributors for timely action and contribution of their valuable research papers. We hope that the present volume would serve the purpose of understanding the population problems in Uttar Pradesh and Bihar.

Harihar Sahoo
F. Ram
B. Paswan
H. Lhungdim
Dipti Govil

1

Why are Uttar Pradesh and Bihar Lagging in Fertility Transition?

P.M. KULKARNI

India is passing through a remarkable fertility transition. While some decline in fertility was seen before 1980, the last three decades have shown a steady fall in fertility throughout the country. According to the latest estimate from the Sample Registration System (SRS), the Total Fertility Rate (TFR) was 2.3 in 2013 (Registrar General, India, 2014). But then this is the national picture which masks huge regional variations. It has long been acknowledged that India's fertility transition has varied spatially (Dyson and Moore, 1983; Bhat, 1996; Guilmoto and Rajan, 2001). The TFR in a large number of states, with about half of India's population, is below the low replacement level of 2.1 and some others are also approaching this level. Fertility transition in some states and in the country has been extensively studied; see, for example, Zachariah (1984), Srinivasan (1995), Bhat (1996), Krishnamoorthy et al. (2005), Ram and Ram (2009), Kulkarni (2011) and the papers in Guilmoto and Rajan (2005). Fertility decline began first in the southern states of Kerala and Tamil Nadu which reached a low TFR as early as 1990, but soon other southern states as well as some western states such as Maharashtra, Punjab, Himachal Pradesh, Jammu and Kashmir and eastern states of West Bengal and Odisha also reached low levels. So did some small states and Delhi. However, fertility in some states in the north-central region is well above replacement level. While these states too have been experiencing transition to low fertility, the TFR is yet to fall below 3. Notable among these are Uttar Pradesh and Bihar, two of the largest states of the country. Fairly reliable data from the Sample Registration System are available since 1971 for Uttar Pradesh and since 1981 for Bihar, and the trends show that the TFR in these states has always remained above the national average (Figure 1). Given their huge population mass, these states have slowed down India's fertility transition.

Figure 1

Trends in Total Fertility Rate, India, Bihar and Uttar Pradesh, 1971–2013

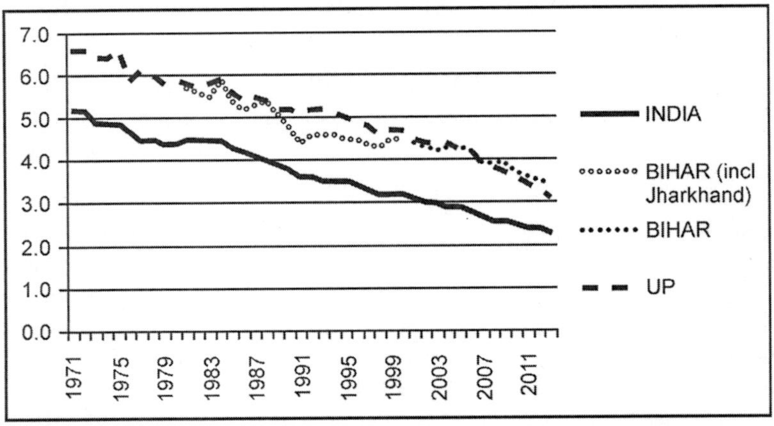

Source: Obtained from Registrar General, India (2009, 2010, 2011, 2012, 2013b, 2014)

The slow pace of fertility transition in these states has traditionally been attributed to their relatively higher child mortality and poorer socio-economic development. The latest estimates show that in 2013 the Infant Mortality Rate (IMR) in Uttar Pradesh was as high as 57 per 1,000 as compared to 40 in India though with a rate of 42, Bihar was close to the national level (Registrar General, India, 2014). While the female literacy rate in India was 65 per cent in 2011, it was only 53 per cent in Bihar and 59 per cent in Uttar Pradesh (Registrar General, India, 2013a). Moreover, 31 per cent of the population of India lived in urban areas in contrast to only 11 per cent of Bihar and 22 per cent of Uttar Pradesh. Demographic literature has well documented the important role socio-economic development plays in demographic transition. Decline in child mortality has been cited as the most important and distal factor in fertility transition (Dyson, 2010). Cochrane (1979) and Jejeebhoy (1995) have highlighted the role of education, especially of females.

In addition to socio-economic conditions and child survival, broadly labelled as demand side factors, the roles of diffusion of a small family norm and contraceptive use are also well recognized (Cleland and Wilson, 1987). In fact, various government and other family planning programmes do make efforts to popularize a small family norm and provide contraceptive services for fertility regulation. India has long had a programme, initially called the 'family planning programme', later the 'family welfare programme' and the 'reproductive and child health programme'. The programme has created awareness about fertility regulation, promoted small family norm, motivated couples to adopt contraception and provided contraceptive services free of cost, and often with small incentives or compensations. Clearly, while the importance of socio-economic changes was recognized, as emphasized in the Bucharest prescription, India did not wait for the socio-economic changes to bring about fertility transition by themselves and actively promoted fertility regulation. The important role played by the programme in some states has been highlighted in many studies; see, for example, Srinivasan (1995), Krishnamoorthy et al. (2005) and Kulkarni (2011). But just as socio-economic development has not been uniform across the country, so has the implementation of the programme. Though conceived, planned, and financed nationally, the programme is administered by states and there have been variations in the implementation. It is well known that contraceptive acceptance was very poor in the states in the north-central region in the initial period. Moreover, the intensification during the emergency and the subsequent setback was also severe in this region. Though the poor acceptance could be blamed on low demand for fertility regulation, evidence has emerged of the inability of the programmes in these states to meet the existing demand. Three rounds of the National Family Health Survey (NFHS) have revealed that the unmet need for family planning is very large in these states (Table 1). It was 25.1 per cent in Bihar and 30.1 in Uttar Pradesh compared to 19.5 per cent in India in 1992–93 (NFHS–1), 24.5 per cent in Bihar and 25.1 per cent in Uttar Pradesh compared to 15.8 per cent in India in 1998–99 (NFHS–2), and 22.8 per cent in Bihar and 21.2 per cent in Uttar Pradesh compared to 12.8 per cent in India in 2005–06 (NFHS–3). Estimates from the District Level Household and Facility Survey, round 3 (2007–08) also give a fairly similar picture (Table 1). Clearly, the population programmes in Bihar and Uttar Pradesh have fallen well short of meeting family planning needs of the population. Therefore, in examining the lag in fertility transition in Uttar Pradesh and Bihar, one needs to see whether it is attributable to shortcomings in development or in programme implementation. This paper is an attempt in this direction.

Table 1

Unmet Need for Family Planning, Large States, India
(% of Currently Married Women with unmet need for Family Planning)

Survey	*NFHS–1*	*NFHS–2*	*NFHS–3*	*DLHS–3*
State/Year	1992–93	1998–99	2005–06	2007–08
Jammu & Kashmir	na	20.0	14.5	14.5
Himachal Pradesh	14.9	8.6	7.2	9.6
Punjab	13.0	7.3	7.3	8.5
Haryana	16.4	7.6	8.3	11.3
Rajasthan	19.8	17.6	14.6	11.4
Uttar Pradesh	30.1	25.1	21.2	23.8
Bihar	25.1	24.5	22.8	25.1
Assam	21.7	17.0	10.5	17.3
West Bengal	17.4	11.8	8.0	9.1
Jharkhand	@	@	23.1	21.3
Odisha	22.4	15.5	14.9	15.2
Chhattisgarh	$	$	10.1	12.6
Madhya Pradesh	20.5	16.2	11.3	13.1
Gujarat	13.1	8.5	8.0	12.2
Maharashtra	14.1	13.0	9.4	10.7
Andhra Pradesh	10.4	7.7	4.7	5.2
Karnataka	18.2	11.5	9.6	10.2
Tamil Nadu	14.6	13.0	8.5	10.0
All India	19.5	15.8	12.8	14.4

Note: NFHS–1, NFHS–2, NFHS–3: National Family Health Survey, rounds 1, 2, 3
DLHS–3: District Level Household and Facility Survey, round 3.
na: Not available; @: Included in Bihar; $: Included in Madhya Pradesh.

Sources: IIPS (1995, 2010), IIPS and ORC Macro (2000), IIPS and Macro International (2007).

The Approach and the Data

Given the deficiency many states, especially Uttar Pradesh and Bihar, face in socio-economic development, it is to be expected that fertility in these states is above the national average. But does the relatively poorer socio-economic development explain the gap in fertility? In order to see this, Total Fertility Rate (TFR) in large states is regressed on three key indicators, namely, Infant Mortality Rate (IMR), female literacy and urbanization (% of population residing in urban areas). The predicted value of TFR for a state gives the expected level of fertility in the state if other conditions are no different from the national conditions. This includes programme and other relevant factors (not accounted for in the regression equation). For a state, if TFR_0 is the actual TFR and TFR_{pred} the TFR predicted from the regression equation for the state, the difference between the predicted TFR and the national TFR, say TFR_N, that is, $TFR_{pred} - TFR_N$ is the gap due to socio-economic difference. For states with poorer development than average, this is expected to be positive, that is, the predicted TFR is expected to be higher than average due to deficiency in development.

Total Fertility Rate for states is obtained from the Sample registration System (SRS). The SRS has been providing annual estimates of the TFR and other the measures of fertility and mortality regularly since 1971 for most large states, and since 1981 for almost all large states with population exceeding ten million (Registrar General, India, 2009, 2010, 2011, 2012, 2013b, 2013c, 2014). Similarly, estimates of the infant mortality rate are also available from the SRS. The estimates are well accepted to be reliable. Decennial censuses give female literacy and urbanization on census dates; the data from the three recent censuses, 1991, 2001, and 2011, are used here since fertility transition was well in progress during this period (Registrar General, India, 1992, 2013a). This makes it possible to regress the TFR on female literacy, urbanization and IMR for the years 1991, 2001 and 2011 allowing predictions of the TFR given the background variables. Kerala with very low level of IMR and very high literacy is an obvious outlier and hence was not included in the regressions. In case some of the explanatory variables did not show a significant effect on TFR, regression equations with only the significant variables were used for prediction.

The programme implementation, including effort and efficiency, is known to vary across states. This is seen from the higher than average unmet need in many states. Meeting this need would raise the contraceptive prevalence rate, in turn lowering the TFR. It is well recognized that it is rarely possible to meet all the need, that is, some unmet need will remain. Westoff and Bankole

(1996) have proposed alternate models of meeting this need one of which labelled 'realistic'. It is possible to compute the prevalence level if need is met realistically following the Westoff-Bankole model; this can be done using the unit level survey data. In order to compute the TFR implied by the new prevalence rate, the Bongaarts model (Bongaarts and Potter, 1983) is invoked. Suppose TFR_0 is the actual TFR of the state, and CPR_0 the contraceptive prevalence rate. The multiplier C_{c0} can be computed from the Bongaarts method; this is given by 1–1.08*u*e where u is the contraceptive prevalence rate and e the average effectiveness of the contraceptive mix. If CPR_1 is the prevalence rate after the unmet need is met realistically, the new value of multiplier C_{c1} can be obtained in a similar manner. The implied TFR, say TFR_1 will then be given by $TFR_1 = TFR_0 * (C_{ci}/C_{c0})$ holding other multipliers of the Bongaarts model constant. However, even at the national level there is some unmet need. Therefore, an adjustment is required to obtain the TFR if the programme in the state operates at the same level as at the national level. This is done by computing a similar ratio of the multiplier at the national level; if C_{c0N} is the multiplier at the national level for the given prevalence rate and C_{c1N} is the multiplier if unmet need is met realistically, the implied TFR (on the assumption of national level programme implementation), say TFR_2, will be given by $TFR_2 = TFR_0 * (C_{c1}/C_{c0})/(C_{c1N}/C_{c0N})$. The difference $TFR_0 - TFR_2$ is then attributable to the programme deficiency relative to the national level. Note that if unmet need in a state is lower than the national level, this will be negative. The unexplained gap, equalling ($TFR_2 - TFR_{pred}$) is due to other unaccounted factors and interaction between socio-economic conditions and programme implementation. Thus, the total gap between the TFR of a state, denoted by TFR_0, and the national TFR, denoted by TFR_N, is decomposed as:

$$TFR_0 - TFR_N = (TFR_{pred} - TFR_N) + (TFR_0 - TFR_2) + (TFR_2 - TFR_{pred}).$$

The three components are attributed to deficiency in socio-economic development, deficiency in programme implementation and residual factors, respectively.

The National Family Health Surveys provide estimates of unmet need for contraception for states in each round; the three rounds were carried out in 1992–93, 1998–99 and 2005–06. Note that these do not correspond to the census years. For the purpose of the decomposition shown above, only the estimates from the third round are used. Moreover, the estimates of the prevalence level implied by meeting the unmet need realistically in the Westoff-Bankole model are obtained from Mohapatra (2010). State estimates of TFR and IMR for the year 2006, roughly corresponding to the NFHS, are available. However, literacy and urbanization refer to census years. But since these change only gradually over the intercensal period, indicators for 2006 were interpolated from the 2001 and 2011 census estimates. Thus, while the predicted values of TFR are computed for the three census years 1991, 2001 and 2011, the decomposition analysis has been carried out only for 2006. The analysis is based on large states, that is, with populations exceeding ten million, as detailed estimates are available for these; Kerala is excluded from the regressions as it is considered an outlier.

Findings

The actual and predicted TFRs for large states are shown in Table 2 for the years 1991, 2001, and 2011 (though three explanatory variables were initially used in the regression equations, only one or two were found to have significant effects and the regression equations were then obtained only on the basis of these). First, the predicted values differ across states. TFR is expected to be much lower than national average; see for example Maharashtra, Himachal Pradesh, Tamil Nadu, Punjab, and West Bengal, relatively developed states (as noted above, Kerala was excluded from the regressions). On the other hand, in Rajasthan, Uttar Pradesh, Bihar and Madhya Pradesh, it is expected to be higher than the average given to their poor development. But the question is whether the predicted TFR is close to the actual; if this is the case, the departure from the national level is explained by departure from the national level of socio-economic development. In many states, predicted TFR was in fact close to the actual TFR. But in some, there is departure from equality (see Figure 2 for the plot for 2011) implying that fertility is not consonant with development in these. At one end, in Andhra Pradesh and Odisha, the residual is consistently negative, that is, the TFR was much lower than predicted. On the other hand, in Uttar Pradesh the TFR was consistently well above the predicted value in 1991, 2001 and 2011, and in Bihar this was so in 2011. In Madhya Pradesh, the gap was very wide in 2001 and moderately wide in 1991 and 2011. In Maharashtra and Gujarat the gap was moderate and in Haryana, wide in 1991 but hardly any after that.

Table 2

Total Fertility Rate, Actual and Predicted, Large States, India, 1991, 2001, 2011

State	*Total Fertility Rate (TFR)*			*Predicted TFR*			*Actual TFR – Predicted TFR*		
	1991	*2001*	*2011*	*1991*	*2001*	*2011*	*1991*	*2001*	*2011*
Jammu & Kashmir			1.8			2.61			–0.81
Himachal Pradesh			1.8			1.76			0.04
Punjab	3.1	2.4	1.8	2.87	2.27	1.83	0.23	0.13	–0.03
Haryana	4.0	3.1	2.3	3.48	2.86	2.29	0.52	0.24	0.01
Rajasthan	4.6	4.0	3.0	4.71	3.77	3.05	–0.11	0.23	–0.05
Uttar Pradesh	5.1	4.5	3.4	4.41	3.90	2.87	0.69	0.60	0.53
Bihar	4.4	4.5	3.6	4.55	4.60	2.87	–0.15	–0.10	0.73
Assam	3.5	3.0	2.4	3.32	2.95	2.49	0.18	0.05	–0.09
West Bengal	3.2	2.4	1.7	3.10	2.56	1.87	0.10	–0.16	–0.17
Jharkhand			2.9			2.65			0.25
Odisha	3.3	2.6	2.2	3.83	3.26	2.65	–0.53	–0.66	–0.45
Chhattisgarh			2.7			2.64			0.06
Madhya Pradesh	4.6	3.9	3.1	4.19	3.28	2.88	0.41	0.62	0.22
Gujarat	3.1	2.9	2.4	2.98	2.70	2.07	0.12	0.20	0.33
Maharashtra	3.0	2.4	1.8	2.75	1.99	1.55	0.25	0.41	0.25
Andhra Pradesh	3.0	2.3	1.8	3.95	3.27	2.58	–0.95	–0.97	–0.78

Cont'd …

... Cont'd

Karnataka	3.1	2.4	1.9	3.24	2.77	2.06	–0.14	–0.37	–0.16
Tamil Nadu	2.2	2.0	1.7	2.81	2.19	1.56	–0.61	–0.19	0.14
India	3.6	3.1	2.4						
R2	0.69	0.72	0.60						
Adjusted R2	0.66	0.69	0.55						

Source: Total Fertility Rate: Registrar General, India (2010, 2013b); other figures are computed from regression equations as described in text.

Figure 2

Predicted TFR vs. Actual TFR, 2011, Large States of India

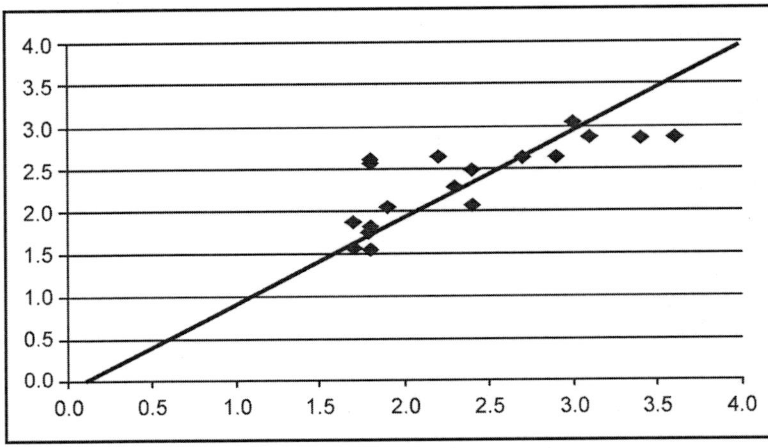

Source: Table 1

The lack of equality of actual and predicted TFR in some states implies that other factors have played some role, and rather large role, in some states. One of these factors is programme implementation. Treating unmet need as proxy for programme implementation deficiency, the gap in the TFR of a state and the national average can be decomposed, as described earlier, into contributions of deficiencies in socio-economic development, programme implementation and other factors, labelled as residual. This has been done for the year 2006 for which reliable data on unmet need, required to carry out the decomposition, are available.

The results are shown in Table 3 only for states that had above average TFR in 2006. Uttar Pradesh and Bihar had the highest TFR, 4.2 in 2006, 1.4 points above the national average of 2.8 for the year. About half of this was attributable to the low level of socio-economic development in these states; 0.67 in Uttar Pradesh and 0.86 in Bihar. But a substantial portion, 0.23–0.27 points was on account of programme deficiency. As noted earlier, unmet need is quite high in these states pointing towards poor implementation of the programme. Four other states, all in the north-central region, have higher than average TFR though the gap is narrow. The above average fertility in Rajasthan is clearly attributable to poor socio-economic development. In Madhya Pradesh too, bulk of the gap is on account of poor development. Deficiency in programme does not seem to be an issue in these two states. In Jharkhand, poorer socio-economic conditions have kept the fertility higher than national level but poorer programme implementation is also a contributing factor. In Chhattisgarh, neither of these two factors makes much of an impact. In fact, unmet need in Chhattisgarh is marginally lower than average (according to both the NFHS–3 and the DLHS–3) implying that programme implementation is fairly good.

Table 3

Decomposition of Gap between State TFR and all-India TFR, Large States with TFR above all-India Level, 2006

State	*TFR (actual)*	*TFR (predicted)*	*TFR (adjusted for unmet need to national level)*	*Total Gap*	*Due to Poorer Socio-economic Development*	*Due to Programme Implementation Gap*	*Residual*
Uttar Pradesh	4.2	3.47	3.97	1.4	0.67	0.23	0.50
Bihar	4.2	3.66	3.93	1.4	0.86	0.27	0.27
Madhya Pradesh	3.5	3.30	3.53	0.7	0.50	–0.03	0.24
Rajasthan	3.5	3.53	3.48	0.7	0.73	0.02	–0.05
Jharkhand	3.4	3.20	3.13	0.6	0.40	0.27	–0.07
Chhattisgarh	3.3	2.98	3.44	0.5	0.18	–0.14	0.46
India	2.8						

Note: See text for the method of decomposition.

But not all of the gap between the state TFR and the national TFR is accounted for by the two factors, socio-economic development and programme implementation, in four of the states. This is particularly so in Uttar Pradesh and Chhattisgarh; Bihar and Madhya Pradesh also show sizable unexplained gap as seen from the residual column of Table 3. This calls for an explanation. It has been well recognized that diffusion has played an important part in fertility transition (Knodel and Prachuabmoh, 1974; Bongaarts and Watkins, 1996; Kulkarni, 2011). Generally, fertility regulation is first adopted by the elite or the upper classes of the population followed by the rest with a lag. Where social interactions are strong, rapid diffusion allows early adoption and consequently fertility declines in all sections in a short time. Has diffusion been poorer in the Uttar Pradesh and Bihar than in the rest of the country? One way to assess this is to see fertility gaps between the upper classes and the lower classes; narrow gap implies high degree of diffusion and vice versa. Since education of woman is the principal background factor influencing fertility, we focus on educational differentials. Table 4 presents these differentials from the third round of the National Family Health Survey, NFHS–3 (carried out during 2005–06) for the six large states with TFR above the national average; for comparison, differentials at the all-India level are also shown in the table. It can be seen that differentials are quite wide in Uttar Pradesh and Bihar. In particular, the gap between the fertility of women with no schooling and those with at least secondary education completed (10 or more years of schooling) is over two points in these states, much wider than elsewhere. For women with at least secondary level education, fertility in these states is only marginally higher than the national level. But TFRs for women with no education are at least one point higher in these states than the national average for this category. This suggests that there is less diffusion across classes in Uttar Pradesh and Bihar as compared to the overall national level.

Table 4

Educational Differentials in Total Fertility Rate in Large States with TFR above the all-India Level, NFHS–3, 2005–06

State	*All*	*Education of Woman*			
		No	< 5 years	5–9 years	10+ years
Uttar Pradesh	3.82	4.61	3.34	3.36	2.36
Bihar	4.00	4.58	*	(3.21)	2.36
Madhya Pradesh	3.12	3.79	(3.11)	2.81	1.94
Rajasthan	3.21	3.71	*	(2.50)	(1.82)
Jharkhand	3.31	3.86	*	(2.86)	(2.04)
Chhattisgarh	2.62	3.23	*	2.35	(1.88)
India	2.68	3.55	2.45	2.23–2.51	2.08–1.80

Source: IIPS and Macro International (2007, 2008a, 2008b, 2008c, 2008d, 2008e, 2008f)

Note: The TFRs in this table are from the NFHS–3 and do not necessarily match those from the Sample Registration System used elsewhere.

Concluding Remarks

India's fertility transition has been characterized by wide regional variations. While transition is undoubtedly in progress throughout the country, some regions have been lagging with implications for unbalanced growth in the foreseeable future. Of course, in a country as large and as diverse as India, where physical as well as socio-economic conditions vary across states and regions of the country, fertility is naturally expected to vary spatially, given the strong relationship between fertility and socio-economic factors well established by extensive demographic research. The poor socio-economic development in some parts, including the large states of Uttar Pradesh and Bihar, has generally been accepted to be the reason for the relatively high fertility, and more specifically, the lag in transition in these. The analysis of data spread over three decades, covering the major period of India's transition to low fertility, lends support to this explanation. Fertility is indeed lower in states better placed in socio-economic conditions. Uttar Pradesh, Bihar, Rajasthan, and Madhya Pradesh with poorer indicators of development have shown consistently higher than average fertility.

But then that is not the entire story. The analysis shows that deficiency in implementation of the population programme has also mattered. This is particularly true of Uttar Pradesh and Bihar (as well as Jharkhand which was part of Bihar earlier). While demand for contraceptive services is not as high in these states as in many others, these states have fallen short of meeting even this demand. Contraceptive acceptance through the programme was high in southern and some western states even in the early 1970s but quite low in the north-central region. When the programme intensified in 1976, during the emergency, the number of sterilizations increased multi-fold in the north-central region from very low levels of the past. Strong pressure tactics were employed during the emergency to raise the number of sterilizations which jumped from 50,722 in 1974–75 to 8,38,071 in 1976–77 in Uttar Pradesh and from 32,394 in 1974–75 to 6,85,636 in 1976–77 in Bihar (Government of India, 1978). This led to widespread resentment and subsequent backlash which was very severe in this region and the programme took a long time to recover. The high unmet need, seen consistently in Uttar Pradesh and Bihar, reflects the inability of the programme to provide adequate services.

What about other factors? Wide educational differentials in fertility indicate that diffusion has not operated much. Diffusion does depend on the degree of social interactions. Wider spread of channels of communication can expedite the process. Over the past two decades, channels of communication have expanded in these states as was elsewhere in the country. But possibly there are constraints to diffusion peculiar to this region, perhaps some cultural factors. Besides, the Indian population programme (family planning or welfare) was also expected to contribute to diffusion. The programme was conceived and developed not only to provide contraceptive services to those who desired to have these but also to motivate couples to adopt a small family norm. Note that the contribution of programme deficiency to the fertility gap as assessed by above measures reflects only the degree of failure of the programme to provide services to those who needed it, but not its failure to create demand. The latter is then part of the residual in the decomposition analysis. The extension approach was adopted by the Indian programme for the purpose of motivation and mass media, and personal campaigns were undertaken and once the target approach was adopted, health and family planning workers, and occasionally other government workers, were assigned quotas of acceptors to be recruited. In that way, it was expected to contribute to lowering family size desires and creating demand. During the intensification of 1976, pressure tactics were used which came under severe criticism. The subsequent setback weakened the motivation campaign, political support to these was lost and the programme administrators became cautious in their efforts. Though motivation did remain a part of the programme in principle, the pressures eased. Besides, the target approach came under criticism especially after the International Conference on Population and Development (ICPD) 1994 and the Swaminathan Committee report and targets were finally formally dropped in 1997. The 2000 population policy also specified addressing unmet need as the top priority. With overall support for a strong neo-Malthusian approach of the kind adopted in the past, weakening the programme's role in motivation has gradually become minimal. Since the programme in Uttar Pradesh and Bihar was weak during the pre-emergency period, and the motivation component of the programme has become weak in the post-emergency period, it has apparently done little to create demand in these states.

Can something be said about the likely trends in the fertility of Uttar Pradesh and Bihar? Socio-economic development is sought to be achieved for its intrinsic value, as a goal in itself, and it also contributes to lowering family size desires and has the added advantage of promoting couple's ability to regulate fertility. Undoubtedly, further development in these states is expected and this will lower fertility. The pace will naturally depend on how rapidly the states will develop. Education of women is a key factor. Over the years, school enrolment of girls is approaching a near universality at the elementary level. But progression to secondary school level has to improve. Raising public expenditure on education has been a long standing demand in India but the actual level of investment has shown little change. There is no doubt that concerted efforts to provide contraceptive services of good quality to the population will lower fertility in these states. Addressing unmet need continues to be the priority of the programme. But will the states be able to enhance the level of service delivery? The persistently high unmet need is a matter of concern. Major changes in the way the programme is administered in these states, known for poor performance for long, are called for. This brings in issues of governance and service delivery. Finally, the causes of poor diffusion in these states need to be studied. What are the impediments? Are some facets of the social structure responsible for preventing speedy diffusion? If so, these need to be understood. At this stage, all one can say is that fertility decline will continue in Uttar Pradesh and Bihar but the transition is expected to be tardy as it has been in the recent past. Therefore, fertility is not likely to reach low replacement level before the mid-2020s and probably even the late 2020s. An unavoidable consequence is that population growth in these states will continue to be high for a long time after it would have become negligible in other parts of the country, creating huge imbalances in interstate population growth.

References

Bhat, P.N.M. 1996. 'Contours of Fertility Decline in India: A District Level Study Based on the 1991 Census', in K. Srinivasan (ed.), *Population Policy and Reproductive Health*. New Delhi: Hindustan Publishing Corporation.

Bongaarts, John and Robert G. Potter. 1983. *Fertility, Biology and Behavior: An Analysis of the Proximate Determinants*. New York: Academic Press.

Bongaarts, John and S. Watkins. 1996. 'Social Interactions and Contemporary Fertility Transitions', *Population and Development Review*, 22: 639–682.

Cleland, John and Christopher Wilson. 1987. 'Demand Theories of the Fertility Transition: An Iconoclastic View', *Population Studies*, 41(1): 5–30.

Cochrane, Susan Hill. 1979. *Fertility and Education: What Do We Really Know?* Baltimore: Johns Hopkins University Press.

Dyson, Tim and Mick Moore. 1983. 'Kinship Structure, Female Autonomy and Demographic Behaviour in India', *Population and Development Review*, 9(1): 35–60.

Dyson, Tim. 2010. *Population and Development: The Demographic Transition.* London: Zed Books.

Government of India. 1978. *Family Welfare Programme in India Yearbook 1976–77.* New Delhi: Ministry of Health and Family Welfare.

Guilmoto, Christophe Z. and S. Irudaya Rajan (eds) 2005. *Fertility Transition in South India.* New Delhi: Sage.

Guilmoto, Christophe Z. and S. Irudaya Rajan. 2001. 'Spatial Patterns of Fertility Transition in Indian Districts', *Population and Development Review*, 27(4): 713–738.

International Institute for Population Studies (IIPS). 1995. National Family Health Survey (NFHS), India, 1992–93. Mumbai: IIPS.

——. 2010. District Level Household and Facility Survey, 2007–08. Mumbai: IIPS.

International Institute for Population Sciences (IIPS) and Macro International. 2007. *National Family Health Survey (NFHS–3), India, 2005–06.* Mumbai: IIPS.

——. 2008a. National Family Health Survey (NFHS–3), India, 2005–06, Bihar. Mumbai: IIPS.

——. 2008b. *National Family Health Survey (NFHS–3), India, 2005–06, Chhattisgarh.* Mumbai: IIPS.

——. 2008c. *National Family Health Survey (NFHS–3), India, 2005–06, Jharkhand.* Mumbai: IIPS.

——. 2008d. *National Family Health Survey (NFHS–3), India, 2005–06, Madhya Pradesh.* Mumbai: IIPS.

——. 2008e. *National Family Health Survey (NFHS–3), India, 2005–06, Rajasthan.* Mumbai: IIPS.

——. 2008f. *National Family Health Survey (NFHS–3), India, 2005–06, Uttar Pradesh.* Mumbai: IIPS.

International Institute for Population Sciences (IIPS) and ORC Macro. 2000. *National Family Health Survey (NFHS–2), India, 1998–99.* Mumbai: IIPS.

Jejeebhoy, Shireen. 1995. *Women's Education, Autonomy, and Reproductive Behaviour: Experience from Developing Countries.* Oxford: Clarendon Press.

Knodel, John and Visid Prachuabmoh. 1974. 'Demographic Aspects of Fertility in Thailand', *Population Studies*, 28: 423–448.

Krishnamoorthy, S., P.M. Kulkarni and N. Audinarayana. 2005. 'Causes of Fertility Transition in Tamil Nadu', in Christophe Z. Guilmoto and S. Irudaya Rajan (eds), *Fertility Transition in South India*. New Delhi: Sage.

Kulkarni, P.M. 2011. 'Towards an Explanation of India's Fertility Transition', *Demography India*, 40(2): 1–21.

Mohapatra, Manoranjan. 2010. Fertility Implications of Addressing Unmet Need for Family Planning in India. M.Phil. Dissertation, Centre for the Study of Regional Development, School of Social Sciences, Jawaharlal Nehru University, New Delhi.

Ram, Usha and F. Ram. 2009. 'Fertility Transition in India: Policy Issues and Programme Challenges', in K.K. Singh, R.C. Yadava and Arvind Pandey (eds), *Population, Poverty and Health: Analytical Approaches*. New Delhi: Hindustan Publishing Corporation.

Registrar General, India. 1992. Census of India 1991, Series–1, India, Final Population Totals: Brief Analysis of Primary Census Abstract. Paper 2 of 1992. New Delhi: Controller of Publications.

——. 2009. Sample Registration System Statistical Report, 2008. Paper No. 1 of 2009. New Delhi: Controller of Publications.

——. 2010. Compendium of India's Fertility and Mortality Indicators 1971–2007: Based on the Sample Registration System (SRS). New Delhi: Office of the Registrar General.

——. 2011. Sample Registration System Statistical Report, 2009. Report No. 1 of 2011. New Delhi: Controller of Publications.

——. 2012. Sample Registration System Statistical Report, 2010. Report No. 1 of 2012. New Delhi: Controller of Publications.

——. 2013a. Census of India 2011: Primary Census Abstract: Data Highlights, India, Series 1. New Delhi: Controller of Publications.

——. 2013b. Sample Registration System Statistical Report, 2011. Report No. 1 of 2013. New Delhi: Controller of Publications.

——. 2013c. Sample Registration System Statistical Report, 2012. Report No. 1 of 2013. New Delhi: Controller of Publications.

——. 2014. Sample Registration System Statistical Report, 2013. Report No. 1 of 2014. New Delhi: Controller of Publications.

Srinivasan, K. 1995. *Regulating Reproduction in India's Population: Efforts, Results, and Recommendations*. New Delhi: Sage.

Westoff, C.F. and A. Bankole. 1996. 'The Potential Demographic Significance of Unmet Need', *International Family Planning Perspectives*, 22(1): 16–20.

Zachariah, K.C. 1984. The Anomaly of Fertility Decline in India's Kerala State: A Field Investigation. Staff Working Paper No. 700, The World Bank, Washington, D.C.

2

Fertility Transition in Bihar and Uttar Pradesh

D.A. NAGDEVE

India had experienced substantial fertility reduction and fertility transition in all the states but the levels and trends of fertility vary considerably in these states. Bihar and Uttar Pradesh among five of the nine high focus states still have fertility rate as high as above three children per woman with considerable variations in the levels and trends of fertility. India's fertility transition may be dependent upon fertility change in the nine high focus states. Fertility transition appeared for the first time during the 1970s in Bihar, Rajasthan, and Uttar Pradesh (UP). During 1970–90 fertility declined by about 1.6 children in Bihar and Rajasthan, but only by about 1.2 in Madhya Pradesh and Uttar Pradesh. Changes in fertility occurred among older women. TFR was higher in UP and lower in Bihar in 1991 compared to 1961. Fertility decline accelerated over time (Ram and Ram, 1997).

The population stabilization of India is mainly decided by the future fertility scenario in Bihar and Uttar Pradesh as these states constitute one-fourth of India's population. Of all the bigger states of India, the decadal growth rate of population during 2001–2011 was the highest: 25.07 per cent in the state of Bihar, followed by 20.09 per cent in Uttar Pradesh (Registrar General and Census Commissioner of India, 2011). Fertility in Bihar and Uttar Pradesh continues to remain well above the replacement level, although it is decreasing at slower pace. The replacement level of fertility and population stabilization in India cannot be achieved without a faster fertility decline in Bihar and Uttar Pradesh (Planning Commission, 2008). The TFR of Bihar declined from 5.7 in 1981 to 3.6 in 2011, whereas in Uttar

Pradesh, during the same period, it declined from 5.8 to 3.4 (Registrar General and Census Commissioner of India, 2013).

A few researchers have studied the fertility transition in Bihar and Uttar Pradesh. Though all the states of India are experiencing fertility transition, the pace of change is not uniform across the states. The fertility level in two of the larger states, namely, Uttar Pradesh and Bihar remains high. The TFR of Bihar declined from 4.4 in 1991 to 3.9 in 2008, whereas in Uttar Pradesh, during the same period, it declined from 5.1 to 3.8 (Registrar General of India, 2009). These states are also lagging in many of the key socio-economic and health indicators and ranked at the bottom of the human development index (Planning Commission, 2011; Mohanty and Ram, 2011).

The fertility transition was more apace in most districts of Uttar Pradesh while it was slow in most districts of Bihar. Factors such as women's years of schooling, age at marriage, the size of the Muslim population and child mortality are the most important predictors of fertility variations across the districts in these states (Das and Mohanty, 2012). The study of rural-urban differentials in India based on the Sample Registration System data of 1972–81 revealed that there was decline in the marital fertility at the older ages and marginal increase in fertility at the younger ages. Urban women were found to have lower fertility than rural women, and voluntary fertility control was the main reason responsible for larger decline in marital fertility (Pathak and Murthy, 1987). Many studies highlighted the importance of women's education as a significant predictor of small family norms and fertility decline regardless of religion, culture and level of development (Vaidyanathan, 1989; Jejeebhoy, 1995; UN, 1995; Parasuraman et al., 1999; Dreze and Murthi, 2001). Evidence also suggests that fertility reduction in recent years in India is largely due to fertility reduction among uneducated and poor women (Bhat, 1996; McNay et al., 2003; Arokiasamy, 2009).

Uttar Pradesh is India's fifth largest state, in terms of land area, with a total area of 2,43,290 square kilometres. Bihar is the twelfth largest state in India, with a total area of 94,163 square kilometres. Uttar Pradesh is the most populous state in India while Bihar is having the third highest population among all the States/Union Territories in India. The population of Bihar and Uttar Pradesh increased from 52 million and 111 million in 1981 to 104 million and 200 million in 2011 respectively. Out of every 100 persons in India, about 16 are from Uttar Pradesh and 9 from Bihar.

The population of Bihar doubled, whereas the population of Uttar Pradesh has increased 1.8 times during 1981 and 2011, an increase of 52 million in Bihar and 89 million in Uttar Pradesh during the last 30 years. The population growth in the Bihar and Uttar Pradesh varies from decade to decade. The decadal growth of population in Bihar has increased from 24.23 per cent in 1981 to 25.33 per cent in 2011, whereas it has decreased from 25.39 per cent in 1981 to 20.09 per cent in 2011 in Uttar Pradesh. The literacy rate in Bihar has increased from 32.1 per cent in 1981 to 61.8 per cent in 2011, whereas Uttar Pradesh has seen an upward trend in literacy from 33.4 per cent in 1981 to 67.68 per cent in 2011. According to 2011 census, male literacy stands at 71.20 per cent while female literacy is at 46.40 per cent in Bihar, whereas male literacy is 77.28 per cent and female literacy is 51.36 per cent in Uttar Pradesh. The sex ratio in Bihar and Uttar Pradesh has increased from 933 and 882 females per 1,000 males in 1981 to 940 and 908 females per 1,000 males in 2011 respectively. The density of population in Bihar and Uttar Pradesh has increased from 402 and 377 persons per square kilometre in 1981 to 1,102 and 828 persons per square kilometre in 2011 respectively. The percentage of urban population in Bihar has decreased from 12 per cent in 1981 to 11 per cent in 2011, while the percentage of urban population in Uttar Pradesh has grown from 18 per cent in 1981 to 22 per cent in 2011.

The states of Uttar Pradesh and Bihar have attracted the attention of demographers and development planners in recent years because they are among the bigger states in India and lagging in many socio-economic and demographic indicators. The marked variations in fertility by residence combined with well-known differences in education provide the opportunity for systematic examination of the levels, trends and the factors contributing to fertility differentials. Therefore, the present paper is an attempt to study fertility transition in Bihar and Uttar Pradesh.

Data and Methodology

The data has been used from the Sample Registration System and an analysis of changes and trends has been conducted from 1981 to 2011.

Vital Rates in Bihar and Uttar Pradesh

The vital rates play an important role in growth of population. The trends in birth, death and infant mortality rate in Bihar and Uttar Pradesh is presented in Table 1. It is revealed from the Table that birth rate in Bihar has declined from 39.1 per thousand population in 1981 to 27.7 per thousand population in 2011. Similarly, the birth rate in Uttar Pradesh has declined from 39.6 per thousand population in 1981 to 27.8 per thousand population in 2011. The percentage change in average birth rate in Uttar Pradesh is slightly higher, 29.8 per cent as compared to 29.2 per cent in Bihar between the periods 1981 and 2011. At the same time, crude death rate in Bihar and Uttar Pradesh has also declined from 13.9 and 16.3 per thousand population in 1981 to 6.7 and 7.9 per thousand population in 2011 respectively. During 1981–2011, the percentage change in average death rate in Bihar is slightly higher, 51.8 per cent as compared to 51.5 per cent in Uttar Pradesh. Infant Mortality Rate (IMR) per thousand live births in Bihar and Uttar Pradesh has steadily declined from 118 and 150 in 1981 to 44 and 57 in 2011 respectively. The percentage change in infant mortality rate in Bihar is slightly higher 62.7 per cent as compared to 62 per cent in Uttar Pradesh between the periods 1981 and 2011. Similarly, the birth rate, death rate and infant mortality rate has declined both in rural and urban areas but birth rate, death rate and infant mortality rate is higher in rural areas than urban areas during 1981–2011. The percentage change in average birth rate, death rate and infant mortality rate between the periods 1971 and 2011 is higher in urban areas than rural areas in both the states.

Table 1

Trends in Birth Rate, Death Rate and Infant Mortality Rate by Residence in Bihar and Uttar Pradesh, 1981–2011

Year	*Bihar*			*Uttar Pradesh*		
	Total	*Rural*	*Urban*	*Total*	*Rural*	*Urban*
	Birth Rate					
1981	39.1	39.7	33.9	39.6	40.8	31.5
1986	36.5	37.2	29.8	37.5	39.1	30.7
1991	30.7	31.3	25.5	35.7	37.2	29
1996	32.1	33.1	23.6	34	35.2	28
2001	31.2	32.3	23.4	32.1	33.2	27
2006	29.9	30.7	23	30.1	31	26
2011	27.7	28.4	21.7	27.8	28.8	23.7
% change during 1981–2011	–29.16	–28.46	–35.99	–29.80	–29.41	–24.76

Cont'd...

...Cont'd

			Death Rate			
1981	13.9	14.7	8	16.3	17.3	9.9
1986	13.8	14.4	8.8	14.6	15.7	10
1991	9.8	10.2	6.3	11.3	12	8.3
1996	10.2	10.6	6.9	10.3	10.7	8.2
2001	8.2	8.5	6.3	10.1	10.6	7.8
2006	7.7	7.8	6.3	8.6	9.1	6.6
2011	6.7	6.9	5.5	7.9	8.3	6.1
% change during 1981–2011	–51.8	–53.06	–31.25	–51.53	–52.02	–38.38
			Infant Mortality Rate			
1981	118	124	60	150	157	97
1986	101	104	68	132	140	88
1991	69	71	46	97	102	74
1996	71	73	54	85	88	67
2001	62	63	52	83	86	62
2006	60	62	45	71	75	53
2011	44	45	34	57	60	41
% change during 1981–2011	–62.71	–64	–43.33	–62	–61.78	–57.73

Note: Bihar excludes Jharkhand in 2006 and 2011; Uttar Pradesh excludes Uttarakhand in 2001, 2006 and 2011.

Source: India, Registrar General, Compendium of India's Fertility and Mortality Indicators 1971–2007; India, Registrar General, Sample Registration System Statistical Report 2011.

Fertility Trends in Bihar and Uttar Pradesh

Trends in age-specific fertility rates per 1,000 women by residence in Bihar and Uttar Pradesh are depicted in Table 2. The age-specific fertility rates are much higher in rural areas than in urban areas, both in Bihar and Uttar Pradesh in all age groups. There is consistent fertility decline by residence among all age groups in Bihar but there is an increase in younger and old age groups in Uttar Pradesh. The age-specific fertility rates declined from 1981 to 2011 in both urban and rural areas of Bihar but in Uttar Pradesh there are few exceptions. The peak age of childbearing is 20–29, with steadily declining fertility rates thereafter. The high fertility is still concentrated in the prime childbearing age of 20–29 years in both urban and rural areas both in Bihar and Uttar Pradesh. Fertility rates declined sharply in

Table 2

Trends in Age-specific Fertility Rate by Residence at Interval of 5 Years in Bihar and Uttar Pradesh, 1981 to 2011 (per 1,000 women)

Age Group	*Bihar*					*Uttar Pradesh*				
	1981	*1991*	*2001*	*2011*	*% change during 1981–2011*	*1981*	*1991*	*2001*	*2011*	*% change during 1981–2011*
					Total					
15–19	114	78.5	53.5	33	–71.05	71	45.3	32.6	26.1	–63.24
20–24	275.5	230.8	244.6	247.5	–10.16	207.7	186.7	181.9	220.3	6.07
25–29	277.4	203.9	233.3	221.4	–20.19	193.8	130.7	129.2	223.1	15.12
30–34	214	165.1	180.9	128.8	–39.81	124.6	54.6	46.1	128.4	3.05
35–39	145	116.1	104.3	58.4	–59.72	55.1	20.8	12.4	51.9	–5.81
40–44	73.1	59.9	54.6	26.3	–64.02	19.5	4.2	3.2	22.4	14.87
45–49	33.2	26.5	15.3	6.3	–81.02	5.3	1.5	0.8	7.2	35.85
					Rural					
15–19	118.9	82.2	56.8	34	–71.40	82.2	47.8	35.9	28.9	–64.84
20–24	276.5	234	255.6	257.4	–6.91	228.8	184.2	195.4	238.5	4.24
25–29	281.8	205.4	238.5	226.4	–19.66	208.4	139.3	131.1	233.8	12.19
30–34	218.4	169.8	189.6	133.2	–39.01	136	62.2	48.3	130.3	–4.19
35–39	151.3	119.4	108.7	61.3	–59.48	59.4	25.5	13.2	55.3	–6.90

Cont'd…

...Cont'd

40–44	74.6	63.4	58.6	28.1	–62.33	20.8	5.8	3.1	24.4	17.31
45–49	33.8	27.6	15.6	6.8	–79.88	6.1	1.7	1.2	7.9	29.51
					Urban					
15–19	78.3	45.7	27.8	24.2	–69.09	46.1	40.6	25.3	13.1	–71.58
20–24	267.6	204.7	176.5	172.2	–35.65	164.6	191.3	153.8	150.3	–8.69
25–29	243.4	190.8	193.5	180.3	–25.92	166.4	117	125.7	185.8	11.66
30–34	177	121.8	118	91.7	–48.19	100.6	41.2	41.8	121.6	20.87
35–39	97.9	87.8	70	33.1	–66.19	45	11.5	11.1	38	–15.56
40–44	61.3	28.9	28.2	12.5	–79.61	16	1	3.6	15.1	–5.63
45–49	27.4	16.8	13.2	2.9	–89.42	3.1	1.1	0	4.8	54.84

Note: Bihar excludes Jharkhand in 2006 and 2011; Uttar Pradesh excludes Uttarakhand in 2001, 2006 and 2011.

Source: India, Registrar General, Compendium of India's Fertility and Mortality Indicators 1971–2007; India, Registrar General, Sample Registration System Statistical Report, 2011.

age group 15–19 and beyond the age of 25, reaching extremely low levels for women of age 40–44 and 45–49 in Bihar, but in Uttar Pradesh it has shown an increase in the age 20–29 and 40–49 in rural areas and in age 25–34 and 45–49 in urban areas. Early child bearing is substantial in both Bihar and Uttar Pradesh, which accounted for 4.57 and 3.84 per cent of births in the age group 15–19 respectively. It was also observed that 69.5 per cent of births occur to women below the age 30 in Bihar compared to 69.1 per cent of births in Uttar Pradesh. Surprisingly, the contribution of early childbearing (age 15–19) is higher 4.68 per cent in urban areas than 4.55 per cent in rural areas of Bihar, but in Uttar Pradesh it is lower: 2.48 per cent in urban areas than 4.02 per cent in rural areas. It is also found that the percentage of births occurring to women below the age 30 in 2011 is 69.3 and 69.73 per cent in rural areas and 72.9 and 66 per cent in urban areas of Bihar and Uttar Pradesh respectively. The percentage change in age-specific fertility rate during 1981–2011 reveals that overall decline in fertility rates is more in urban areas compared to rural areas in both Bihar and Uttar Pradesh. The fertility decline is slower in the middle age groups 20–29 for both rural and urban areas in Bihar but it is increased in age groups 20–29 in rural areas and in age groups 25–34 in urban areas of Uttar Pradesh. The minimum decline of 10 per cent has been noticed in the age group 20–24 in Bihar but it has increased by 6 per cent in Uttar Pradesh. Similar picture is observed in both rural and urban areas of Bihar and Uttar Pradesh.

The total fertility rate declined considerably from 1981 to 2011 in Bihar and Uttar Pradesh. The trends of total fertility rate by residence in Bihar and Uttar Pradesh from 1981–2011 is presented in Table 3. From beginning the TFR of Uttar Pradesh is found to be higher than the Bihar up to 2001 but it is lower in Uttar Pradesh than Bihar in 2011. But the rate of decline was different and it was slower in Bihar as compared to Uttar Pradesh during 1981–2011. The pace of fertility decline is accelerated during the period 1981–91, with an estimated TFR of 5.7 per woman in 1981 to 4.4 in 1991 in Bihar compared to a TFR of 5.8 per woman in 1981 to 5.1 in 1991 in Uttar Pradesh. The pace of fertility decline is decelerated, with an estimated TFR of 4.4 in 1991 and 2001 in Bihar but TFR in Uttar Pradesh declined from 5.1 in 1991 to 4.5 in 2001. In 2011, it further declined to 3.6 in Bihar and 3.4 in Uttar Pradesh. The fertility decline also shows an accelerated fall in both Bihar and Uttar Pradesh during 1981–91 but there is no fertility decline during

1991–2001 in Bihar. However, the rate of fertility decline remained stable in Uttar Pradesh during 1991–2001. The fertility declined rapidly in Uttar Pradesh compared to Bihar and a steep drop during the 2001–2011 decade observed both in Bihar and Uttar Pradesh. The annual decline in fertility during the period 1981–2011 was higher, 1.38 per cent in Uttar Pradesh than 1.23 per cent in Bihar. The comparison of the TFR between 1981–91 and 1991–2001, shows that the rate of decline in the TFR is lower during 1991–2001 (no decline) compared to 2.28 per cent during 1981–1991 in Bihar but in Uttar Pradesh the rate of decline in the TFR is lower during 1991–2001 (1.18% per year) compared to 1.21 per cent during 1981–1991. Similarly, the comparison of the TFR between 1991–2001 and 2001–2011 in both Bihar and Uttar Pradesh indicates that the rate of decline in the TFR is lower during 1991–2001 compared to 2001–2011. There was no fertility decline during 1991–2001 compared to 1.82 per cent per year during 2001–2011 in Bihar. Similarly, the rate of decline in the TFR is lower during 1991–2001 (1.18% per year) compared to 2.44 per cent per year during 2001–2011. On an average, women in Bihar give birth to four children (3.6) as compared to six children (5.7) in 1981, whereas women in Uttar Pradesh give birth to three children (3.4) as compared to six children (5.8) in 1981.

Table 3

Trends in Total Fertility Rate by Residence at Interval of 5 Years in Bihar and Uttar Pradesh, 1981 to 2011

Year	*Bihar*			*Uttar Pradesh*		
	Total	*Rural*	*Urban*	*Total*	*Rural*	*Urban*
1981	5.7	5.8	4.8	5.8	6.1	4.1
1986	5.2	5.3	4.2	5.4	5.8	4
1991	4.4	4.5	3.5	5.1	5.4	3.7
1996	4.5	4.6	3.2	4.9	5.1	3.7
2001	4.4	4.6	3.1	4.5	4.8	3.4
2006*	4.2	4.3	3	4.2	4.4	3.2
2011*	3.6	3.7	2.6	3.4	3.6	2.6
Index of TFR						
1981	100	100	100	100	100	100
1986	91.23	91.38	87.50	93.10	95.08	97.56
1991	77.19	77.59	72.92	87.93	88.52	90.24

Cont'd ...

... Cont'd

1996	78.95	79.31	66.67	84.48	83.61	90.24
2001	77.19	79.31	64.58	77.59	78.69	82.93
2006	73.68	74.14	62.50	72.41	72.13	78.05
2011	63.16	63.79	54.17	58.62	59.02	63.41
% Decline in TFR						
1981–1991	–22.81	–22.41	–27.08	–12.07	–11.48	–9.76
1991–2001	0.00	2.22	–11.43	–11.76	–11.11	–8.11
2001–2011	–18.18	–19.57	–16.13	–24.44	–25.00	–23.53
1981–2011	–36.84	–36.21	–45.83	–41.38	–40.98	–36.59
% Annual Decline in TFR						
1981–1991	–2.28	–2.24	–2.71	–1.21	–1.15	–0.98
1991–2001	0.00	0.22	–1.14	–1.18	–1.11	–0.81
2001–2011	–1.82	–1.96	–1.61	–2.44	–2.50	–2.35
1981–2011	–1.23	–1.21	–1.53	–1.38	–1.37	–1.22

Note: Bihar excludes Jharkhand in 2006 and 2011; Uttar Pradesh excludes Uttarakhand in 2001, 2006 and 2011.

Source: India, Registrar General, Compendium of India's Fertility and Mortality Indicators 1971–2007; India, Registrar General, Sample Registration System Statistical Report, 2011.

The TFR of rural Bihar was 5.8 and in the urban areas it was 4.7 in 1981, thus having a difference of 19 per cent, whereas the TFR of rural Uttar Pradesh was 6.1 and in the urban areas it was 4.1, thus having a difference of 33 per cent. It declined to 3.7 in rural areas and 2.6 in urban areas of Bihar in 2011, difference of 30 per cent whereas in Uttar Pradesh it declined to 3.6 in rural areas and 2.6 in urban areas in 2011, difference of 28 per cent. The percentage of annual decline in the TFR was 1.21 and 1.37 in rural areas, and in urban areas it was 1.53 and 1.22 during 1981–2011 in Bihar and Uttar Pradesh respectively. In the recent decade (i.e. 2001–2011), the fertility decline in rural Bihar and Uttar Pradesh has been faster (an average annual decline of 1.96 and 2.50 per cent in the TFR) as compared to 1.61 and 2.35 per cent in urban areas respectively. The difference between rural and urban TFRs in Bihar has increased from 19 per cent in 1981 to 30 per cent in 2001, whereas in Uttar Pradesh it declined from 33 per cent in 1981 to 28 per cent in 2011.

Marital Fertility Trends in Bihar and Uttar Pradesh

Age at marriage of females is a key factor that influences fertility. Based on the distribution of live births by age of married females, age-specific marital fertility rates (ASMFRs) are calculated. Trends in age-specific marital fertility rates per 1,000 women by residence in Bihar and Uttar Pradesh are depicted in Table 4. There is consistent marital fertility decline by residence among all age groups except age group 15–24. The age-specific marital fertility rates declined from 1984 to 2011 in Bihar and Uttar Pradesh. Marital fertility in both Bihar and Uttar Pradesh is much higher in rural areas than in urban areas in all the age groups and its peak is in the age group 20–24 years. A perceptible decline in marital fertility is seen in female age group of 30 years and above, both in rural and urban areas of Bihar and Uttar Pradesh. The high marital fertility is still concentrated in the prime childbearing age of 20–29 years in both urban and rural areas of Bihar and Uttar Pradesh. Marital fertility rates increased in age group 15–24 and it declined sharply beyond the age of 25, reaching extremely low levels for women of age 40–44 and 45–49. Early marital fertility is substantial in Bihar and Uttar Pradesh, which accounted for 23 per cent of births in the age group 15–19 in Bihar and 24 per cent of births in the age group 15–19 in Uttar Pradesh. It was also observed that 78 per cent of births in Bihar and 81 per cent of births in Uttar Pradesh occur to women below the age of 30. Surprisingly, the contribution of early marital fertility (age 15–19) is higher: 27 per cent in urban areas than 22 per cent in rural areas of Bihar, whereas the contribution of early marital fertility (age 15–19) is higher: 4 per cent in rural areas than 2 per cent in urban areas of Uttar Pradesh. But a higher 84 per cent of births occurred to women below the age 30 in urban areas compared to 78 per cent of births in women below the age 30 in rural areas of Bihar in 2011. On the contrary, higher 70 per cent of births occur to women below the age 30 in rural areas and 66 per cent of births occur to women below the age 30 in urban areas in Uttar Pradesh. The percentage change in age-specific marital fertility rate during 1981–2011 reveals that overall decline in fertility rates is more in urban areas compared to rural areas in both Bihar and Uttar Pradesh. The decline is perceptible for the higher age groups 40–49 in both urban and rural areas of Bihar but the decline is perceptible for the early marital fertility (age 15–19) and for the higher age groups 40–49 in both urban and rural areas of Uttar Pradesh. During 1984–2011, the marital fertility declined by 77 per cent each in the age groups 40–49 in urban areas in Bihar and Uttar Pradesh as compared to 75 per cent in rural areas of Bihar and 74 per cent in rural areas of Uttar Pradesh. It is slower

Table 4

Trends in Age-specific Marital Fertility Rate at Interval of 5 Years by Residence in Bihar and Uttar Pradesh, 1984–2011

Age Group	Bihar					Uttar Pradesh				
	1984	1991	2001	2011	% change during 1984–2011	1984	1991	2001	2011	% change during 1984–2011
					Total					
15–19	202.4	188.9	186.7	235.3	16.25	211.4	222.7	212.2	271	28.19
20–24	300.8	273.9	310	344.6	14.56	312.2	329.3	351.3	383.9	22.97
25–29	258.4	214.2	245.3	235.8	–8.75	283.9	266	266.3	253.6	–10.67
30–34	215.8	171.7	184.7	132.4	–38.65	226.6	203.1	195.5	133.6	–41.04
35–39	135.9	122.9	108	60.4	–55.56	139.9	132.7	122.4	54.2	–61.26
40–44	86.8	65.6	58.2	27.7	–68.09	77.2	72.1	58.2	24	–68.91
45–49	52.2	30.9	17	6.8	–86.97	39.4	28.4	23.8	8	–79.70
					Rural					
15–19	199.8	189.2	189.2	234.7	17.47	203.1	216.5	212.5	28.9	–85.77
20–24	297	270.8	311.7	347.5	17.00	313	325.2	350	238.5	–23.80
25–29	259.8	214.8	248.7	238.1	–8.35	292.9	276.7	268	233.8	–20.18
30–34	220.1	176.7	193.5	136.6	–37.94	238.8	214.9	204.6	130.3	–45.44
35–39	141.2	126.3	112.5	63.4	–55.10	149.9	146	128	55.3	–63.11

Cont'd…

...Cont'd

40–44	90.5	69.6	62.5	29.6	–67.29	81.4	76.7	63.4	24.4	–70.02
45–49	55.2	32	17.3	7.3	–86.78	41.1	30.5	25.4	7.9	–80.78
					Urban					
15–19	241.6	184.7	155.2	244.2	1.08	285.9	292.5	210.2	13.1	–95.42
20–24	345.4	305.9	295.4	315.3	–8.71	308.6	351.2	358.6	150.3	–51.30
25–29	245.9	208.8	217.5	214.1	–12.93	247.4	223.5	257.9	185.8	–24.90
30–34	176.6	127.2	121.2	96	–45.64	173.2	156.4	151.2	121.6	–29.79
35–39	91.4	93.1	72.6	34.6	–62.14	98.9	78.9	95	38	–61.58
40–44	49.7	31.5	29.9	13.4	–73.04	55.2	52.7	35.5	15.1	–72.64
45–49	21.4	19.8	14.6	3.1	–85.51	31.2	18.5	16.5	4.8	–84.62

Note: Bihar excludes Jharkhand in 2006 and 2011; Uttar Pradesh excludes Uttarakhand in 2001, 2006 and 2011.

Source: India, Registrar General, Compendium of India's Fertility and Mortality Indicators 1971–2007; India, Registrar General, Sample Registration System Statistical Report, 2011.

in the early age groups (15–19 and 20–24) for both the rural and urban areas in Bihar, whereas it is slower in middle age groups 20–29 in rural areas and 25–34 age groups in urban areas of Uttar Pradesh. The increase in marital fertility of 28 per cent and 16 per cent in age group 15–19 and 23 per cent and 15 per cent in age group 20–24 has been noticed in Uttar Pradesh and Bihar respectively.

The total marital fertility rate (TMFR) declined considerably from 1984 to 2011 in both Bihar and Uttar Pradesh. The trends of total marital fertility rate from 1984–2011 in Bihar and Uttar Pradesh is presented in Table 5. From beginning the TMFR of Uttar Pradesh is found to be higher than the Bihar. But the rate of decline was slightly higher in Bihar than Uttar Pradesh. During the period 1984–86, marital fertility seems to have decreased from a TMFR of 6.3 and 6.4 per woman in 1984 to 6 and 6.3 in 1986 in Bihar and Uttar Pradesh respectively. It further decreased to 5.3 and 6.3 in 1991 and to 5.3 and 5.9 in 1996 but it increased to 5.5 and 6.1 in 2001 in Bihar and Uttar Pradesh respectively. The pace of fertility decline is accelerated, with an estimated TFR of 5.7 in 2006 and further it declined to 5.6 in 2011 in Uttar Pradesh but there was no further decline in Bihar. The marital fertility decline also shows a moderate fall through the 1980s, decelerated in Bihar and accelerated in Uttar Pradesh during 1991–2001 and a steep drop during the recent decade. The annual decline in marital fertility during the period 1984–2011 was 0.65 per cent for Bihar and 0.46 per cent for Uttar Pradesh. The comparison of the TMFR between 1984–91 and 1991–2001, shows that the rate of decline in the TMFR is lower during 1991–2001 (an increase of 0.38 per cent per year) compared to 2.27 per cent during 1984–1991 in Bihar, whereas the rate of decline in the TMFR is lower during 1984–1991 (0.22 per cent per year) compared to 0.32 per cent during 1991–2001 in Uttar Pradesh. Similarly, the comparison of the TMFR between 1991–2001 and 2001–2011 indicates that the rate of decline in the TMFR is higher in the recent decade (0.55 per cent per year) compared to an increase of 0.38 per cent during 1991–2001 in Bihar, whereas the rate of decline in the TMFR is higher in the recent decade (0.82 per cent per year) compared to 0.32 per cent during 1991–2001 in Uttar Pradesh. On an average, married women in Bihar and Uttar Pradesh gave birth to five children (5.2) and six children (5.6) as compared to six children (6.3 in Bihar and 6.4 in Uttar Pradesh) in the early 1980s respectively.

Table 5

Trends in Total Marital Fertility Rate by Residence in Bihar and Uttar Pradesh, 1984–2011

Year	*Bihar*			*Uttar Pradesh*		
	Total	*Rural*	*Urban*	*Total*	*Rural*	*Urban*
1984	6.3	6.3	5.9	6.4	6.6	6
1986	6	6.1	5.7	6.3	6.5	5.7
1991	5.3	5.4	4.9	6.3	6.4	5.9
1996	5.3	5.4	4.5	5.9	6	5.6
2001	5.5	5.7	4.5	6.1	6.3	5.6
2006	5.2	5.2	4.8	5.7	5.8	5.7
2011	5.2	5.3	4.6	5.6	5.7	5.5
Index of TMFR						
1984	100	100	100	100	100	100
1986	95.24	96.83	96.61	98.44	98.48	95.00
1991	84.13	85.71	83.05	98.44	96.97	98.33
1996	84.13	85.71	76.27	92.19	90.91	93.33
2001	87.30	90.48	76.27	95.31	95.45	93.33
2006	82.54	82.54	81.36	89.06	87.88	95.00
2011	82.54	84.13	77.97	87.50	86.36	91.67
% Decline in TMFR						
1984–1991	–15.87	–14.29	–16.95	–1.56	–3.03	–1.67
1991–2001	3.77	5.56	–8.16	–3.17	–1.56	–5.08
2001–2011	–5.45	–7.02	2.22	–8.20	–9.52	–1.79
1984–2011	–17.46	–15.87	–22.03	–12.50	–13.64	–8.33
% Annual Decline in TMFR						
1984–1991	–2.27	–2.04	–2.42	–0.22	–0.43	–0.24
1991–2001	0.38	0.56	–0.82	–0.32	–0.16	–0.51
2001–2011	–0.55	–0.70	0.22	–0.82	–0.95	–0.18
1984–2011	–0.65	–0.59	–0.82	–0.46	–0.51	–0.31

Note: Bihar excludes Jharkhand in 2006 and 2011; Uttar Pradesh excludes Uttarakhand in 2001, 2006 and 2011.

Source: India, Registrar General, Compendium of India's Fertility and Mortality Indicators 1971–2007; India, Registrar General, Sample Registration System Statistical Report, 2011.

The TMFR of rural Bihar in 1984 was 6.3 and in the urban areas it was 5.9, thus having a difference of 6 per cent whereas the TMFR of rural Uttar Pradesh in 1984 was 6.4 and in the urban areas it was 6, thus having a difference of 9 per cent. It declined to

Table 6

Age-specific Fertility Rates and Total Fertility Rates by Education in Bihar and Uttar Pradesh, 2011

Age Group	*Educational level*								
	Illiterate	*Literate*							
		Total Literate	*Without any formal education*	*Below primary*	*Primary*	*Middle*	*Class X*	*Class XII*	*Graduate and above*
				Bihar					
15–19	67.6	19.2	72.9	35.4	20.9	13.4	8.2	7.9	0
20–24	325.9	185.7	254.8	253.8	199.3	191	117.5	113.4	92.6
25–29	263.1	172.5	186.5	188.2	204.2	182.9	159.8	91.1	119.7
30–34	160.2	84.5	108.4	93.6	96	88.1	66.1	40	73.6
35–39	75.4	28.7	53.5	30	20.9	25.9	19.9	16	24.8
40–44	35.3	10.5	19	13.1	11.6	8.9	3	9.3	0
45–49	7.8	3	3.3	4.3	6.1	2.5	0	0	0
TFR	4.7	2.5	3.5	3.1	2.8	2.6	1.9	1.4	1.6
				Uttar Pradesh					
15–19	55.6	22.3	107.2	99	40.5	16.1	13	10.8	0
20–24	263.3	205.8	332.4	326.6	290.4	202.9	148.9	119.4	128.9

Cont'd…

...Cont'd

25–29	229.8	218.6	243.3	255.2	247.5	236.1	211.1	176	150.6
30–34	143.9	111.8	130.8	113.7	107.4	125.8	99	92.3	112.8
35–39	61.9	37.2	59.2	66.5	45.1	33.6	7	18.7	26.3
40–44	29.2	11	21.1	18.1	10.7	11.8	5.5	2.2	7.1
45–49	8.4	4.8	27	3.9	4.7	1.6	0	0	0

Note: Bihar excludes Jharkhand in 2011; Uttar Pradesh excludes Uttarakhand in 2011.

Source: India, Registrar General, Sample Registration System Statistical Report, 2011.

5.3 in rural areas and 4.6 in urban areas of Bihar in 2011, difference of 13 per cent. Similarly, TMFR declined to 5.7 in rural areas and 5.5 in urban areas of Uttar Pradesh in 2011, difference of 4 per cent. The percentage of annual decline in the TMFR during 1984–2011 was 0.59 and 0.46 in rural areas and in urban areas it was 0.82 and 0.51 in Bihar and Uttar Pradesh respectively. In the recent decade (i.e. 2001–2011), the marital fertility decline in rural Bihar has been faster (an average annual decline of 0.70 per cent in the TMFR) as compared to an increase of 0.22 per cent in urban areas of Bihar. On contrary, the marital fertility decline in urban Uttar Pradesh has been faster (an average annual decline of 0.95 per cent in the TMFR) as compared to 0.82 per cent in rural areas of Uttar Pradesh. The difference between rural and urban TMFRs in Bihar has increased from 6 per cent in 1984 to 13 per cent in 2011, whereas it declined in Uttar Pradesh from 9 per cent in 1984 to 4 per cent in 2011.

Fertility by Level of Education of the Women

Female education has a direct impact on fertility. To ascertain levels of fertility by educational status of the women age-specific fertility rate and total fertility rate by educational status of the women in Bihar and Uttar Pradesh have been depicted in Table 6. The data reveals considerable differences in Bihar and Uttar Pradesh with the literates in Uttar Pradesh generally reporting higher levels of fertility than in Bihar for all age groups. Fertility attains the peak in the age-group 20–24 years both in Bihar and Uttar Pradesh except for the women having education level primary, class 10, graduate and above in Bihar and education level middle, class 10, class 12, graduate and above in Uttar Pradesh. 'Illiterate' women have higher levels of age-specific fertility rates both in Bihar and Uttar Pradesh than the 'Literate'. Within the 'Literate' group there is a general decline in the fertility rates with the increase in the educational status both in Bihar and Uttar Pradesh, barring a few exceptions.

Pattern of Higher Order Births

The distribution of live births by order of birth gives an idea about the total number of children ever born to the eligible women and it gives a broad idea for the preference of small family. The examination of the trends in the pattern of higher order births (four and above) also indicates a decline in fertility of Bihar and Uttar Pradesh. The change in the higher order births is good indicator of fertility change and also helps to assess the overall fertility impact of contraceptive prevalence. Since the main focus of family planning programme in India is to reduce higher order births, changes in the proportion of higher order births over a period of time is expected to reflect changes in the fertility levels. The proportion of lower order births are expected to increase as a result of the reduction in higher order births when fertility declines from high to low levels. The distribution of live births by order of births in Bihar and Uttar Pradesh is given in Table 7. From the Table it may be observed that, the percentage of births of four children and above in Bihar and Uttar Pradesh has declined from 34 per cent and 32.7 per cent in 1991 to 24.6 and 18.8 per cent in 2011 respectively. As expected, the percentage of first order births and second order births has been increased from 25 per cent and 21.4 per cent in Bihar than 26 per cent and 22.6 per cent in Uttar Pradesh in 1991 to 32 per cent and 25 per cent in Bihar as compared to 35.6 per cent and 28.7 per cent in Uttar Pradesh in 2011 respectively. The percentage of 3 order births in Bihar and Uttar Pradesh has decreased from 19.6 per cent and 18.7 per cent in 1991 to 18.4 per cent and 17 per cent in 2011 respectively. It may also be noticed that the percentage of birth order up to 2 has increased from 46.4 per cent and 48.6 per cent in 1991 to 57 per cent and 64.3 per cent in 2011, whereas the percentage of birth order 3 and above in Bihar and Uttar Pradesh has declined from 53.6 per cent and 51.4 per cent in 1991 to 43 per cent and 35.8 per cent in 2011 respectively. This shows the evidence of fertility decline in Bihar and Uttar Pradesh.

Table 7

Percentage Distribution of Live Births by Order of Birth in Bihar and Uttar Pradesh, 1991–2011

Year	*Bihar*				*Uttar Pradesh*			
	1	*2*	*3*	*4+*	*1*	*2*	*3*	*4+*
				Total				
1991	25	21.4	19.6	34	26	22.6	18.7	32.7
1996	24.8	21.1	19	35.1	23.8	20.6	18.1	37.5
2001	25.1	23.1	18.8	33	25.7	21.3	18.2	34.9
2006	26.8	23.9	18.1	31.3	29.7	23.2	17.9	29.1
2011	32	25	18.4	24.6	35.6	28.7	17	18.8

Cont'd ...

...Cont'd

				Rural				
1991	24.8	21.2	19.8	34.2	25.6	22.5	18.9	33.1
1996	24.4	20.9	19.1	35.6	23.4	20.4	18.5	37.8
2001	24.8	22.6	18.9	33.7	25.1	21.3	18.2	35.4
2006	26.4	23.7	18.3	31.7	28.8	23.1	18.1	30.1
2011	31.4	25	18.5	25.1	35	28.4	17.4	19.3
				Urban				
1991	26.9	22.7	18.5	32	28	23.1	17.8	31.1
1996	28.9	23.9	18.7	28.6	26.4	21.8	15.9	35.8
2001	28.7	27.7	17.7	25.9	29	21.6	17.7	31.7
2006	31.3	26.3	16	26.5	34.2	24	17.2	24.6
2011	38.8	25.1	17.9	18.2	38.8	30.4	14.9	15.9

Note: Bihar excludes Jharkhand in 2006 and 2011; Uttar Pradesh excludes Uttarakhand in 2001, 2006 and 2011.

Source: India, Registrar General, Compendium of India's Fertility and Mortality Indicators 1971–2007; India, Registrar General, Sample Registration System Statistical Report, 2011.

Summary and Conclusions

The analysis revealed that the total fertility rate in Bihar and Uttar Pradesh declined from 5.7 and 5.8 in 1981 to 3.6 and 3.4 in 2011 respectively, according to Sample Registration System estimates. Bihar and Uttar Pradesh had experienced reduction in fertility but still these states are having higher fertility and the levels and trends of fertility vary considerably. The results confirm the persistence of differences in fertility and it varies by residence and education. The pattern of fertility decline was not uniform in rural and urban areas and rural areas were lagging behind in both Bihar and Uttar Pradesh. It also shows that fertility is declining slowly in Bihar and Uttar Pradesh. It also shows a faster decline during 1981–91 and moderate fall during 1991–2001 and a steep drop during the 2001–2011 in both Bihar and Uttar Pradesh. A strong negative association was observed between the education level of women and fertility, both in rural and urban areas of Bihar and Uttar Pradesh. The fertility decline was mainly due to the education, decrease in higher order births of three and above and decrease in fertility among older women in age group 30 and above. In spite of fertility differentials, the decline has been observed in rural and urban areas including the illiterate. The causes of decline may be different among population of the Bihar and Uttar Pradesh. There is need to analyse in greater detail the factors that have contributed to the rapid decline in fertility during 1981–91 and recent decade. From the above analysis, it may be concluded that, the fertility differentials exist in Bihar and Uttar Pradesh because of variations in socio-economic development including education. There is a negative relationship between education and fertility. This indicates the education of women is contributed to lower fertility. Therefore, education of the girls needs to be encouraged. There is a need to give more thrust on rural areas with high fertility for achieving below replacement fertility in Bihar and Uttar Pradesh.

References

Arokiasamy, P. 2009. 'Fertility Decline in India: Contributions by Uneducated Women Using Contraception', *Economic and Political Weekly*, 44(30): 55–64.

Bhat, P.N.M. 1996. 'Contours of Fertility Decline in India: A District Level Study Based on the 1991 Census', in K. Srinivasan (ed.), *Population Policy and Reproductive Health*. New Delhi: Hindustan Publishing Corporation, 96–117.

Das, Malay and S.K. Mohanty. 2012. 'Spatial Pattern of Fertility Transition in Uttar Pradesh and Bihar: A District Level Analysis', *Genus*, 68(2): 81–106.

Dreze, J. and M. Murthi. 2001. 'Fertility, Education and Development: Evidence from India', *Population and Development Review*, 27(1): 33–63.

Jejeebhoy, S.J. 1995. *Women's Education, Autonomy, and Reproductive Behaviour: Experience from Developing Countries*. Oxford: Clarendon Press.

McNay, K., P. Arokiasamy and R.H. Cassen. 2003. 'Why are Uneducated Women in India Using Contraception? A Multilevel Analysis', *Population Studies*, 57(1): 21–40.

Mohanty, S.K. and F. Ram. 2011. 'Spatial Patterns of Poverty Reduction and Fertilities Transition in India', *Population Review,* 50(1): 62–78.

Parasuraman, S., T.K. Roy, D. Radha Devi, B. Paswan, P. Arokiasamy and S. Unisa. 1999. *Role of Women's Education in Shaping Fertility in India: Evidence from NFHS*. Mumbai: IIPS.

Pathak, K.B. and P.K. Murthy. 1987. 'Rural Urban Fertility Differential in India', *Jansankhya*, 5(1): 41–59.

Planning Commission. 2008. *Report of the Working Group on Population Stabilization of the Eleventh Five year Plan* (2007–2012). New Delhi: Government of India, Planning Commission.

Planning Commission. 2011. *India Human Development Report 2011, Towards Social Inclusion*. Institute of Applied Manpower Research, Government of India, Oxford: Oxford University Press.

Ram, U. and F. Ram. 1997. 'Fertility Transition in Uttar Pradesh and its Neighbouring States', in Kamla Gupta and Arvind Pandey (eds), *Population and Development in Uttar Pradesh*. New Delhi: B.R. Publishing Corporation, 199–216.

Registrar General and Census Commissioner of India. 2011. Provisional Population Total: Paper 1 of 2011. India Series 1, Census of India 2011. New Delhi, India: Registrar General and Census Commissioner.

——. 2013. Sample Registration System Statistical Report, 2011. New Delhi, India: Registrar General and Census Commissioner.

Registrar General of India. 2009. Compendium of India's Fertility and Mortality Indicators 1971–2007 Based on the Sample Registration System (SRS). New Delhi, India: Registrar General.

United Nations (UN). 1995. Women's Education and Fertility Behaviour: Evidence from the Demographic and Health Surveys. United Nations, New York.

Vaidyanathan, K.E. 1989. 'Status of Women and Family Planning: The Indian Case', *Asia-Pacific Population Journal*, 4(2): 3–18.

3

Fertility Transition in Empowered Action Group States

RAVI B.P. VERMA

Fertility reduction and improving maternal and child health in India are still important unresolved issues for government of India, demographers and social scientists. In particular, since 1952, India has been undertaking several initiatives to reduce the total fertility rate at the replacement level of 2.1 children per woman by 2017 under the 12th Five-Year Plan (Government of India, 2002, 2012). It is observed that the fertility rate in all states and India have been declining, but the progress of change has been noted to be slow by several researchers and falling short of national and Millennium Development Goals targets (George, 2010; Paul et al., 2011; Verma, 2013; Verma et al., 2012a, 2012b; Verma, Sinha, Kumar and Sinha, 2010). For example, in 2009 a group of researchers observed that adolescent-specific reproductive health services still continue to be scarce and inadequate, and only target the married adolescents. However, the government's recent enactment of policies to address the information and service needs of adolescents is encouraging. National programmes to keep girls in school hold promise for decreasing early marriages; since childbearing outside marriage is rare, delays in marriage will go a long way toward reducing adolescent childbearing (Moore et al., 2009; Bajpai et al., 2009). Thus, as consequences of social and economic development, government's strong commitments, couples are adopting family planning methods (particularly sterilization) and showing increasing desire for small family norm in the country. As of 2013, fourteen states in India have already achieved their fertility below or at the replacement level. Theses states are Chandigarh, Goa, Punjab, Himachal Pradesh, Tamil Nadu, Kerala, Andhra Pradesh, Delhi, West Bengal, Maharashtra, Sikkim, Karnataka, Jammu & Kashmir and Tripura. Fertility rate among women with 10 years or more of education completed is also at replacement level. These are partial indication of the success of the fertility reduction programme in India, concentrated in some parts/sections of the country.

In fact, statewide variations in fertility reduction are very strong in India. Particularly, the empowered action group (EAG) states (Bihar, Chhattisgarh, Jharkhand, Odisha, Madhya Pradesh, Rajasthan, Uttarakhand and Uttar Pradesh) have made relatively very slow progress. These states represent about 42 per cent of total population of India in 2011 where the challenges to achieve the goals of fertility is very serious, particularly in Uttar Pradesh and Bihar. In 2009, it has been observed, 'opinions in India regarding TFR prospects in Uttar Pradesh see TFR of 2.1 or lower is a distant dream' (Haub, 2009). Also, in 2002 the same view was mentioned by another expert that, 'Bihar and UP sustained levels of below replacement fertility are probably several decades off' (Dyson, 2002). Does it know the fact that there are too many obstacles in these states to achieve this goal? These obstacles could be due to social inequities, disparities in health systems between and within these states, demographic transition and other factors such as inadequate infrastructure, corruption (mismanagement of funds), and failure in implementing the planned initiatives. Therefore, the purpose of this paper is to review the progress made in the areas of fertility over the period 2000 to 2013 for Empowered Action Group (EAG) states in India. How far are these states behind the national goals of fertility reduction? When will they achieve the goals of fertility? To answer these questions, the author has projected the year for achieving the goal of replacement level fertility for each of EAG states and India, using two methods; geometric rate of change in total fertility rate based on the recent years derived from the Sample Registration System (2011) and ratio method applied to the UN's fertility projections.

The analysis of fertility data is done for four periods, 1998–99, 2005–06 and 2006 to 2010, 2010–13. The fertility indicator is compared with the national figure and also with southern states i.e. Andhra Pradesh, Kerala, Tamil Nadu and Karnataka.

Data and Methods

The geometric rate of change in total fertility rate derived from Sample Registration System is computed to compare the average rate of progress per year, over the years 2005–06 to 2006–2010 for each state and India. This average rate of change has been used to estimate the level of fertility for the year 2013. The year for achieving the target of fertility at 2.1 children per woman aged 15–49 years is also estimated based on the average geometric rate of change in total fertility rate over the years 2005–06 to 2006–2009. This has been designated as the medium scenario of projected year for achieving the target of fertility at 2.1.

Figure 1

Fertility Rates for India, 1950–55 to 2005–10 (Estimated) and 2010–15 to 2095–2100 (Four Projected Scenarios by the United Nations)

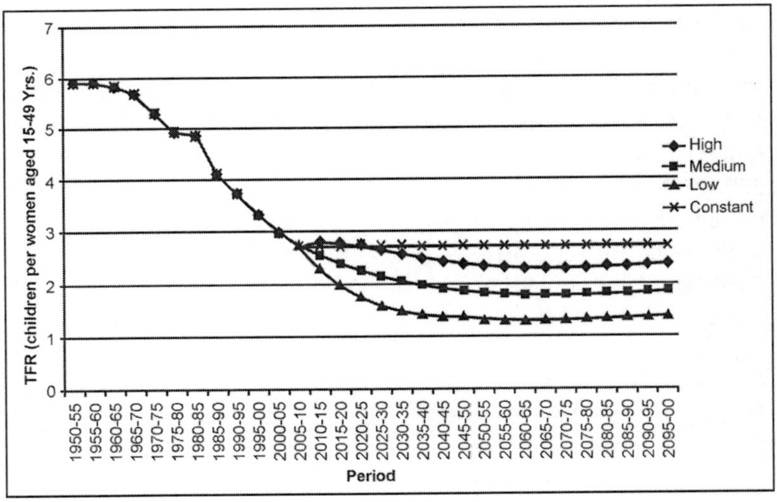

Source: United Nations (2011).

An attempt has also been made to project two additional scenarios (High and Low) of the year for achieving the targets of fertility at 2.1 children per woman for all EAG states based on the projections of fertility made by the United Nations in 2011 for India. The UN-projection of fertility for the World Population Prospects, 2010 is the latest projection of fertility that provides four sets of scenarios for India from 1950 to 2100 (UN, 2011). They are presented in Figure 1. These projections are based on the Bayesian

Hierarchical forecasting model, using the data from 1950 to 2010. It is based on ARIMA model, providing the confidence interval. These new projected fertility data have been used to generate the fertility assumptions for selected states in India with below replacement level, 2010–2100 (Verma et al., 2012a).

Methods of projecting the fertility used by some scholars for states in India vary in nature, Gompertz Curve to regression method (Bhat, 2002b; Natrajan and Jayachandran, 2000). Using these methods they have developed one or two scenarios of fertility (High and Medium). In all these projections, the difference between the base year and the first projected TFR has been found to be very large. Also, the projected TFRs for all states are almost the same at 1.6 children per woman. The ratio method was found to be used by one scholar for projecting population at the state level (Government of India, 2011). Moreover, all these projections of fertility by states and India were not sound, because they were based on the fertility data from Sample Registration System (SRS) for the period 1986 to 1998 which were underestimated by 2 per cent for India as a whole (Rutherford and Mishra, 2001). Therefore, these projections of fertility for India are not used in this paper.

The ratios of fertility rate of each state over India for each year were computed to understand the trends (increase and decrease/constant) in ratios of TFR over the national average. Later, the average ratio of TFR for the last five years for the selected states was computed. For states with higher fertility rates over the nation, the relative ratio would be more than one. For these cases, it is assumed that these ratios would converge to one over the 50 years. Assuming that, the relative ratios for the interval years are estimated by the geometric rate of growth method. For states with lower fertility rate over the nation, the average relative ratio of TFR over the period 2006–2010 is assumed to be constant to project the TFR. These relative ratios were later multiplied to the two sets of projection of TFR provided by the UN (2011) Medium and Low for India, as the fertility in the EAG states is largely expected to decline in future.

Fertility Levels and Trends

Total Fertility Rate (TFR) measures the number of children born to a woman if she follows the age-specific fertility schedule. Table 1 shows the TFRs for the periods starting from 1971 to 2013 for India and selected 30 states and union territories. In the year 2013, the estimated

Table 1

Total Fertility Rate, India and States, 1971 to 2013

India/states/ Years	SRS			NFHS–1	NFHS–II	NFHS–III	SRS						Estimated
	1971	1981	1991	1992–93	1998–99	2005–06	2005	2006	2007	2008	2009	2010	2013
Chandigarh													1.23
Andhra Pradesh	4.8	4.0	3.0	2.6	2.3	1.8	2	2	1.9	1.8	1.9	1.8	1.66
Goa	na	na	1.6	1.9	1.8	1.8						1.5	1.42
Tamil Nadu	3.9	3.4	2.2	2.5	2.2	1.8	1.7	1.7	1.6	1.7	1.7	1.7	1.64
Himachal Pradesh	na	na	3	3	2.1	1.9	2.2	2	1.9	1.9	1.9	1.8	1.64
Kerala	4.1	2.8	1.8	2	2	1.9	1.7	1.7	1.7	1.7	1.7	1.8	1.65
Punjab	5.2	4	3.1	2.9	2.2	2.0	2.1	2.1	2	1.9	1.9	1.8	1.61
Sikkim					2.8							1.9	1.74
Delhi	na	na	1.8	3	2.4	2.1	2.1	2.1	2	2	1.9	1.9	1.71
Karnataka	4	3.6	3.1	2.9	2.1	2.1	2.2	2.1	2.1	2	2	2.0	1.79
Maharashtra	4.6	3.6	3	2.9	2.5	2.1	2.2	2.1	2	2	1.9	1.9	1.72
Tripura					1.9							2.3	2.01
West Bengal	na	4.2	3.2	2.9	2.3	2.3	2.1	2	1.9	1.9	1.9	1.8	1.71
Assam	5.7	4.1	3.5	3.5	2.3	2.4	2.9	2.7	2.7	2.6	2.6	2.5	2.24

Cont'd...

...Cont'd

Jammu & Kashmir	na	na	Na	na	2.7	2.4	2.4	2.3	2.3	2.2	2.2	2.0	1.8
Gujarat	5.6	4.3	3.1	3	2.7	2.4	2.8	2.7	2.6	2.5	2.5	2.5	2.25
Odisha	4.7	4.3	3.3	2.9	2.5	2.4	2.6	2.5	2.4	2.4	2.4	2.3	2.17
Uttaranchal					2.6							2.37	2.17
Haryana	6.7	5	4	4	2.9	2.7	2.8	2.7	2.6	2.5	2.5	2.3	2.15
India	5.2	4.5	3.6	3.4	2.9	2.7	2.9	2.8	2.7	2.6	2.6	2.5	2.32
Chhattisgarh					2.8		3.4	3.3	3.1	3	3	2.8	2.52
Manipur	na	na	2.5	2.8	3	2.8						2.67	2.42
Mizoram	na	na	Na	2.3	2.9	2.9						2.82	2.54
Arunachal Pradesh	na	na	4.1	4.3	2.5	3.0						2.88	2.62
Madhya Pradesh	5.6	5.2	4.6	3.9	3.4	3.1	3.6	3.5	3.4	3.3	3.3	3.2	2.95
Rajasthan	6.3	5.2	4.6	3.6	3.8	3.2	3.7	3.5	3.4	3.3	3.3	3.1	2.83
Jharkhand					2.8		3.5	3.4	3.2	3.2	3.2	3.0	2.76
Nagaland	na	na	2.3	3.3	3.5	3.7						3.14	2.84
Meghalaya	na	na	4.1	3.7	4.6	3.8						3.27	2.92
Uttar Pradesh	6.6	5.8	5.1	4.8	4.1	3.8	4.2	4.2	3.9	3.8	3.7	3.5	3.21
Bihar	na	5.7	4.4	4	3.7	4	4.3	4.2	3.9	3.9	3.9	3.7	3.43

total fertility rate in India was 2.3 children per woman, considerably higher than the replacement level fertility. There was a strong statewide variation in the total fertility rate, ranging from 1.23 in Chandigarh to 3.43 in Bihar (Table 1). The states were grouped into three groups based on fertility level (Low, Medium and High).

TFR	*Number of States*	*Name of States*
Low: TFR Under or equal to 2.1	14	Chandigarh, Goa, Punjab, Himachal Pradesh, Tamil Nadu, Kerala, Andhra Pradesh, Karnataka, Delhi, Jammu & Kashmir, West Bengal, Maharashtra, Sikkim, Tripura.
Medium: TFR between 2.1 to 2.3	5	Haryana, Uttarakhand, Odisha, Gujarat, Assam.
High: TFR above 2.3	11	Manipur, Chhattisgarh, Mizoram, Arunachal Pradesh, Jharkhand, Rajasthan, Nagaland, Meghalaya, Madhya Pradesh, Uttar Pradesh, Bihar.

Fertility Change

Table 2 shows the per cent relative change in TFR per annum for the EAG States, Southern States and India for the years 1998–99 to 2005–06, and 2005–06 to 2009–10. During the years, 1998–99 and 2005–06, the total fertility rate in India had declined by 1.0 per cent per annum. In contrast, the average per cent relative rate of fertility decline among EAG states was much smaller (0.3% per year). Among the southern states, the rate of decline in fertility rate was much faster (1.7% per year). It has been noted that the fertility rate from the NFHS–II (1998–99) was found to be underestimated, particularly in Bihar. Thus, the positive rates of change in fertility for Bihar and Jharkhand for the years, 1998–99 to 2005–06 are not acceptable for further analysis. For the years, 2005–06 to 2009–10, the per cent relative rate of fertility change is negative, and also considerably higher than the years 1998–99 to 2005–06 in all EAG states. On average, the rate of decline in fertility among EAG states (2.7%) is considerably higher than that for India (2.1%), and southern states (0.7%).

In view of the unstable rate of change in TFR over these periods 1998–99 to 2005–06 and 2005–06 to 2009–10 for the EAG States in India, the projection of the year to achieve the TFR at 2.1 for these states is a complex process. However, in the section 4, three scenarios of the projected year of the TFR reaching at 2.1 for the EAG states and India are presented.

Table 2

Per cent Relative Change in TFR Per Annum for the EAG States, Southern States and India for the Years 1998–99 to 2005–06 and 2005–06 to 2009–10

EAG	*NFHS*		*SRS*		*Per cent Relative Change per Annum*	
	1998–99	*2005–06*	*2005–06*	*2009–10*	*1998–99 to 2005–06*	*2005–06 to 2009–10*
Bihar	3.7	4	4.25	3.8	1.16	–2.21
Chattisgarh (1)	0	0	0	3.4	na	na
Jharkhand	2.8	3.3	3.45	3.1	2.55	–2.12
Odisha	2.5	2.4	2.55	2.4	–0.57	–1.62
Madhya Pradesh (1)	3.4	3.1	3.55	3.3	–1.26	–1.75
Rajasthan	3.8	3.2	3.6	3.2	–2.26	–3.04
Uttaranchal (2)	2.6	2.6	0	2.2	0.00	na
Uttar Pradesh (2)	4.1	3.8	4.2	3.6	–1.05	–2.89
EAG States	3.3	3.2	3.6	3.1	–0.3	–2.9
India	2.9	2.7	2.9	2.6	–0.99	–2.20
Andhra Pradesh	2.3	1.8	2	1.9	–3.1	–1.50
Kerala	2	1.9	1.7	1.8	–0.71	0.59
Tamil Nadu	2.2	1.8	1.7	1.7	–2.60	0.00
Karnataka	2.1	2.1	2.15	2	0.00	–1.40
Southern states	2.15	1.9	1.9	1.8	–1.7	–0.7

Notes: (1) Until 1998–99, Chhattisgarh was the part of the Madhya Pradesh. (2) Until 1998–99, Uttarakhand/Uttaranchal the part of Uttar Pradesh. Therefore, the data used in this table are based on the adjusted boundary changes.

Projection of Year to Achieve the Goal of TFR at 2.1

Table 3 shows the projected year to achieve the goal of 2.1 TFR by EAG states, Southern states and India. The geometric rate of change in TFRs for each EAG state and India are based on the TFRs derived from the Sample Registration System for 2005–6 and 2009–10. First, these rates used the projected year to achieve the goal of TFR at 2.1 children per woman. Results indicate that under the current geometric rate of change in TFR, India should achieve the replacement level fertility by 2019, very close to the year (2017) planned under 12th Five-Year Plan of Government of India (Mathews et al., 2009). This is also very close to the year projected

Table 3

Total Fertility Rates for the EAG and Southern States and India

States	*SRS* 2005–06	*SRS* 2009–10	*Per cent Relative Change per annum 2005–6 to 2009–10*	*Geometric Rate of Change Method Year to achieve TFR at 2.1*	*Year Projected under Geometric Method*	*Mid-Year Projected under ratio method applied to UN low projection of TFR 2011*	*Mid-Year Projected under ratio method applied to UN medium projection of TFR 2011*
EAG							
Bihar	4.25	3.8	–2.21	26	2,036	2,027.5	2,042.5
Chhattisgarh (1)	0	3.4	na				
Jharkhand	3.45	3.1	–2.12	18	2,028	2,022.5	2,037.5
Odisha	2.55	2.4	–1.62	7	2,017	2,015.5	2,022.5
Madhya Pradesh (1)	3.55	3.3	–1.75	25	2,035	2,022.5	2,037.5
Rajasthan	3.6	3.2	–3.04	14	2,024	2,025.5	2,037.5
Uttarakhand (2)	0	2.2	na				
Uttar Pradesh (2)	4.2	3.6	–2.89	18	2,028	2,027.5	2,042.5
All EAG	3.6	3.1	–2.9	13	2,023		
India	2.9	2.6	–0.99	20	2,019	2,017.5	2,032.5
Southern States							
Andhra Pradesh	2	1.9	–1.50				

Cont'd...

...Cont'd

Kerala	1.7	1.8	0.59
Tamil Nadu	1.7	1.7	0.00
Karnataka	2.15	2	–1.40
All Southern States	1.9	1.8	–0.7

Notes: (1) Until 1998–99, Chhattisgarh was the part of the Madhya Pradesh. (2) Until 1998–99, Uttarakhand was the part of Uttar Pradesh. Therefore, the data used in this table are not based on the adjusted boundary changes.

Sources: Sample Registration System

under the ratio method applied to the low assumption of fertility by the UN (2011). In contrast, under the ratio approach applied to the medium projection of fertility by the UN (2011), India would attain the TFR 2.1 during 2030 to 2035.

On average, the projected years based on the geometric rate of change for India and EAG states (except Rajasthan) using the SRS data were intermediate between those derived by the ratio method applied to the low and medium assumptions of fertility projections by the UN. India would achieve the fertility decline at 2.1 between 2019 and 2033 over all three scenarios. In contrast, the EAG states would attain the TFR of 2.1 at much later dates, ranging from 2023 to 2043 under the medium assumption, and from 2015 to 2027 under the low assumption of fertility projections for India. Under the geometric rate of change in TFR from SRS, they would attain the target of fertility decline at 2.1 children per woman between 2017 and 2036 (Table 3).

Table 4

Comparison of the Projected Year to Achieve TFR at 2.1 by some Researchers and Institutions for India and some EAG States

Researchers and Organizations	*Methods and Data Sources*	*Projected Year*	*TFR*
	India		
Verma (2013)	Ratio method based on low assumption of fertility projection by the UN (2011)	2018	1.96
	Geometric rate of change in TFR from SRS from 2000–05 to 2006–10	2019	2.1
	Ratio method based on medium assumption of fertility projection by the UN (2011)	2033	2.06
Verma, Sinha and Sinha (2010)	Based on arithmetic rate of change in TFR for the two periods, 1998–99 and 2005–06 (NFHS II and III)	2028	2.1
Ram (2011)	Expert judgement supported by rationale	2023	2.3
	Using projections of fertility by others	2050	2.1
RGI (2007)	Using Bhat's approach	2021	2.1
PFI/PRB: Scenario A	Population Reference Bureau	2056–61	2.4
PFI/PRB: Scenario B	Regression method, SRS 1971–96, see Natarajan and Jayachandran (2001)	2036–41	2.41
USCB (2009)	United States Census Bureau, Logistic Curve, SRS data	2034	2.1

Cont'd ...

... Cont'd

Selected EAG states showing the projected year to achieve fertility at 2.1					
	Bihar	*Jharkhand*	*Madhya Pradesh*	*Rajasthan*	*Uttar Pradesh*
Bhat (2002b)	2021	2018	2025	2021	2027
Verma (2013)					
Ratio method: Low scenario based on UN fertility projection under low assumption	2027	2022	2022	2025	2027
Geometric method, SRS (Medium scenario)	2038	2029	2036	2029	2029
Ratio method: High scenario based on UN fertility projection under medium assumption	2043	2038	2040	2038	2043

Table 4 shows the comparison of projected year to achieve replacement level fertility by different institutions and researchers for India and EAG states. The projection by Bhat (2002b) based on the Gompertz curve using the historical data on TFR from 1975 to 1995 from the SRS for the large states, indicated that India will achieve TFR 2.1 in the year 2021. This estimate by Bhat was used by the Registrar General of India for population projections of India and states, 2006–2026. This was also used to validate the estimates of fertility by districts in India based on the 2011 Census of India by Guilmoto and other researchers (Narwal and Gram, 2013). In contrast to Bhat estimate, the projection of TFR by other researchers and institutions varied to a great extend ranging from 2019 (Verma, 2013) to 2059 (Population Foundation of India and Population Reference Bureau, Scenario A). However, the year projected by the ratio method applied to the low assumption of fertility by the UN (2011) for India and all EAG states except Bihar were similar to those projected by Bhat (2002b).

However, the selection of low scenario of the year for fertility decline at 2.1 based on the low assumption of fertility projection by the UN in future may go wrong under the current pace of economy of the country. The Indian economy in 2013 is characterized as slow growth, high inflation, risky government finance, and a trembling currency that is the worst performing in emerging markets (CNN, 2013). Under the same circumstances, the projected year of fertility decline by the geometric method using the SRS fertility data under the medium scenario may also go wrong, unless the initiatives for improvement for social and economic change proposed under the 12th Five-Year Plan would be implemented and monitored properly. Moreover, it is also known that compared with the national average and some southern states, the socio-economic indicators of the EAG states are much lower. Couples in these states start 'childbearing' early, complete childbearing late, have a large number of children within short interval and also desire a larger number of children, with strong preference for son. Female literacy rate is also low in these states. These EAG states would take longer time to narrow down the gap in these indicators such as high fertility rates, strong son's preference and low female literacy. Given the large population among EAG states, the development of these states will affect the overall progress of the nation. Therefore, it seems that there are so many uncertainties to take into account on the recent rate of change in TFR for EAG states.

Under the current socio-economic environment prevailing in the EAG states, it would be better to rely more on the scenario with the ratio-method applied to the medium scenario of fertility projected by the UN (2011) for India. In the next 22 years, it is expected that the fertility would be close to or under the replacement level for all EAG states except in Uttar Pradesh, Bihar and Madhya Pradesh.

Conclusions, Discussions and Suggestions

Fertility is declining in all the states in India. However, the pace of decline is relatively much slower in Uttar Pradesh, Bihar and other EAG states. Three scenarios of fertility decline in EAG states and India are developed to project the year to achieve the replacement level of fertility, 2.1 children per woman. The first scenario of the projected year is based on the geometric rate of change in fertility derived from the Sample Registration System over the period 2006–2010. The second and third scenarios are based on the average relative ratio of fertility for the EAG states to the nation over the period, 2006–2010, multiplying them with the low and medium assumptions of fertility for India projected by the UN (2011). It is observed that under the geometric rate of change in TFR from SRS data and the ratio method applied to the low assumption of fertility by the UN (2011), the total fertility rate in India would decline to 2.1 by 2017 or 2019. Similarly, according to both methods, all the EAG states would achieve their fertility at the replacement level in later years. In view of the slower socio-economic environment prevailing in the EAG states and India, it is suggested to take the scenario of the projected year of fertility at the replacement level based on the ratio-method applied to the medium projection of fertility by the UN (2011). According to this method, it is expected that India would achieve the fertility rate at 2.1 by 2032. The EAG states except Bihar, Madhya Pradesh and Uttar Pradesh would achieve it between 2022 and 2037. The projected years of fertility to be at 2.1 are much longer for Bihar, Uttar Pradesh in 2042 and Madhya Pradesh in 2039.

Discussions

This study supports that the future decline in TFR at 2.1 in these three states (Bihar, Uttar Pradesh and Madhya Pradesh) could be a distant dream as stated by Haub (2009). This could be due to slow changes in some determinants of fertility changes in these states (Verma et al., 2012b; Verma, Sinha and Sinha, 2010). Using data from the NFHS–II and NFHS–III, Verma, Sinha and Sinha (2010) have found that there was a minimal change in the prevalence of early marriages, teenage fertility and son preference over the seven years. Compared to the female sterilization, the spacing methods such as pill, IUD and condom were not popular in India. The prevalence of these three spacing methods in 2005–06, India was as low as 3.1 per cent, 1.7 per cent and 2.4 per cent respectively. In general, the change in female sterilization contributed considerably in reducing the fertility level, particularly in the high fertility states. However, the percentages of currently married women aged 15–44 using female sterilization based on the DLHS survey in 2007–2008 are considerably lower in Uttar Pradesh (16.5%) and Bihar ((25.0%), as compared to that of Andhra Pradesh (60.3%).

However, fertility change could be accelerated more in India and EAG states through: (1) lowering the prevailing high proportion of unmet need of family planning methods, (2) declining infant and child mortality, and (3) increasing female literacy. Some studies related to these three aspects are reviewed.

Unmet Need of Family Planning Methods

Data on the percentage of unmet need of family planning methods based on the DLHS I, II and III have indicated that in general, there were some changes in the proportion of unmet need of total family planning method among married women aged 15–49 over the periods 1998–99 to 2002–004. In India, total unmet need declined from 25.3 to 21.3 per cent and thereafter it remained almost constant at 21.3 per cent. A decline in the proportion of unmet need of total family planning method was observed for all EAG states over the periods, 1998–99 and 2002–04. During the period 2002–04 and 2007–08 the unmet need declined considerably in three EAG states only, Madhya Pradesh (21 to 19.3%), Rajasthan (21.8 to 17.9%) and Uttarakhand (26.9 to 20.8%). In contrast, the proportion of unmet need had gone up considerably in Odisha (19 to 24.0%). Among the southern states there had been a considerable decline in the proportion of unmet need for family planning. In Andhra Pradesh, during the period 2002–04 to 2007–08, unmet need declined from 11.7 to 6.5 per cent. It was also observed that the proportion of unmet need for spacing methods was higher than the limiting method.

As stated by Ram (2011), the higher proportion of unmet need of family in the high fertility states implies that the family planning programmes have not reached the poor, uneducated and others who need them most. People in these states still desire more than two children on average, due primarily to feelings of insecurity associated with the survival of their children.

Infant and Child Mortality Under 5 Years

Studies on mortality among infants and children under 5 years showed a reduction has occurred in the rates (Ram et al., 2013; Narwal and Gram, 2013). Ram et al. (2013) reported that 'at current rates of progress, MDG4 will be met by India around 2020, by the richer states around 2015 and by the poor states around 2023. Accelerated programme to reduce mortality during all the neonatal period and at ages 1–59 months is needed in most Indian districts. The results found large variation in mortality between 589 districts in India. Only about one-third of Indian districts are on track to achieve the UN Million Development Goal 4 of reducing under-5 mortality, while another third will only achieve it after 2020. This latter third is also home to 41 per cent of India's live births, but 56 per cent of all child deaths. Additionally, female mortality exceeded male mortality in nearly all states in India, totalling 74,000 excess girl deaths.

Another study by Narwal and Gram (2013) analysed the effect of National Health Rural Mission on the rate of reductions in Infant Mortality Rate in India and states. Their main findings are 'The infant mortality rate in rural India declined from 74 to 55/1,000 live births between 2000 and 2009, with AARR of 3.0 per cent (95% CI=2.6%–3.4%) and the urban-rural gap in infant mortality narrowed (p=0.036). However, there was no evidence (p=0.49) that AARR in rural India increased post-NRHM (3.4%, 95% CI 2.0–4.7%) compared to pre-NRHM (2.8%, 95% CI 2.1%–3.5%). States varied widely in rates of infant mortality reduction. Projections of infant mortality rates suggested that only eight states might be on track to help India achieve MDG4 by 2015. These eight states are: Dadar and Nager Haveli, Tamil Nadu, Maharashtra, Chhattisgarh, Uttarakhand, Jharkhand, Manipur and Daman & Diu. Thus, the risks of survival of infant and children under 5 years in India and some states are still a matter of concern, which may be one of the leading causes of high fertility in the EAG states. Consequently, based on the DLHS 2007–08, it is observed that the percentage of married women, aged 15–49 with two children who want no more children are relatively lower in Uttar Pradesh (56%) and Bihar (44%) than in West Bengal (80%).

Female Literacy

The literacy among females needs to be improved further. It is good to learn that more initiatives are planned to improve the health and education in India under the 12th Five-Year Plan by the Planning Commission of India.

Further Suggestions for Improvement

In order to improve the lagged situation of fertility decline among EAG states in India, it is suggested to pursue more monitoring and evaluation of services at the district level. Also, more care is needed to provide services of family planning, initiatives undertaken by Janani Suraksha Yojana (JSY) to reach poor, schedule and backward castes; and making more efforts to improve.

Uttar Pradesh, Bihar and Madhya Pradesh require some special attention for improvement. One could propose the improvement plan by identifying the problem at the districts level. For example, Kumari et al. (2013) has ranked the districts of the EAG states and Assam based on some demographic, health indicators. 46 per cent of districts in Uttar Pradesh and Bihar are underdeveloped. Similarly, the percentage of underdeveloped districts in Uttar Pradesh was found to be the highest, 53 per cent among all districts of the EAG states. More strong actions for improvement should be focused in these districts. It is good to find that under the 12th Five-year plan, the Planning commission of government of India has planned to identify and focus the development issues at the underdeveloped district level (Government of India, 2012). I hope, by the next thirty years, there will be no regional disparity in India with respect to fertility, and some socio-economic indicators. All states would feel to be inclusive of the development in India.

Acknowledgement

Thanks to the reviewer of this paper for providing some constructive suggestions and making editorial changes in the earlier draft.

References

Bajpai, N., J.D. Sachs and R.H. Dholakia. 2009. *Improving Access, Delivery and Efficiency of the Public Health System in Rural India: Mid-term Evaluation of the National Rural Health Mission*. New York: Center on Globalization and Substantial Development, The Earth Institute at Columbia University.

Bhat, P.N.M. 2002a. 'Completeness of India's Sample Registration System: An Assessment through General Growth Balance Method', *Population Studies*, 56(2): 119–113.

——. 2002b. India's Changing Dates with Replacement Fertility: A Review of Recent Fertility Trends and Future Prospects. Paper presented at the 'Expert Group Meeting on Completing the Future Fertility Transition', New York: United Nations Population Division, 376–391.

CNN. 2013. India's Economic Growth Slowest Since 2009. http://money.cnn.com.

Dyson, Tim. 2002. 'On the Future of Human Fertility in India', in *Completing the Fertility Transition*, United Nations, New York, USA, 392–408.

George, M.V. 2010. 'The Fertility Decline in India's Kerala State: A Unique Example of Below Replacement Fertility in a High Fertility Country', *Canadian Studies in Population*, 37(3–4): 563–609.

Government of India. 2002. National Population Policy 2000. New Delhi: Ministry of Health and Family Welfare.

——. 2011. Family Welfare Statistics in India. New Delhi: Ministry of Health and Family Welfare.

——. 2012. 12th Five-Year Plan, 2012–2017: Social Sectors. www.12thplan.gov.in.

Guilmoto, Christopher and Irudaya Rajan. 2013. *Fertility at District Level in India: Lessons from the 2011 Census*. Paris: Working Paper, Centre of Population and Development, IRD/CEPED.

Haub, Carl. 2009. *Fertility in India: Trends and Prospects*. Washington, D.C.: Population Reference Bureau.

Kumari, Anchala, Arun Kumar Sinha and Ravi B.P. Verma. 2013. 'Ranking of Districts of EAG States Using the Composite Index'. Presented at the IASSH Conference in Chennai, December 26–28.

Mahmood, Aslam and Amitabh Kundu. *Demographic Projections for India and States, 2001–2051: Regional Variations*. New Delhi: Jawaharlal Nehru University. http://nrip.iwmi.org.

Mathews, Z., Sabu S. Padmadas, Inge Hutter, Juiet McEachran, and James J. Brown. 2009. 'Does Early Childbearing and a Sterilization-focused Family Planning Programme in India Fuel Population Growth?', *Journal of Demographic Research*, 20(28): 693–720.

Moore, A., S. Singh, U. Ram, L. Remez and S. Audam. 2009. *Adolescent Marriage and Childbearing in India: Current Situation and Recent Trends*. New York: Guttmacher Institute.

Narwal, Rajesh and Lu Gram. 2013. 'Has the Rate of Reduction in Infant Mortality Increased in India Since the Launch of National Rural Health Mission? Analysis of Time Trends 2000–2009 with Projection to 2015', *International Journal of MCH and AIDS*, 2(1): 139–152.

Natarajan, K.S. and V. Jayachandran. 2000. *Population Growth in 21st Century, India*. New Delhi: Population Foundation of India.

Paul, Vinod Kumar, Harshpal Singh Sachdev, Dileep Mavalankar, Prema Ramachandran, Mari Jeeva Sankar, Nita Bhandari, Vishnubhatla Sreenivas, Thiagarajan Sundraraman, Dipti Govil, David Osrin and Betty Kirkwood. 2011. 'Reproductive Health, and Child Health and Nutrition in India: Meeting the Challenge', *The Lancet*, 377(9762): 332–349.

Ram, U., P. Jha, F. Ram, K. Kumar, S. Awasthi, A. Shet, J. Pader, S. Nansukusa and R. Kumar. 2013. 'Neonatal, 1–59 Month, and Under–5 Mortality in 597 Indian Districts, 2001 to 2012: Estimates from National Demographic and Mortality Surveys', *Lancet Global Health 2013*, 1(4): 219–226.

Ram, Bali. 2011. 'Fertility Decline and Family Change in India: A Demographic Perspective', *Journal of Comparative Family Studies*, 43: 11–40.

Registrar General and Census Commissioner of India. 2006. Population Projections for India and States, 2001–2026. Report of the Technical Group on Population Projections Constituted by the National Commission on Population, New Delhi.

Rutherford, R.D. and Vinod Mishra. 2001. An Evaluation of Recent Fertility Trends in India. National Health Survey Subject Report 19. Mumbai: International Institute for Population Sciences.

Sample Registration System. 2011. Maternal and Child Mortality and Total Fertility Rates. New Delhi: Registrar General of India, Government of India.

——. 2012. *Special Bulletin*, 47(2). New Delhi: Registrar General of India, Government of India.

United Nations (UN). 2011. *World Population Prospects: The 2010 Revision*. Department of Economic and Social Affairs, Population Division.

Verma, Ravi B.P. 2013. A Review of Fertility Trends and Maternal Health in India, 2000–2013. Presented at the conference of Indian Association of Social Sciences and Health held at SRM University in Chennai, December 26–28.

Verma, Ravi B.P., Arun K. Sinha and Dilip Kumar. 2012a. Fertility Projections for Selected Large States in India with Below Replacement Level, 2010–2100. Presented at the annual meeting of Canadian Population Society held at the Wilfred Laurier University and the University of Waterloo, Kitchener and Waterloo, May 30–June 1.

——. 2012b. High Fertility Trend and Maternal Health in India, 1999–2009. Presented at the conference on Bihar Foundation organized by Bihar Government in Patna, February.

Verma, Ravi B.P., Arun K. Sinha and Ravi R. Sinha. 2010. High Fertility Trend and Maternal Health in India, 1999–2009: A Review of Progress. Presented at the annual meeting of the Concordia University, Montreal, Quebec, Canada. Also presented at the conference on Bihar Foundation organized by Bihar Government in Patna, February 2012.

Verma, Ravi B.P., Arun K. Sinha, Dilip Kumar and Ravi R. Sinha. 2010. Medium Fertility Trend and Maternal Health in India, 1999–2009: A Review of Progress. Presented at the meeting of the 19th International Conference on Interdisciplinary Mathematical and Statistical Techniques held at Patna University, December 18–20.

4

Marriage and Age at First Birth among Women in EAG States of India

PRIYA BHAKAT

It is well known that natural population growth depends primarily on two factors, fertility and mortality. In some societies marriage defines the onset of the socially acceptable time for sexual activity and childbearing. As such, marriage is not only the most predominant context for childbearing but also one of the most important determinants of fertility (Bongaarts, 1983). The higher the age at marriage, the shorter is the reproductive span. In India, procreation starts only after marriage; the legal age at marriage for women is 18 years and for men is 21 years (Prohibition of Child Marriage Act, 2006). The marriage below this age is termed as child marriage and it is considered to be a violation of human rights (UNICEF, 2007). Getting married below the legal age is very common in the developing world, especially in India.

Worldwide, 70 million women aged 20–24 had been married before they reached age 18 (ICRW, 2012). According to ICRW report, more than 40 per cent of world's child marriage takes place in India. In India, the prevalence of marriage before the 18th birthday ranks 13th among the top 20 'hot spot' countries for child marriage, with 47 per cent of women marrying before the age of 18 (UNICEF, 2013). Early marriage is always associated with early childbearing. In many societies where reproduction is primarily confined within marriage, the changes in respect of marriage age and the resultant reduction in proportion of women remaining in married state are directly linked to fertility and thus, determine the future trend of demographic transition (Goswami, 2012). On an average, women who marry early will have a longer period of exposure to the risk of pregnancy, often leading to higher fertility. Thus, early marriage typically coincides with early pregnancy which poses great health risks for a young mother and for her infant.

According to NFHS–III survey, 47.3 per cent of women aged 20–24 were married by age 18. Of these, 2.6 per cent were married before they turned 13; 22.6 per cent were married before they were 16; and 44.5 per cent were married when they were between 16 and 17. The DLHS 3 report shows that Bihar has the lowest mean age at marriage followed by Rajasthan, Jharkhand, Uttar Pradesh and Madhya Pradesh. All these states come under the Empowered Action Group (EAG) states. The EAG states were created under the Ministry of Health and Family Welfare (MOHFW), especially to ensure population stabilization and intersect oral convergence.

The major objectives of this study are:

1. To map the spatial and temporal variation in age at marriage and age at first birth in EAG states of India.
2. Estimate the gap between mean age at marriage and age at first birth for females and assess the hazard ratio attributable to changes in socio-economic and demographic factors in EAG states.

Data Source and Methodology

The study utilizes data obtained from Census of India. Census doesn't provide data on age at first birth, so for further analysis National Family Health Survey (NFHS), District Level Health Survey (DLHS) and Annual Health Survey (AHS) data has been used.

Singulate Mean Age at Marriage (SMAM) propounded by Hajnal in 1953, has been calculated using data from Census 1961 to 2011. SMAM is the average length of single life expressed in years among those who marry before age 50. Cox Proportional Hazard Model has been applied to assess relationship between covariates and survival time (Age at Marriage and Age at First Birth). It deals with making inferences about event rates. The data from DLHS III has been utilized. The covariates considered were Age at Marriage for females and their Age at First Birth and independent variable was Current Age of respondent, Place of Residence, Religion and Caste of respondent, Highest Years of Schooling, Work Status, Husband's highest years of schooling, Wealth Index and

Contraceptive Prevalence. Descriptive statistics (mean and t test/f-test, bi-variate analysis) has also been applied. The data has been analysed through SPSS.

Results and Discussion

Temporal Trend

Table 1 shows the variation in SMAM for females in the EAG states of India. According to 1961 census, in Bihar, women used to remain single till age 14.3 which increased to 19.7 in 2011 census. In Madhya Pradesh, SMAM increased from 13.9 in 1961 census to 20.5 in 2011 census. Odisha recorded the highest SMAM and Rajasthan has the lowest among all the EAG states. Rajasthan and Uttar Pradesh have shown no changes in SMAM based on 2001–2011 census data. Except for Uttarakhand, the newly formed (formed in 2000) states – Chhattisgarh and Jharkhand have shown increase in SMAM over years.

Table 1

Temporal Variation of SMAM for EAG States (1961–2011)

States	*Singulate Mean Age at Marriage (Females)*								
	1961	*1971*	*1981*	*1991*	*NFHS 1*	*NFHS 2*	*2001*	*NFHS 3*	*2011*
Bihar	14.3	15.3	16.6	17.5	18.0	18.8	18.6	19.0	19.7
Chhattisgarh	–	–	–	–	–	–	20.1	20.3	21.3
Jharkhand	–	–	–	–	–	–	19.5	19.1	20.4
Madhya Pradesh	13.9	15.0	16.6	17.8	17.4	18.9	19.1	20.1	20.5
Odisha	16.4	17.3	19.1	20.2	20.7	21.2	21.7	21.3	22.0
Rajasthan	14.2	15.1	16.1	17.5	18.4	18.3	18.5	19.3	18.5
Uttarakhand	–	–	–	–	–	–	21.6	21.7	21.2
Uttar Pradesh	14.5	15.5	16.7	18.0	18.6	19.0	19.6	20.3	19.6

Source: Computed from Census and NFHS data.

Associated with the increasing trend in mean age at marriage for females another notable feature is indicated by the consequent increase in trend of age at first birth (Table 2). It must be noted that while there is an increase in age at marriage for all the EAG states, Rajasthan, Bihar and UP has shown a slight fall in mean age at first birth in different time periods. This explains the fact that in India there is an intense pressure on new brides to have a child shortly after marriage.

Table 2

Temporal Variation of Age at First Birth for EAG States

States	*Mean Age at First Birth*				
	NFHS 1 (1992–93)	*NFHS 2 (1998–99)*	*NFHS 3 (2005–06)*	*DLHS 3 (2007–08)*	*AHS (2010–11)*
Bihar	18.8	18.8	18.5	19.3	21.5
Chhattisgarh	–	–	18.6	19.3	21.5
Jharkhand	–	–	18.4	20.8	21.6
Madhya Pradesh	18.9	18.5	19.4	19.5	21.5
Odisha	18.8	19.1	19.6	21.2	22.8
Rajasthan	20.3	19.5	19.1	19.9	21.7
Uttarakhand	–	–	20.0	21.7	22.2
Uttar Pradesh	19.6	19.0	19.1	20.6	21.9

Source: National Family Health Survey, District Level Health Survey, Annual Health Survey.

Spatial Variation

The AHS data estimates reveal that the mean age at marriage for females vary from as low as 16.8 years in Bhilwara district of Rajasthan to as high as 24.0 years in Jagatsinghapur district of Odisha. A clear view of map suggests that a significant number of districts are characterized by mean age at marriage of 18–20 years. Three districts of Bihar (Gaya, Nawada and Jamui) and one of Rajasthan (Bhilwara) has shown mean age at marriage of females below 18 years. Among the districts which recorded highest level of mean age at marriage for females above 23 years includes Kendrapara, Puri, Cuttack and Jagatsinghapur of Odisha and Dehradun of Uttarakhand.

Marriages among females below legal age vary from 3 per cent in Uttarakhand to 21.9 per cent in Rajasthan. It is as low as 0.5 per cent in Jagatsinghapur district of Odisha to as high as 53.9 per cent in Bhilwara district of Rajasthan. The traditional problem of marrying the daughters before the legal age of 18 years is still quite significant in districts of Rajasthan, Bihar, Jharkhand, Madhya Pradesh and UP. A total of 14 districts, seven of each in Rajasthan and Bihar have shown above 30 per cent of women marrying below legal age.

Figure 1

Mean Age at Marriage (Female) 2010–11 (EAG States)

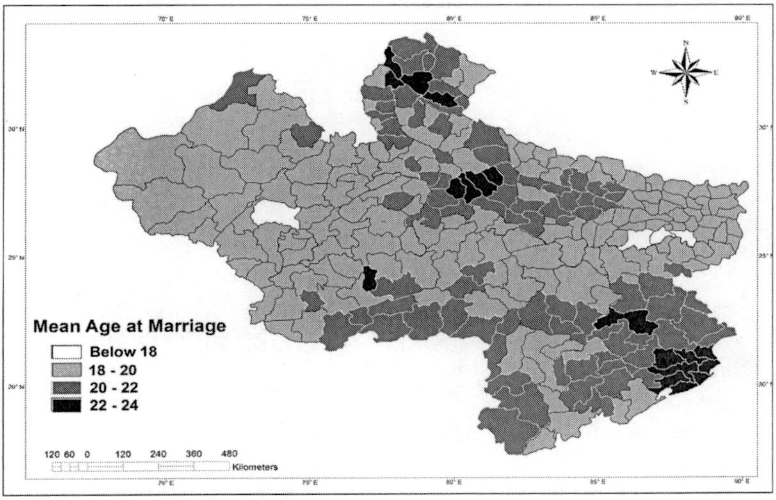

Source: Annual Health Survey 2010–11.

Figure 2

Marriage Among Females below Legal Age (18 Years) 2010–11 (EAG States)

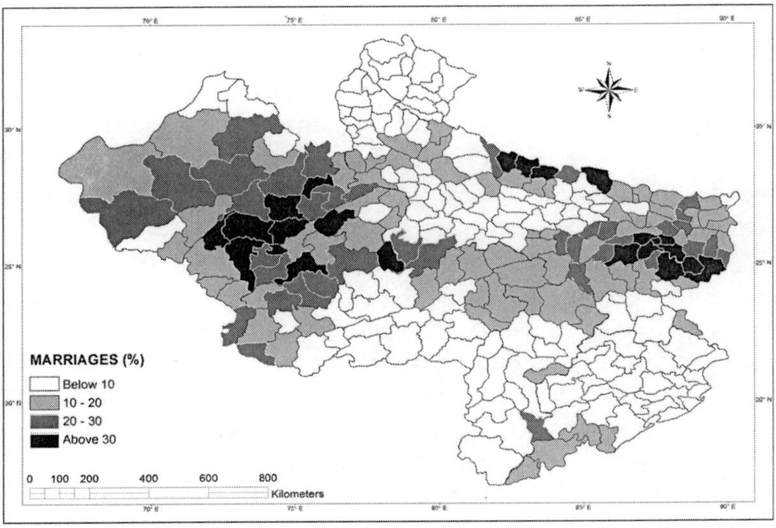

Source: Annual Health Survey 2010–11.

Figure 3

Currently Married Women Age 20–24 Years Married before Legal Age (18 Years) 2010–11 (EAG States)

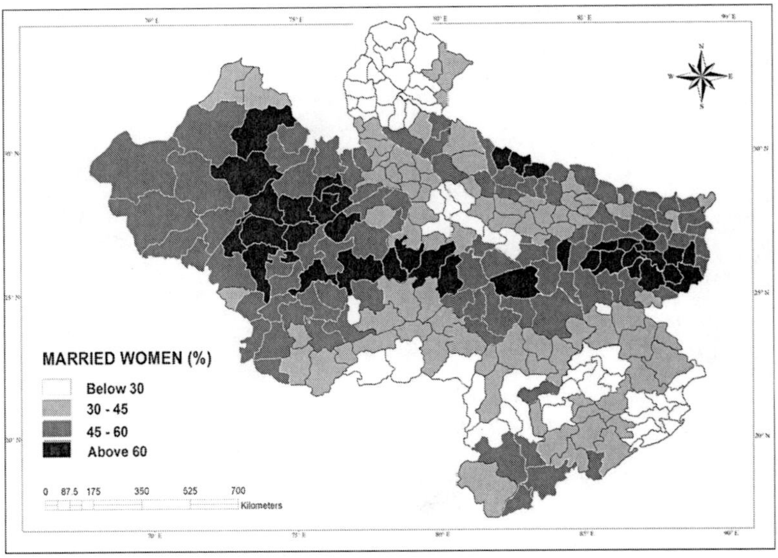

Source: Annual Health Survey 2010–11.

A comparison of the Figures 2 and 3 clearly indicates that there was decline in the percentage of women marrying below the legal age. Almost 57 per cent of currently married woman aged 20–24 in Rajasthan, 55 per cent in Bihar, 48 per cent in Madhya Pradesh, 39 per cent in Uttar Pradesh, 31 per cent in Odisha and 25 per cent in Uttaranchal got married before the legal age of 18 years.

Teenage pregnancy and motherhood is an important subject in societies where the marriage of girls takes place at very early age. The age at which a woman first engages in sexual intercourse after marriage usually marks the beginning of her exposure to child-bearing. In India, women (particularly young women) virtually have very limited role in making reproductive decisions. The highest median age of first live birth is 22.8 in Odisha. The lowest is recorded in Bihar. The median age at first birth among women aged 15–49 years varied from 20 years in Bharwani district of Madhya Pradesh to 24.7 years in Jagatsinghapur district of Odisha.

Figure 4

Median Age at First Live Birth of Women Aged 15–49 Years 2010–11 (EAG States)

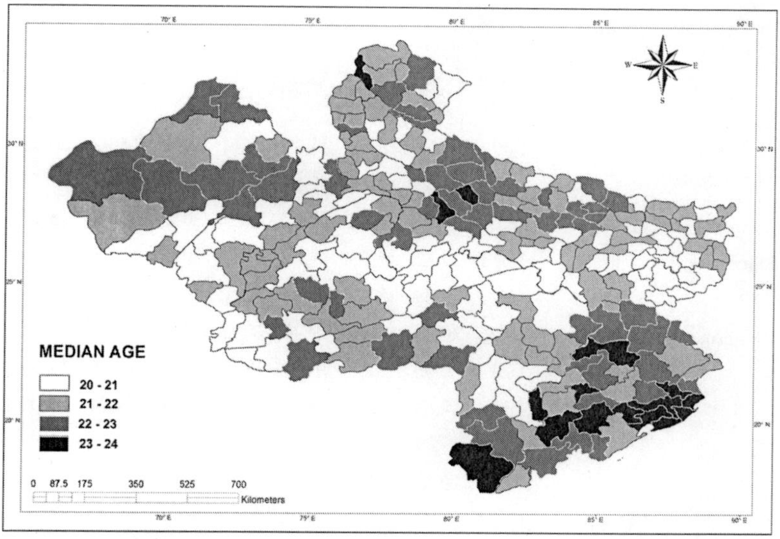

Source: Annual Health Survey 2010–11.

Mean Age at Marriage and First Birth

Married women of current age group 15–24 shows higher mean age at marriage than other age groups. However, Table 3 shows that women of current age group 35–49 show larger gap between age at marriage and first birth compared to women of present age 15–24. Women marrying at a younger age are expected to have longer first birth interval not only due to physiology, but also due to delayed cohabitation and lower sexual frequency (Dommaraju, 2009). The mean age at female marriage for Hindus and Muslims were nearly similar and varied from 15 years in Rajasthan to 19 years in Uttarakhand, whereas it is comparatively high in other religions in all the EAG states. The females from Scheduled Caste have shown lower mean age at marriage followed by Scheduled Tribes. It is significantly low in Bihar, Uttar Pradesh, Rajasthan and Madhya Pradesh. Higher proportions of SC females have become mothers by the age of 19 years. Several studies reported that female education has a strong effect in changing age at marriage than male education. The present study also showed that there has been a rise in age at

Table 3

Mean Age at Marriage and First Birth by Background Variables for EAG States of India

Independent Variables	Category	Odisha		Jharkhand		Bihar		Uttarakhand	
		Marri-age	Birth	Marri-age	Birth	Marri-age	Birth	Marri-age	Birth
Current Age of respondent	15 – 24	18.78	20.44	18.64	20.29	18.80	19.81	15.92	20.54
	25 – 34	18.69	20.47	17.25	19.55	18.94	20.78	15.82	19.72
	35 – 49	18.08	19.91	17.40	20.33	18.30	20.87	15.64	18.93
Place of residence	Rural	18.14	20.12	16.93	19.44	18.43	20.54	15.38	19.80
	Urban	19.08	20.78	18.47	20.42	19.67	21.41	17.37	20.44
Religion	Hindu	18.26	20.23	16.90	19.48	18.64	20.71	15.67	19.91
	Muslim	18.32	20.00	16.83	19.09	18.31	20.22	16.36	19.88
	Others	18.14	19.69	18.10	20.15	20.31	22.09	18.84	21.09
Caste	SC	17.74	19.71	16.63	19.18	17.76	19.75	15.43	19.67
	ST	17.47	19.39	17.81	19.99	17.78	19.83	15.04	19.67
	General & Others	18.88	20.22	17.87	19.44	18.90	20.97	16.04	20.06
Highest years of schooling	No schooling	17.12	19.01	12.5	15.7	–	–	15.24	20.56
	Primary	18.43	20.35	17.27	19.49	18.46	20.45	16.54	19.88
	Secondary	21.16	22.68	19.28	21.06	20.05	22.15	19.13	21.49
	Higher	24.83	26.22	–	–	22.75	24.09	22.86	24.00
Work Status	Not Working	18.64	20.77	17.45	19.87	19.83	21.14	19.47	21.65
	Working	20.24	21.60	18.35	20.11	21.44	22.42	19.85	21.84
Husbands Highest year of schooling	No schooling	17.20	19.20	17.33	20.00	–	–	15.12	19.87
	Primary	18.07	20.09	16.89	19.34	18.06	20.24	16.52	19.68
	Secondary	20.08	21.70	17.96	20.08	19.38	21.28	17.00	20.37
	Higher	20.59	21.89	18.44	19.97	20.59	22.53	17.71	20.12
Wealth Index	Poor	17.65	19.72	16.94	19.48	17.60	20.03	14.98	19.80
	Middle	18.55	20.42	16.85	19.28	18.10	20.35	15.27	19.70
	Rich	19.64	21.33	18.16	20.18	19.09	20.99	16.92	20.21

(continued form facing page)

Uttar Pradesh		*Rajasthan*		*Madhya Pradesh*		*Chhattisgarh*	
Marri-age	*Birth*	*Marri-age*	*Birth*	*Marri-age*	*Birth*	*Marri-age*	*Birth*
16.48	18.75	16.97	19.50	16.23	18.55	17.58	19.81
16.34	19.61	16.81	19.43	16.00	19.63	16.40	19.38
15.45	19.74	15.93	18.61	15.12	20.24	15.78	19.20
15.55	19.25	16.21	19.09	15.31	19.51	15.09	19.21
17.66	20.38	18.02	20.32	17.78	20.32	16.77	19.77
15.92	19.47	16.39	19.22	16.50	19.65	17.07	19.27
17.51	19.77	17.75	19.75	16.86	19.57	16.03	19.17
19.47	21.56	20.09	21.89	19.35	21.28	17.87	20.45
15.38	19.20	16.04	18.96	14.84	19.25	15.37	18.80
15.90	19.00	16.69	19.30	15.40	19.02	15.34	19.01
16.24	19.78	16.77	19.38	16.97	19.76	16.47	19.39
15.31	18.83	15.20	17.22	15.42	19.41	15.05	19.07
16.55	19.54	17.03	19.40	16.43	19.71	15.89	19.36
19.78	21.87	20.75	22.48	18.97	21.41	18.0	20.71
23.69	24.93	22.04	23.72	23.29	25.92	18.86	20.65
19.66	21.38	19.39	21.67	18.73	20.46	17.33	19.02
20.13	22.65	20.87	22.73	20.31	21.76	18.03	19.41
15.77	19.76	14.07	17.67	15.05	19.63	15.88	18.51
15.75	19.29	16.24	19.05	15.45	19.40	16.00	19.04
17.46	20.41	18.41	20.61	16.82	20.33	17.27	19.89
18.21	20.53	18.58	19.87	18.46	20.16	–	–
15.31	19.10	16.02	18.98	15.57	19.20	16.71	19.02
15.68	19.37	16.23	19.06	15.37	19.43	16.51	19.36
17.45	20.29	18.18	20.45	17.10	20.22	18.12	20.14

Source: Computed from District Level Health Survey (2007–08) data.

marriage with increase in husband's education but the change is very modest. Mean age at marriage and first birth was comparatively high in Uttarakhand among working women. Unlike all other states Rajasthan, Bihar and Jharkhand had shown almost similar mean age at marriage and first birth for both working and non-working women. Poverty is considered as the one of the most important causes behind early marriage (Ghosh, 2011). Among the poor section, the mean age at marriage among girls was below 18 years in all the EAG states. It varied from 14.9 in Rajasthan to 17.7 in Odisha. Interestingly, the mean age at marriage among the rich section was also below legal age for Rajasthan (16.9), Madhya Pradesh (17.5) and Uttar Pradesh (17.1). The fact that early marriage is practised among the financially secured family indicates that poverty is not always the dominant factor and that cultural traditions can be a strong influence.

Hazard Ratio Analysis for Age at Marriage

This section includes the result of survival analysis of age at marriage (Table 4) for the eight EAG states of India. It is found that the risk of getting married at an early age differs not only among the states but also among the age groups. In Odisha, Chhattisgarh, UP and Uttarakhand women of age group 15–24 are at lower risk of getting married at an early age, compared to women in age group 35–49. However, in Madhya Pradesh and Rajasthan, the risk was greater among women in the age group 15–24. It highlights the conservative nature of the state that still values long held beliefs and attitudes. Over years the mean age at marriage has been advancing in both rural as well as in urban areas. It is observed that women in urban areas are witnessing late marriages compared to their rural counterparts in all the EAG states of India. In Bihar, Madhya Pradesh and UP, Muslim women are at a higher risk of getting married before legal age. Hindu women are more likely to get married early in Jharkhand and Odisha. Age at marriage also varied across different castes. Results shows that in Bihar, Jharkhand and Uttar Pradesh, the general and other castes were at a higher risk of getting married at an early age compared to Scheduled Castes and Scheduled Tribes. Scheduled Tribes have a different living style and norms which are less guided by the preoccupations with sexual purity. However, it is found that STs in Madhya Pradesh, Chhattisgarh, Rajasthan and Uttarakhand were at a higher risk of

Table 4

Hazard Ratio of Age at Marriage for EAG States of India

Independent Variables	*Category*	*Bihar*	*Jharkhand*	*Madhya Pradesh*	*Chhattisgarh*	*Odisha*	*Rajasthan*	*Uttar Pradesh*	*Uttaranchal*
Age (35–49®)	25–34	1.513	0.162**	0.138***	1.024	0.187**	0.956*	1.413**	0.054***
	15–24	1.763	1.845	1.414*	0.384*	0.151	1.875*	0.703***	0.114**
Residence (Rural®)	Urban	0.851**	0.861*	0.854*	0.911	1.069	0.930**	0.735***	0.941
Religion (Hindu®)	Muslim	1.768***	0.872***	1.750**	0.816	0.954	0.951*	1.691**	0.927
	Others	0.881	0.797***	0.546***	0.328***	0.946	0.667***	0.246***	0.907
Caste (General & Others®)	SC	0.976	0.949	0.968	1.039*	1.107*	0.984	0.912	1.327
	ST	0.901	0.809	1.899**	1.832***	0.875***	1.111***	0.738*	1.804*
Schooling (No schooling®)	Primary	0.884	0.609	0.508**	0.577	0.744**	0.615*	0.719***	0.321***
	Secondary	0.544***	0.344	0.202***	0.172***	0.220***	0.316***	0.364***	0.079*
	Higher	0.759	–	0.174**	0.130**	0.158*	0.259***	0.003***	0.145
Work (No®)	Working	1.819	1.256	0.562	0.350	0.054**	1.508	0.473	0.038**
Husband Schooling (No schooling®)	Primary	0.969	1.521	0.874	1.165	0.768	1.583	0.949	1.323
	Secondary	0.967	1.584	0.812	0.937	0.654*	1.490	0.932	1.579
	Higher	–	1.193	0.811	1.050	0.659	1.993	0.665	1.266
Wealth (poor®)	Middle	0.986**	1.015*	1.035	1.012	0.954	1.001	0.993*	1.260**
	Rich	0.992*	1.124**	1.009	0.005	1.015	1.013	0.904***	1.229**

Source: Computed from District Level Health Survey (2007–08) data.

Note: (1) ® is the reference category. (2) *** is the coefficient which is significant at one per cent level of significance. (3) ** is the coefficient which is significant at five per cent level of significance. (4) * is the coefficient which is significant at ten per cent level of significance.

marrying early compared to others. The hazard ratio has shown significant decline in early marriage with an increase in highest years of schooling among women. It is found that working women are more likely to delay their marriage compared to that of non-working women. However, Rajasthan showed that working women are at higher risk of getting married early compared to that of non-working women. It can be said that traditional values surpass economic reasons and parents feel more secure when their daughters are married.

Poverty is one of the major factors underpinning early age at marriage. In Bihar and UP, hazard ratios show that women from poor section were at a higher risk of marrying at an early age compared to the women in rich section of the society. In Jharkhand and Uttarakhand, women from rich and middle income group were more likely to get married at an early age compared to the poor section. Increased wedding expenses and dowry associated with a daughter's marriage sometimes lead to postponement of marriage as parents are unable to accumulate resources and financial support in order to provide appropriate dowry and pay for the wedding (Caldwell et al., 1983; Schlegel, 1993).

Hazard Ratio Analysis for Age at First Birth

Marriage is the normative proxy for exposure to the risk of fertility. Postponement of first birth can make an important contribution to overall fertility decline. In India, the transition from wife to mother usually occurs about two years after marriage, as young couples are expected to have their first child soon after starting their life together. Unplanned childbearing among adolescents is not uncommon. Table 5 shows that in Bihar and Jharkhand, women in younger and middle ages are at a higher risk of giving birth at an early age compared to the women in older age group, whereas it is just the opposite in Uttar Pradesh and Madhya Pradesh. Urban women are at a lower risk of birth at an early age compared to the rural ones in Uttar Pradesh. In Bihar and Uttarakhand, women in urban areas are more likely to have early childbirth compared to rural areas. In some cases, the first birth in rural India might be delayed because of temporary separation of the partners as of social customs of *Gauna*.[1] The coefficient suggests that Muslim women are at a higher risk of having their first child at an early age. In general, polygamy associated with low level of contraceptive usage leads to

Table 5

Hazard Ratio of Age at First Birth for EAG States of India

Independent variables	*Category*	*Bihar*	*Jharkhand*	*Madhya Pradesh*	*Chhattisgarh*	*Odisha*	*Rajasthan*	*Uttar Pradesh*	*Uttarakhand*
Age (35–49®)	25–34	1.706	1.854**	0.065*	0.768	0.641	0.759	0.854*	0.775
	15–24	1.610*	1.153*	0.014*	0.225	0.526	0.212	0.384	0.632**
Residence (Rural®)	Urban	1.024*	0.969	0.965	1.077	0.989	1.102	0.830**	1.455*
Religion (Hindu®)	Muslim	1.068**	0.861	1.183*	0.913	1.198*	0.842	1.995**	1.062
	Others	0.933***	0.956	0.898	0.332*	0.954	0.828	0.264**	0.867
Caste (General & Others®)	SC	0.860	0.821	0.843*	1.117	1.159*	1.095*	0.992	1.177
	ST	1.333	1.761**	1.023	1.020	0.916	1.202	0.760	1.825***
Schooling (No schooling®)	Primary	1.636	0.910**	0.399	0.982***	0.688	0.463***	0.796	0.934***
	Secondary	0.794	0.517***	0.122***	0.213***	0.257***	0.346***	0.308*	0.365***
	Higher	1.099	–	0.109***	1.373	0.299***	0.934*	0.014	0.228
Work (No®)	Working	1.020	1.153	0.446	0.375	0.153	1.463	0.821*	0.652**
Husband Schooling (No schooling®)	Primary	0.317*	0.841	0.785**	0.923	0.506	1.443*	1.515	0.758
	Secondary	0.350*	0.470	1.737	2.287	0.428	1.313*	1.611	0.881***
	Higher	–	0.724	1.486	1.165	0.315	1.112	1.110	1.115
KAP-GAP (Yes®)	No	1.018	1.314***	1.530**	1.400***	1.134	1.129	1.265***	1.836
Wealth (poor®)	Middle	0.888	1.138	1.126	0.991	1.136	1.125	1.097	1.017
	Rich	0.829	1.039	1.144	0.905	0.951	1.137	0.943*	1.504

Source: Computed from District Level Health Survey (2007–08) data

Note: (1) ® is the reference category. (2) *** is the coefficient which is significant at one per cent level of significance. (3) ** is the coefficient which is significant at five per cent level of significance. (4) * is the coefficient which is significant at ten per cent level of significance.

early birth and high fertility (Rustagi et al., 2010). Scheduled Castes and Scheduled Tribes are more likely to give birth at an early age compared to General and Other Castes in all the states except Odisha and Rajasthan. Female education lowers the risk of early marriage and early age at first birth (Goswami, 2012). Programmes to keep girls in school hold promise for decreasing early marriages; since childbearing outside marriage is rare, delays in age at marriage will go a long way toward reducing adolescent childbearing (Moore et al., 2009). The significant values clearly indicate the effect of education on age at first birth in all the states. Even women who are employed prefer to have their first childbirth after attaining stability in their professional life (Loughran and Zissimopoulos, 2009; Miller, 2011; Chandler et al., 1994: Blackburn et al., 1993; Taniguchi, 1999). In Odisha working women are 0.153 times less likely to give birth at an early age. Although husband's education is not a very significant factor but it is also one of the positive influential factor in delaying marriage and first child birth in Odisha.

Early marriage is associated with reduced level of autonomy and self-efficacy. The use of contraceptive in order to delay first pregnancy is far less prevalent among those who married early compared to those who married late (UNFPA, 2012). In addition, young women married early are at a higher risk of miscarriage or stillbirth. Wealth Index states that women from rich background are less likely to give birth at an early age compared to women in poor section. Adolescent-specific reproductive health services continue to be scarce and inadequate. However, the government's recent enactment of policies to address the information and service needs towards married and unmarried adolescents is encouraging.

Conclusion

Despite prohibition of child marriage as enacted in Child Marriage Restraint Act of 1929, marriages of minors still occur, particularly among illiterate and from rural areas. This paper shows that child marriage and early childbearing is an accepted cultural practice and is practised widely in all the EAG states of India, specifically in rural areas. Rajasthan and Bihar have shown the lowest age at marriage for females. Overall literacy rate and even female literacy rate is high in Odisha and Uttaranchal compared to other EAG states and once education is controlled, women in Rajasthan and Bihar would also behave similarly to the women in Odisha and Uttaranchal. Age at marriage and age at First Birth based on Religion, Caste, and Wealth Index has shown varied results for different states. Insufficient knowledge and lack of access to contraception is an important underlying factor for early birth among women in EAG states.

Given the severity of child marriage and early childbearing, Government of India has adopted several policies to combat this practice. Some of them are National Population Policy (2000), National Policy for the Empowerment of Women (2001), National Plan of Action for Children (2005) and Prohibition of Child Marriage Act (2006). National and State level cash incentive schemes such as Balika Samridhi Yojana[2] and Janani Suraksha Yojana[3] to discourage child marriage and early child bearing is very common in India. However, the social system still encourages child marriage and early childbearing. Lack of birth certificates among girls curbs the right to refuse to marry even when they are younger than the legal age of marriage. A strict policy should be adopted to prevent teenage girls from being forced into marriage and early motherhood. This will help India in reducing maternal and infant mortality rates and also in stabilizing its population. There is general lack of knowledge and awareness of laws among Indian women which generally stems from illiteracy (Sagade, 2005). Along with government initiatives, consensus of all section of the society is also needed for eradicating the problem of child marriage from its root, which is possible only when there is nearly 100 per cent literacy.

Notes

1. *Gauna* is a north Indian custom and the ceremony associated with the consummation of marriage. It is associated with the custom of child marriage. The ceremony takes place several years after marriage. Before the ceremony the bride stays at her natal home.
2. Balika Samridhi Yojana was launched by Government of India w.e.f. 15–8–97.
3. Janani Suraksha Yojana was launched on 12th April 2005, by the honourable Prime Minister, implemented in all states and UTs with special focus on low performing states.

References

Agyei, W.K.A. and J. Mbamanya. 1989. 'Determinants of Cumulative Fertility in Kenya', *Journal of Biosocial Science*, 21(2): 135–144.

Axinn, W.G. and A. Thornton. 1996. 'The Influence of Parents' Marital Dissolution on Children's Attitudes Toward Family Formation', *Demography*, 33: 66–81.

Becker, G.S. 1991. *A Treatise on the Family*, Enlarged Edition. Cambridge: Harvard University Press.

Bernardi, L. 2003. 'Channels of Social Influence on Reproduction', *Population Research and Policy Review*, 22(5–6): 427–555.

Blackburn, M.L., D.E. Bloom and D. Neumark. 1993. 'Fertility Timing, Wages, and Human Capital', *Journal of Population Economics*, 6(1): 1–30.

Bongaarts, J. 1983. 'The Proximate Determinants of Natural Fertility', *Population Development Review*, 2: 105.

Bumpass, L.L. and J.A. Sweet. 1972. 'Differentials in Marital Stability', *American Sociological Review*, 37: 754–766.

Caldwell, J.C., P. Caldwell, B.K. Caldwell and I. Pieris. 1998. 'The Construction of Adolescence in a Changing World: Implications for Sexuality, Reproduction, and Marriage', *Studies in Family Planning*, 29: 137–153.

Caldwell, J.C., P.H. Reddy and P. Caldwell. 1983. 'The Causes of Marriage Change in South India', *Population Studies*, 37: 343–361.

Casterline, J.B., L. Williams and P. McDonald. 1986. 'The Age Difference between Spouses: Variations in Developing Countries', *Population Studies*, 40(3): 353–374.

Chandler, T.D., Y. Kamo and J.D. Werbel. 1994. 'Do Delays in Marriage and Childbirth Affect Earnings?', *Social Science Quarterly*, 75(4): 838–853.

Choe, M.K., S. Thapa and V. Mishra. 2005. 'Early Marriage and Early Motherhood in Nepal', *Journal of Biosocial Science*, 37(2): 143–162.

Coale, A. 1989. 'Marriage and Childbearing in China Since 1940', *Social Forces*, 67(4): 833–850.

Davis, K. 1955. 'Institutional Patterns Favoring High Fertility in Underdeveloped Areas', *Eugenics Quarterly*, 2: 33–39.

Desai, S. and L. Andrist. 2010. 'Gender Scripts and Age at Marriage in India', *Demography*, 47(3): 667–687.

Dommaraju, P. 2009. 'Timing of First Birth in India', *Genus*, 65(1): 81–101.

Feng, W. and Y. Quanhe. 1996. 'Age at Marriage and the First Birth Interval: The Emerging Change in Sexual Behavior among Young Couples in China', *Population and Development*, 22(2): 299–320.

Geraldine, R.C. 2008. 'Before She's Ready 15 Places Girls Marry by 15', *World Vision*.

Ghosh, B. 2011. 'Child Marriage, Society and the Law: A Study in a Rural Context in West Bengal, India', *International Journal of Law, Policy and the Family*, 25(2): 199–219.

Goldman, N. 1981. 'Dissolution of First Unions in Colombia, Panama and Peru', *Demography*, 18: 659–680.

Goswami, B. 2012. An Investigation into the Pattern of Delayed Marriage in India. Working Paper 275, The Institute for Social and Economic Change, Bengaluru.

International Center for Research on Women (ICRW). 2012. Child Marriage Fact and Figures. Retrieved from http://www.icrw.org/child-marriage-facts-and-figures.

International Institute for Population Sciences (IIPS) and Macro International. 2007. *National Family Health Survey (NFHS–3), India, 2005–06*. Mumbai: IIPS.

International Institute for Population Sciences (IIPS) and ORC Macro. 2000. *National Family Health Survey (NFHS–2), India, 1998–99*. Mumbai: IIPS.

Islam, M.M. and M. Mahmud. 1996. 'Marriage Patterns and Some Issues Related to Adolescent Marriage in Bangladesh', *Asia-Pacific Population Journal*, 11(3): 27–42.

Jejeebhoy, S. and S.S. Halli. 2005. 'Marriage Patterns in Rural India: Influence of Socio-cultural Context', in C.B. Lloyd, J.R. Behrman, N.P. Stromquist and B. Cohen (eds), *The Changing Transitions to Adulthood in Developing Countries: Selected Studies*. Washington, D.C.: National Academies Press, National Research Council, 172–199.

Kapadia, K. 1966. *Marriage and Family in India*. Bombay: Oxford University Press.

Loughran, D.S. and J.M. Zissimopoulos. 2009. 'Why Wait? The Effect of Marriage and Childbearing on the Wages of Men and Women', *Journal of Human Resources*, 44(2): 326–349.

Marini, M.M. 1978. 'The Transition to Adulthood: Sex Differences in Educational Attainment and Age at Marriage', *American Sociological Review*, 43: 483–507.

McDonald, P., L. Ruzicka and J. Caldwell. 1980. Interrelations between Nuptiality and Fertility: Evidence from the World Fertility Survey. World Fertility Conference, London, 77–137.

Miller, A.R. 2011. 'The Effects of Motherhood Timing on Career Path', *Journal of Population Economics*, 24(3): 1071–1100.

Moore, A.M., S. Singh, U. Ram, L. Remez and S. Audam. 2009. *Adolescent Marriage and Childbearing in India: Current Situation and Recent Trends*. New York: Guttmacher Institute.

Nanda, P., S. Kapoor, S. Mukherjee, M. Hersh, S. Basu and R. Bhargava. 2011. Delaying Marriage for Girls in India: Formative Research to Design Interventions for Changing Norms. International Centre for Research on Women, Report to UNICEF.

Prohibition of Child Marriage Act 2006. Ministry of Law and Justice, New Delhi.

Reneflot, A. 2006. 'A Gender Perspective on Preferences for Marriage among Cohabiting Couples', *Demographic Research*, 15: 311–328.

Rustagi, N., D.K. Taneja, R. Kaur and G.K. Ingle. 2010. 'Factors Affecting Contraception among Women in a Minority Community in Delhi: A Qualitative Study', *Health and Population: Perspectives and Issues*, 33(1): 10–15.

Sagade, J. 2005. *Child Marriage in India: Socio-legal and Human Rights Dimensions*. New Delhi: Oxford University Press.

Santhya, K.G., U. Ram, R. Acharya, S.J. Jejeeboy, F. Ram and A. Singh. 2010. 'Associations between Early Marriage and Young Women's Marital and Reproductive Health Outcomes: Evidence from India', *International Perspectives on Sexual and Reproductive Health*, 36(3): 132–139.

Schlegel, A. 1993. 'Dowry: Who Competes for What?', *American Anthropologist*, 95: 155–57.

Sheela, J. and N. Audinarayana. 2009. 'Determinants of Female Age at First Marriage in Tamil Nadu: An Analysis of NFHS Data', *The Journal of Family Welfare*, 46(2): 25–32.

Singh, S.N. 1989. 'Age of Females at Effective Marriage in Rural Areas of Eastern Uttar Pradesh', in S.N. Singh, M.K. Premi, P.S. Bhatia and A. Bose (eds), *Population Transition in India*. Delhi: B.R. Publishing Corporation, 81–88.

South, S.J. 2001. 'The Variable Effects of Family Background on the Timing of First Marriage: United States, 1969–93', *Social Science Research*, 30: 606–626.

Taniguchi, H. 1999. 'The Timing of Childbearing and Women's Wages', *Journal of Marriage and the Family*, 61(4): 1008–1019.

UNFPA. 2012. *Marrying Too Young: End Child Marriage*. New York.

UNICEF. 2007. *Gender, Rights and Civic Engagement Section: Division of Policy and Practice*. New York.

——. 2013. *Ending Child Marriage: Progress and Prospects*. New York.

5

Factors Affecting Induced Abortion in India and Uttar Pradesh

Findings from DLHS–3

SHEWLI SHABNAM

With the growing concern for reproductive health of women, the study of abortion phenomena has drawn serious attention of the researchers and policy-makers worldwide (Mishra et al., 1997). Abortion is defined as termination of pregnancy before the foetus has become viable, i.e. capable of living independently (Park, 2009). A foetus is assumed to be viable after 28 weeks of pregnancy. An abortion may occur spontaneously in the course of pregnancy (miscarriage or spontaneous abortion) or it can take place due to deliberate outside intervention (induced abortion) (IIPS, 2007). Induced abortions may be safe or unsafe. Unsafe abortion is a procedure for terminating an unintended pregnancy carried out either by persons lacking the necessary skills or in an environment that does not conform to minimal medical standards or both (AGI, 1999). An estimated 2.1 million unsafe abortions took place worldwide in 2008, almost all in developing countries, and deaths due to unsafe abortion remained close to 13 per cent of all maternal deaths of that year (WHO, 2011). The high incidence of unsafe abortions in developing countries presents a severe public health crisis since they lead to deaths, serious health complications and long-term disabilities of women that place an enormous burden on the family and the country's health care system. Abortions that occur outside legal framework are usually unsafe, as they are frequently performed by unskilled providers in unhygienic conditions and involve dangerous methods. Even if it is performed by a qualified doctor, a clandestine abortion (outside the condition of law) carries additional risk for women, as medical back up may not be immediately available in an emergency situation or women may not receive appropriate post-abortion care if complications occur (Singh et al., 2009). Therefore, the women's organizations have long been advocated for making abortion legal and accessible to all women in need.

Among the developing nations, India became the first country to legalize induced abortion under the Medical Termination of Pregnancy (MTP) Act, 1971 (which came into effect from April1, 1972). Besides medical, eugenic, socio-economic and humanitarian ground, this act specified contraceptive failure as a legitimate ground for abortion, thus legalizing abortion on demand. Yet, since 1972, the proportion of women seeking abortion from unauthorized sources has not declined (Mohan and Goyal, 2000). There are many reasons for it. Three decades after legalization, in India, two safe abortions are performed for every three unsafe ones simply because most abortion clinics are located in urban centres while 70 per cent of Indian women live in a rural setting (Lancet editorial, 2009). Besides, many women unaware of the legal status of abortion and seeking for clandestine abortion fall prey to unsafe abortions in private clinics (Khan et al., 1996). In fact, according to Duggal and Ramachandran (2004), certified and legal abortion facilities accounted for only 24 per cent of all private abortion facilities in India. Following MTP Act, only qualified doctors (qualification specified in MTP Act) can perform abortions in clinics or hospitals maintained by the government or in non-governmental institutions which possess a licence from the Chief Medical Officer of the district. The required number of doctors and institutions for abortions are far less than the demand for abortion. It also exacerbates the incidence of unsafe abortion.

Estimates of prevalence of abortions (both spontaneous and induced) in India are scarce. Only the Ministry of Health and Family Welfare, Government of India provides annual estimate of reported MTP cases. But it is believed that there is a large extent of under-reporting with respect of induced abortions (Casterline, 1989). Karkal (1991) estimated that in India three illegal abortions occurred per one legal abortion and 4–5 illegal abortions were performed for every MTP in urban area (cited in Mishra et al., 1997). According to the government estimation, there were 12,510 institutions approved for MTPs in India in 2007–08 where 6,41,786 MTPs were performed (Ministry of Health and Family Welfare, Government of India, 2009). On the other hand at the Consortium on National Consensus for Medical Abortion in India held in

AIIMS, New Delhi in 2008 it was declared that in India, on an average, 11 million abortions take place annually and each year around 20,000 women die due to abortion-related complications. It simply indicates that every year around 5 million abortions are done in unapproved medical institutions. Khan et al. (1996) also estimated that annually 5–6 million abortions are conducted by private practitioners in India. A large number of these abortions are done in rural areas having inadequate facilities in unhygienic conditions by untrained village practitioners. These are the basic reasons for continued high levels of maternal morbidity and mortality in India. The official statistics from 1998 showed that complications of abortion were responsible for about 9 per cent of total maternal deaths in rural India (Ministry of Health and Family Welfare, Government of India, 2003). As one the Millennium Development Goals (MDGs) target to reduce maternal mortality ratio by three quarters between 1990 and 2015 and reduction in maternal mortality cannot be achieved without reducing unsafe abortion, special attention is required to reduce the number of abortions and ensure safe abortion in India, the country with the highest number of maternal mortality in the world (WHO, 2010).

In this backdrop we are interested to know the level and patterns of induced abortion in India. Which are the states where induced abortion is comparatively higher? What are factors associated with induced abortion in India? Using the data of a nationwide population-based survey (District Level Household Survey–3) we have tried to find out the answers. In India the reasons for seeking abortion reported in various studies ranged from proximate determinants such as a desire to limit family size or space pregnancies, seeking abortion for medical reasons to distal determinants such as poverty, violence and belief system (Visaria et al., 2004). Various studies show that achieving desired sex composition of children is one of the important factors of induced abortion in India (Das, 1987; Bandewar, 2003; Visaria et al., 2004; Unisa et al., 2007) and consequently sex-selective abortion is regarded as the most important cause of declining child sex ratio in India (Retherford and Roy, 2004; Jha et al., 2006, 2011). As sex-selective abortion is a crime in India, therefore, there may be a tendency among women to report induced abortions as spontaneous. In this context we should look at the spontaneous abortion rates along with induced abortion rates in the states where child-sex ratio is very low. In India 27 per cent of the induced abortion is found in one state, namely, Uttar Pradesh. Therefore, the factors responsible for induced abortion in Uttar Pradesh have also been analysed in this paper.

The specific objectives of the present study are:

1. To examine the variations in the level of induced and spontaneous abortions among the states of India.
2. To identify the factors associated with induced abortion in India and Uttar Pradesh.

Methods

This study is based on the data from the third round of District Level Household and Facility Survey (DLHS–3). DLHS–3 is a nationwide sample survey (excluding the state of Nagaland) conducted in India in 2007–08 covering 7,20,320 households. From these households 6,43,944 ever-married women age 15–49 were interviewed and information was collected on women's characteristics, immunization and childcare, contraception and fertility preferences, reproductive health etc. However, this study is based on information from 2,25,225 currently-married women who were pregnant within three years prior to the survey. They were asked if they have experienced pregnancy termination, and if so, the number of induced or spontaneous abortions. In the traditional cultural context of India, unmarried women have not been asked about abortion. To understand the level of spontaneous and induced abortion, abortion ratios have been calculated for all the states. Abortion ratio is defined as the number of abortions per 100 pregnancies. Both bivariate and multivariate techniques have been used to determine the factors influencing induced abortion. All the analyses are done using SPSS version 20.0.

Results

Level of Induced and Spontaneous Abortions in India

Table 1 presents induced and spontaneous abortion ratios for India. At the national level the spontaneous and induced abortion ratios are 4.1 and 1.5 per 100 pregnancies respectively. Based on DLHS–3, in India, the highest induced abortion ratio is found in Manipur (3.8) followed by Delhi (3.6) and Assam (3.1). Other states/union territories (UTs) where induced abortion ratios are found above the national level are Punjab, Haryana, Chandigarh, Uttar Pradesh, Tripura, West Bengal, Maharashtra, Goa, Kerala, Pondicherry (now Puducherry) and Tamil Nadu. The highest spontaneous abortion ratio is observed in Haryana (9.5 per 100 pregnancies). High level of spontaneous abortion ratio (above 6.0 per 100 pregnancies) is also found in Delhi (8.2), Tamil Nadu (6.6) and Kerala (6.2).

Table 1

Abortion Ratios in India, 2007–08

State/Union Territories	*Total Pregnancies**	*No of Abortions per 100 Pregnancies*	
		Induced	*Spontaneous*
Jammu & Kashmir	7,155	1.1	3.3
Himachal Pradesh	3,407	0.4	2.1
Punjab	8,057	1.7	5.9
Chandigarh	268	1.9	4.9
Uttaranchal	5,409	0.5	1.2
Haryana	11,195	2.9	9.5
Delhi	3,717	3.6	8.2
Rajasthan	16,443	0.5	3.0
Uttar Pradesh	57,919	2.1	5.3
Bihar	31,228	0.8	3.7
Sikkim	1,753	0.6	2.8
Arunachal Pradesh	3,833	0.6	1.6
Manipur	5,027	3.8	5.1
Mizoram	3,675	0.1	2.7
Tripura	1,968	2.4	3.5
Meghalaya	4,254	0.3	0.4
Assam	13,574	3.1	4.0
West Bengal	8,478	2.8	3.7
Jharkhand	14,704	0.4	2.0
Odisha	9,586	1.2	2.7
Chhattisgarh	8,303	0.8	4.0
Madhya Pradesh	21,737	0.5	2.7
Gujarat	10,250	0.5	2.1
Daman & Diu	851	1.4	2.9
Dadra & Nagar Haveli	473	0.2	1.1
Maharashtra	14,950	2.4	4.4
Andhra Pradesh	6,691	0.7	3.9
Karnataka	10,441	1.0	4.1
Goa	514	2.9	3.5
Lakshadweep	558	0.2	5.0
Kerala	4,193	2.6	6.2
Tamil Nadu	9,086	2.7	6.6
Puducherry	1,251	2.7	5.5

Source: Computed from unit level data of DLHS–3.

* Pregnancies in three years preceding the survey of currently married women age 15–49 years

Figure 1

Spatial Variation of Induced Abortion Ratio in India, 2007–08

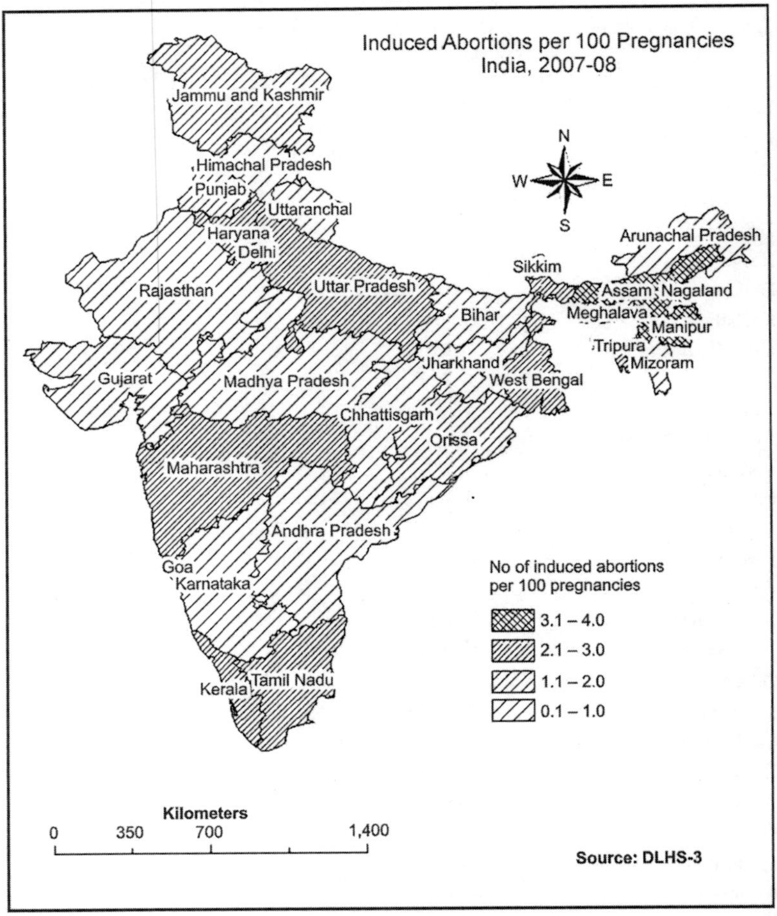

Figure 1 show the regional variation of induced abortion ratios in India. It is evident from Figure 1 that the induced abortion ratio is low (1 or below per 100 pregnancies) in the states starting from Gujarat in the west to Bihar and Jharkhand in the east. Among the four states of south India, Kerala and Tamil Nadu show abortion ratio between 2.1 and 3.0 while in Andhra Pradesh and Karnataka it is 1.0 or below. The states of eastern and north-eastern India also show differential level of induced abortion ratio. While in Manipur and Assam it is above 3.0, in Arunachal Pradesh and Mizoram it is as low as 1.0 or less. Among the northern states, induced abortion rate is comparatively higher in Haryana, Delhi and Uttar Pradesh.

Figure 2

Spatial Variation of Spontaneous Abortion Ratio in India, 2007–08

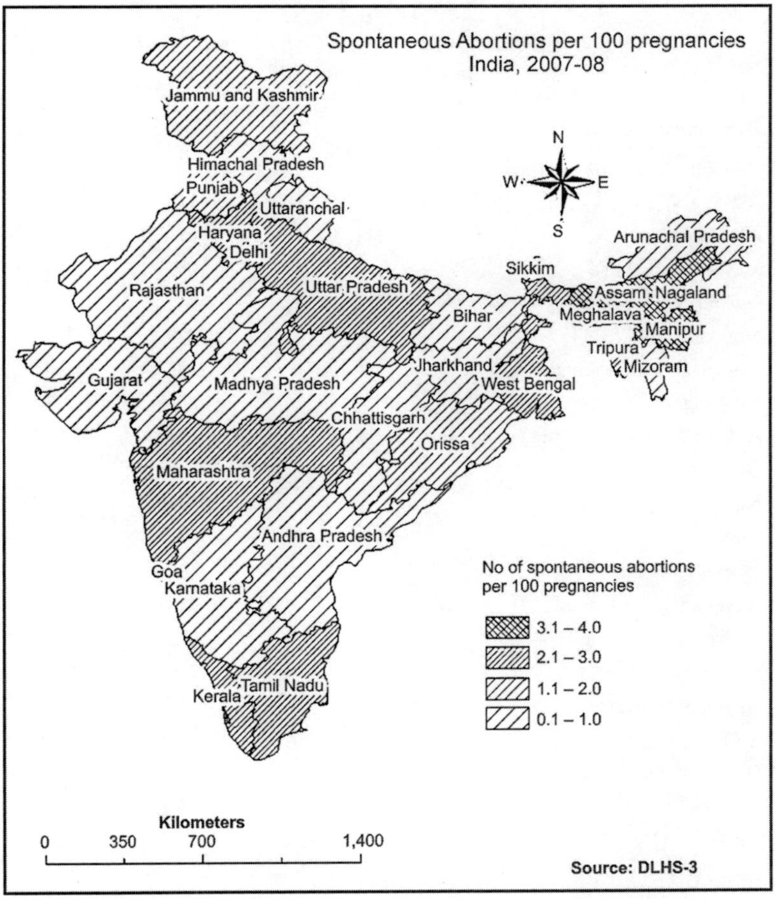

The regional pattern of spontaneous abortion can be identifiable from Figure 2. Spontaneous abortion ratio is comparatively higher (above 6.0 per 100 pregnancies) in two states of north India (Haryana and Delhi) and two states of south India (Kerala and Tamil Nadu). These states also show comparatively higher induced abortion ratios. The abortion ratio between 2.1 and 4.0 prevails in the region starting from Gujarat in the West to Odisha in the east.

Wide variation in spontaneous abortion ratios is found among the states in south India. It is also true for the states of north and north-east India. Therefore, it can be said that no striking spatial pattern in abortion has been observed in this study.

Table 2

Distribution of Women by Background Characteristics – India and Uttar Pradesh, 2007–08

Background Characteristics of Women	*India*	*Uttar Pradesh*
Age of mother at birth/abortion		
<20 years	11.6	11.5
20–29 years	69.7	63.5
30 years and above	18.7	24.9
Number of living children with their composition of sex		
No living child	2.9	3.2
No son, at least 1 daughter	23.7	18.4
No daughter, at least 1 son	26.4	21.1
At least 1 son and at least 1 daughter	47.0	57.3
Unmet need		
No	64.4	55.6
Yes	35.6	44.4
Years of schooling		
Never attended school	41.6	62.0
< 5 years	7.3	4.3
5–9 years	29.2	22.0
10 years and above	21.8	11.7
Religion		
Hindu	74.9	80.3
Muslim	15.1	19.3
Others	10.1	0.5
Caste		
Scheduled caste (SC)	18.6	21.2
Scheduled tribe (ST)	16.9	1.6
Others	64.5	77.2
Type of locality		
Rural	71.7	84.4
Urban	28.3	15.6

Cont'd...

...Cont'd

Knowledge about determination of sex before birth		
Yes	59.4	61.0
No	22.4	20.4
Don't know	18.2	18.6
Wealth Index		
Poorest	18.0	22.8
Poorer	19.0	21.4
Middle	19.5	20.2
Richer	21.1	19.3
Richest	22.4	16.3

Source: Computed from unit level data of DLHS–3.

Note: Percentages are calculated using sample weights.

Factors Associated with Induced Abortion in India and Uttar Pradesh

As we are more concerned about induced abortion, in this section we intend to throw a light on the correlates of induced abortion. Let us first look at the distribution of women included in the analysis by background characteristics (Table 2). Majority of the women in India and in Uttar Pradesh were from rural background, in age group 20–29 years at the time of birth/abortion and most of them reported to have had no unmet need for contraception at the time of survey. At national level around 47 per cent women had at least one son and one daughter. In case of Uttar Pradesh this proportion rose to 57.3 per cent. Around 40 per cent women in India and 62 per cent women in Uttar Pradesh never attended school. In Uttar Pradesh the proportion of Scheduled Tribes and the women other than Hindu and Muslim religion were considerably small (less than 1.6 per cent and 0.5 per cent respectively). In case of India, these percentages were 16.9 and 10.1 respectively. However, in both Uttar Pradesh and India three in five women possessed knowledge about determination of sex before birth. In India, 18 per cent women belonged to the poorest category compared to 22.8 per cent in Uttar Pradesh. On the other hand, 22.4 per cent women in India were from the richest category while only 16.3 belonged to that category in Uttar Pradesh.

The bivariate analysis (Table 3) reveals that no contradictory results are found between India and Uttar Pradesh except one. In case of India, the percentage of induced abortion was lower among women with at least one living son and at least one living daughter (3.7%) compared to those with no living child (5.7%). But in Uttar Pradesh among the women with at least one living son and at least one living daughter, the percentage of induced abortion was 5.0 and among those who had no living child, 4.8 per cent of them reported to have had induced abortion. In all other cases, similar findings are seen for both India and Uttar Pradesh. Induced abortion was found higher among women aged 30 years or above and who reported no unmet need. In Uttar Pradesh the percentage of women experiencing induced abortion was 3.5 times higher among the richest compared to the poorest (4 times higher in case of India). Our analysis reveals that the percentage of abortion also rises with increasing level of mother's education. Higher proportions of induced abortion was observed among Hindus than Muslims, among those who were neither Scheduled Caste (SC) nor Scheduled Tribe (ST) than SCs/STs, and in urban areas than in rural areas. Induced abortion was found higher among women who knew that sex of the baby could be identified before birth than those who did not know it.

Table 3

Percentage of Currently Married Women Age 15–49 who Experienced Induced Abortion in Three Years Preceding the Survey by Background Characteristics, India and Uttar Pradesh, 2007–08

Background Characteristics of Women	*India*		*Uttar Pradesh*	
	% of Women	*Sample Size*	*% of Women*	*Sample Size*
Age of mother at abortion				
<20 years	1.3	27,031	1.2	4677
20–29 years	3.1	1,55,534	4.0	25,733
30 years and above	5.2	42,636	6.5	10,070
No of living children with their composition of sex				
No living child	5.7	6,536	4.8	1,289
No son, at least 1 daughter	2.5	52,438	2.9	7,467
No daughter, at least 1 son	3.1	58,323	3.7	8,538
At least 1 son and at least 1 daughter	3.7	1,07,853	5.0	23,186
Unmet need				
No	3.9	1,42,716	5.3	22,479

Cont'd...

...Cont'd

Yes	2.1	82,489	3.1	18,004
Years of schooling				
Never attended school	2.1	1,00,255	3.4	25,077
< 5 years	2.8	17,001	4.9	1,733
5–9 years	3.8	64,766	5.5	8,887
10 years and above	5.0	43,105	6.9	4,758
Religion				
Hindu	3.5	1,70,117	4.4	32,552
Muslim	3.2	32,507	4.1	7,735
Others	2.2	22,579	6.3	195
Caste				
Scheduled caste (SC)	2.8	42,094	3.1	8,599
Scheduled tribe (ST)	1.5	39,447	2.4	623
Others	3.9	1,39,415	4.7	31,155
Type of locality				
Rural	2.7	1,82,605	3.9	34,250
Urban	4.9	42,600	6.5	6,233
Knowledge about determination of sex before birth				
Yes	4.0	1,29,766	4.9	24,706
No	2.5	51,536	3.4	8,240
Don't know	2.0	43,901	3.3	7,537
Wealth Index				
Poorest	1.4	45,697	2.4	9,235
Poorer	1.9	47,266	2.9	8,648
Middle	2.7	45,720	3.5	8,166
Richer	4.0	45,513	5.5	7,854
Richest	5.8	40,965	8.5	6,580

Source: Computed from unit level data of DLHS–3.

Note: Percentages are calculated using sample weight.

Multivariate technique, namely, binary logistic regression model has been used to identify the net impact of various demographic and socio-economic factors on induced abortion. During DLHS–3, a woman was asked 'Did any of your pregnancy terminate in spontaneous or induced abortion?' If she said 'Yes' for induced abortion, it is coded as '1' and if the answer was 'No' it is coded as '0'. In the present analysis binary logistic regression model has been used as the dependent variable 'women's experience of induced abortion' is dichotomous in nature. The result has been shown as adjusted odds ratio with the level of significance (Table 4).

Table 4

Logistic Regression Results of Experiencing Induced Abortion by Currently Married Women Aged 15–49, India and Uttar Pradesh, 2007–08

Background Characteristics of Women	*India Exp(B)*	*Uttar Pradesh Exp(B)*
Age of mother at abortion		
<20 years ®	1	1
20–29 years	1.994***	2.996***
30 years and above	4.015***	5.971***
No of living children with their composition of sex		
No living child®	1	1
No son, at least 1 daughter	.420***	.579***
No daughter, at least 1 son	.517***	.741*
At least 1 son and at least 1 daughter	.636***	.888
Unmet need		
No®	1	1
Yes	.614***	.633***
Years of schooling		
Never attended school®	1	1
< 5 years	1.308***	1.376**
5–9 years	1.465***	1.304***
10 years and above	1.329***	1.129
Religion		
Hindu®	1	1
Muslim	.792***	.730***
Others	.613***	.801
Caste		
Scheduled caste (SC) ®	1	1
Scheduled tribe (ST)	.721***	.794
Others	1.168***	1.253**
Type of locality		
Rural®	1	1
Urban	1.072*	1.048
Knowledge about determination of sex before birth		
Yes®	1	1
No	.772***	.778***

Cont'd...

...Cont'd

Don't know	.806***	.832*
Wealth Index		
Poorest®	1	1
Poorer	1.251***	1.219*
Middle	1.708***	1.488***
Richer	2.304***	2.296***
Richest	2.911***	3.367***
N	2,20,782	40,342

Note: *p<0.05, **p<0.01, ***p<0.001; ® Reference category.

Source: Computed from unit level data of DLHS–3.

It is evident from Table 4 that in both India and Uttar Pradesh induced abortion is significantly associated with various background characteristics of women such as mother's age at the time of abortion, unmet need, years of schooling of mothers, religion, caste, wealth index and knowledge about determination of sex before birth. Controlling for other factors, compared to women with age at abortion below 20 years, those with age at abortion 20–29 years or 30 years & above was more likely to report induced abortion. The probability of induced abortion was found lower among the women with at least one living son and at least one living daughter than those who had no living child. However, the result is significant in case of India (p<0.001) but not in case of Uttar Pradesh. Contrary to our expectation, those with unmet need were less likely to report induced abortion than who had unmet need. The result is significant both for India (p<0.001) and Uttar Pradesh (p<0.001). Women's years of schooling significantly increases the risk of induced abortion. After covariate adjustment it is found that Muslim women were less likely to experience induced abortion than Hindu women in India (OR .792, p<0.001) and in Uttar Pradesh (OR .730, p<0.001). In case of India compared to scheduled caste women, women from scheduled tribe were significantly less prone to induced abortion. The result is not significant in case of Uttar Pradesh as the sample size of scheduled tribe population is very small in this state. On the other hand, in both India and Uttar Pradesh, non-SC/ST women were significantly more likely to experience induced abortion than scheduled caste women. In our analysis it is observed that with increasing wealth index the chances of reporting induced abortion has increased significantly. After covariate adjustment, compared to the rural areas induced abortion was more likely to occur in urban areas. However, the result is significant for India but not for Uttar Pradesh. When other factors are adjusted for, those who did not know about sex determination test, were significantly less likely to report induced abortion than those who knew it.

Discussion

The present study shows that in India spontaneous and induced abortion ratios are 4.1 and 1.5 per 100 pregnancies respectively. It is quite possible that because of the restriction on sex-selective abortion in India, many respondents may conceal the actual number of induced abortions they had (IIPS, 2010). In the social context of India, question on premarital sex-related abortions was not asked during the DLHS–3 survey. Thus, the induced abortion ratio on reality may be quite high than the estimation we have got. Let us consider the case of Haryana where the child sex ratio is distinctly biased against girls for a long time. Here, the numbers of induced and spontaneous abortions per 100 pregnancies are found to be 2.9 and 9.5 respectively. It is not hard to assume that some of the induced abortions have been reported as spontaneous. Based on a sample survey in Haryana, Unisa et al. (2007) also came to the similar conclusion.

It is found that the odds of induced abortion increases with maternal age at abortion. Similar findings are recorded by Pallikadavath and Stones (2006). They have suggested that the need for spacing at higher age might have triggered the decision to obtain an abortion. The present study finds that abortion is higher among women with no living children. Perhaps if a newly married woman at a very young age becomes pregnant, she may accept abortion to avoid unwanted pregnancy. Visaria et al. (2007) from a multicentric study on abortion found that despite the pressure on young brides to prove their fertility, some women in Tamil Nadu, Andhra Pradesh, Gujarat and Maharashtra cited immediate conception after marriage as a reason for abortion.

It is difficult to explain why the probability of experiencing induced abortion is found the lowest among women with at least one daughter but no son, because strong son preference exists in India and as India is showing declining trend in fertility, it is more likely that after the birth of one or two daughters women will go for sex selective abortion in order to get a son. The opposite trend, that is, sex selective abortion in favour of female child is not common in the country. In case of India compared to women with no children, women with at least one son and at least one daughter have significantly lower odds of reporting induced abortion. It can be argued that women with more children do not conform to small family norm. Here it should also be mentioned that it is not possible to identify the causal relationship between the number and sex composition of living children and the incidence of induced abortion. The observed family composition could be an effect of induced abortion. Another study (Pallikadavath and Stones, 2006) from India suggested that at the national level, unintended pregnancy rather than the sex of the previous child was the driver of abortion in India. A qualitative study from Nepal (Thapa and Padhye, 2001) have also found that it was not the sex of the children but the intention to limit or space births was the most common reason of induced abortion. Research in other South Asian countries has also revealed that mistimed and unwanted pregnancies are the foremost causes of seeking abortion in those countries (Kamran et al., 2011; Gazdar et al., 2012).

Women having no unmet need have reported higher odds of experiencing induced abortion. It is quite possible that many of them could have had unmet need earlier that led to unwanted pregnancies which have finally been aborted. Women's education and family wealth are significantly positively associated with induced abortion. Several studies, e.g. Singh et al. (2006), Pallikadavath and Stones (2006), Unisa et al. (2007), Maharana (2011) support this hypothesis. Rich educated women mostly prefer small family size. They have greater access to information and abortion services than poor uneducated women. So in case of unwanted pregnancy, they can easily adopt abortion.

Religion may have an impact on abortion through differential norms regarding abortion and family size. As a result, abortion rates vary among various religious groups. The scheduled tribes are the most disadvantaged social group in India. Because of socio-economic backwardness they have lesser access to abortion. Also, small family norm is less prevalent among them compared to other caste. Therefore, among various caste groups, proportion of abortion is the lowest among scheduled tribes. Visaria (2007) has also found that in Gujarat, upper-caste women were openly or covertly pressurized to go for abortions to have male child if the first child was a daughter but such pressure was much less among the lower castes.

As the facilities of abortion are more available in urban areas, women living in urban areas have higher odds of induced abortion than women living in rural areas. According to Pallikadavath and Stones (2006), this may also reflect a lower demand for abortions in rural areas due to limited exposure to the media. As expected, knowledge about prenatal sex determination is positively associated with induced abortion.

Conclusion

This study has several limitations. First, the survey did not include unmarried women. Second there is a chance of recall bias. Third, there may be a deliberate tendency of women to report induced abortion as spontaneous abortion. In spite of these shortcomings, this study provides a vivid picture of abortion scenario in India and helps to understand various socio-economic and demographic correlates of induced abortion in India and in Uttar Pradesh. The states where abortion rates are high need special attention. Son preference and unmet need for contraception are regarded as two important causes of induced abortion in India, but this study does not provide clear evidence in support of these hypotheses. Therefore, further research is needed to explore the role of sex-selective abortions and unmet need for contraception behind the declining child sex ratio in India.

References

Alan Guttmacher Institute (AGI). 1999. *Sharing Responsibility: Women, Society and Abortion Worldwide*. New York: AGI.

All India Institute of Medical Sciences (AIIMS). 2008. *Consortium on National Consensus for Medical Abortion in India*. Department of Obstetrics and Gynaecology, New Delhi: AIIMS.

Bandewar, S. 2003. 'Abortion Services and Providers' Perceptions: Gender Dimensions', *Economic and Political Weekly*, 38(21): 2075–2081.

Casterline, J.B. 1989. 'Collecting Data on Pregnancy Loss: A Review of Evidence from WFS', *Studies in Family Planning*, 20(2): 81–95.

Das, N. 1987. 'Sex Preference and Fertility Behaviour: A Study of Recent Indian Data', *Demography*, 24(4): 517–530.

Duggal, R. and V. Ramachandran. 2004. 'Urgent Concerns on Abortion Services', *Economic and Political Weekly*, 39(10): 1025–1026.

Fredrich, B. 2007. 'Eliminating Unsafe Abortion Worldwide', *Lancet*, 370: 1295–1296.

Gazdar, H., A. Khan and S. Qureshi. 2012. Causes and Implications of Induced Abortion in Pakistan: A Social and Economic Analysis. Research Report. Karachi, Pakistan: Collective for Social Science Research.

International Institute for Population Sciences (IIPS). 2007. *District Level Household Survey–3 Under Reproductive and Child Health Project, 2007–08.* Interviewer's Manual: India, Mumbai: IIPS.

——. 2010. *District Level Household and Facility Survey (DLHS–3), 2007–08: India*. Mumbai: IIPS.

Jha, P., R. Kumar, P. Vasa, N. Dhingra, D. Thiruchelvan et al. 2006. 'Low Male-to-Female Sex Ratio of Children Born in India: National Survey of 1.1 Million Households', *Lancet*, 367: 211–218.

Jha, P., M.A. Kesler, R. Kumar, F. Ram, U. Ram et al. 2011. 'Trends in Selective Abortions of Girls in India: Analysis of Nationally Representative Birth Histories from 1990 to 2005 and Census Data from 1991–2011', *Lancet*, 377: 1921–1928.

Kamran, I., S. Arif and K. Vassos. 2011. 'Concordance and Discordance of Couples in a Rural Pakistani Village: Perspectives on Contraception and Abortion: A Qualitative Study', *Global Public Health*, 6(1): 38–51.

Karkal, M. 1991. 'Abortion Laws and the Abortion Situation in India', Issues in Reproductive and Genetic Emgineering, 4(3): 223–230.

Khan, M.E., S. Barge and G. Philip. 1996. 'Abortion in India: An Overview', *Social Change*, 26(3 & 4): 208–225.

Lancet editorial. 2009. 'Unsafe Abortions: Eight Maternal Deaths Every Hour', *Lancet*, 374: 1301.

Maharana, B. 2011. 'Correlates of Spontaneous and Induced Abortion in India: An Investigation Using a Nationwide Large Scale Survey Data'. Paper presented at the Annual Meeting of Population Association of Anerica, 31 March – 2 April 2011, Washington DC.

Ministry of Health and Family Welfare, Government of India. 2003. *Family Welfare Programme in India: Year Book 2001*. Department of Family Welfare, New Delhi.

——. 2009. *Family Welfare Statistics in India: 2009*. New Delhi: MoHFW.

Mishra, U.S., M. Ramanathan and S.I. Rajan. 1997. Induced Abortion Potential among Indian Women. Working Paper, Centre for Development Studies, Trivandram (now Tiruvananthapuram).

Mohan, R. and R.S. Goyal. 2000. 'The Changing Pattern of Medical Termination of Pregnancies in Rajasthan and India: A Comparative Analysis', *The Journal of Family Welfare*, 46(1): 39–46.

Pallikadavath, S. and R.W. Stones. 2006. 'Maternal and Social Factors Associated with Abortion in India: A Population-based Study', *International Family Planning Perspectives*, 32(3): 120–125.

Park, K. 2009. *Park's Textbook of Preventive and Social Medicine*, 20th edition. Jabalpur: M/S Banarsidas Bhanot.

Registrar General and Census Commissioner of India. 2011. Census of India 2011: Provisional Population Totals. Paper 1 of 2011, India, Series 1.

Retherford, R.D. and T.K. Roy. 2004. 'Effects of Family Composition on Sex-selective Abortion in Punjab, India', *Genus*, 60(3/4): 71–97.

Singh, S. et al. 2006. *Unintended Pregnancy and Induced Abortion in the Philippines: Causes and Consequences*. New York: Guttmacher Institute.

——. 2009. *Abortion Worldwide: A Decade of Uneven Progress*. New York: Guttmacher Institute.

Thapa, S. and S.M. Padhye. 2001. 'Induced Abortion in Urban Nepal', *International Family Planning Perspectives*, 27(3): 144–147.

Unisa, S., S. Pujari and R. Usa. 2007. 'Sex-selective Abortion in Haryana: Evidence from Pregnancy History and Antenatal Care', *Economic and Political Weekly*, 42(1): 60–66.

Visaria, L. 2007. 'Sex-selective Abortion in Gujarat and Haryana: Some Empirical Evidence', in L. Visaria and V. Ramachandran (eds), *Abortion in India: Ground Realities*. New Delhi: Routledge.

Visaria, L., V. Ramachandran, B. Ganatra and S. Kalyanwala. 2004. 'Abortion in India: Emerging Issues from Qualitative Studies', *Economic and Political Weekly*, 39(46–47): 5044–5052.

——. 2007. 'Abortion Use and Practice: Evidence, Challenges and Emerging Issues', in L. Visaria and V. Ramachandran (eds), *Abortion in India: Ground Realities*, 1st edition. Delhi: Routledge, 1–26.

World Health Organization (WHO). 2010. *Trends in Maternal Mortality: 1990 to 2008: Estimates Developed by WHO, UNICEF, UNFPA and the World Bank*. Geneva: WHO.

——. 2011. *Unsafe Abortion: Global and Regional Estimates of the Incidence of Unsafe Abortion and Associated Mortality in 2008*, 6th edition. Geneva: WHO.

6

Family Planning Use and Unmet Need among Scheduled and Non-Scheduled Population in Bihar

Empirical Evidence from DLHS–3

RATI PARIHAR, B. PASWAN AND AKASH WANKHEDE

The fertility level of world has been declining since 1950s. India, being the second largest country in the world in terms of population, was worried about it population growth in the wake of mortality decline and subsequent rise in life expectancy in the post-independence period. This was the reason that led India to adopt its first-ever official family planning programme. India is first country in the world to adopt family planning programme officially in the year 1952. The result was obvious in the form of the beginning of fertility decline in India in the first half of 1960s. However, the achievement in family planning programme in India was not up to the mark specially in some northern and central Indian states including Bihar which could not be the part of the process until 1980. In fact, their current total fertility rates are still relatively very high. High fertility levels not only have several adverse implications for societies but also for individuals. Since these states constitute a great chunk of India's population, they are the major players that would determine future socio-economic and demographic situation of the country. Hence, quick and substantial reduction in fertility in low resource settings, such as these states, is a highly desirable goal.

Previous conducted studies, however, show that one of the ways to reduce such a high fertility rate is contraception. Application of the Bongaarts (1978) model of proximate determinants to the National Family Health Survey (NFHS) data indicates that the total fertility in India is mainly determined by the level of contraceptive methods (Jain, 1997; Visaria, 2002). The prevalence of contraceptive use explores the level of fertility in the respective region. The area with high prevalence of contraceptive will definitely have low level of fertility, and that with low prevalence will have high level of fertility.

Family planning being a viable solution to control such fast growing populations, not only helps in spacing and limiting the number of children, but also improves maternal and child health, empowers women and boosts economic development. The National Rural Health Mission programme initiated by government in 2005 also promotes contraceptive use on voluntary basis through comprehensive programmes to increase the use of family planning methods in the country; however, a large proportion of women from reproductive ages who want to stop or space childbearing are unable to use family planning methods. Demographers and health specialists refer to these women as having an 'unmet need' for family planning. *Unmet need refers to fecund women who either wish to postpone the next birth (spacers) or who wish to stop child bearing (limiters) but are not using a contraceptive method. This concept clearly indicates a gap between a woman's reproductive intention and contraceptive behaviour.* It is generally true that there is wide variation in use and unmet need for family planning by region and socio-economic characteristics of population. The findings from district level household survey (DLHS–3), 2007–2008, reveals that the unmet need for family planning at national level in India is 21 per cent, showing a slow decrease from 25 per cent in 2003–2004. In Bihar the total unmet need for contraception either for spacing or limiting is 36 per cent. The same figures for spacing and limiting are 13.0 and 23.0 per cent respectively.

Literature Review

Many studies in the past in India and elsewhere have found that women with unmet need for family planning constitute a significant fraction of all married women of reproductive age. According to an estimate, more than 100 million sexually active women in developing countries would like to adopt family planning but they are not able to do so. Asia, owing to its huge population, is by far the region with the greatest number of women with unmet need of contraception. Kishore estimated that India has about 31 million of women with unmet need for family planning (Kishore, 2007), despite the existence of the National Policy on Family Planning since the year 1983.

A baseline survey conducted in 1983 in two districts of rural Gujarat showed that family planning practice was low among the scheduled caste, still lower among the scheduled tribes, in comparison to the other caste groups (IIPS and PRC, 1985). Another study carried out in 1990–91 in the four districts of Maharashtra did not show much difference in the extent of family planning practice between the scheduled caste and other caste groups. The practice was, however, less among the scheduled tribes (Roy et al., 1991).

Devi et al. (1996) studied that unmet need for family planning is especially high among women residing in rural areas, women whose husbands are illiterate, illiterate women, Muslim women, Scheduled Tribe women and women not exposed to messages of family planning. Unmet need for family planning was high among the women who did not have any media exposure or did not discuss about family planning with their husbands (Srivastava et al., 2011). Proportion of unmet need for family planning is much higher among the women who reside in the rural areas, at the younger ages and women having less than three children. Educational level of the women and work status is found to be highly significant with respect to their unmet need (Laya, 2012). Unmet need for contraception is higher in the younger age group. With the increase in the educational level, the prevalence of spacers in the unmet need has significantly increased and that of limiters decreased. The prevalence of spacers significantly decreases and limiters increases with the increase in number of living children (Bhattacharya et al., 2006). Roy et al. (2011) studied that the gap between contraceptive need and practice requires increase in contraceptive options by incorporation of natural and traditional methods which are safe, simple and should be provided by healthcare providers.

Need of the Study

Bihar is the focus of this study for several reasons. It is the third most populated state of India with approximately 9 per cent (about 10 crores population as per census, 2011) of the total population of India. It is the poorest state of the country, with the exception of Odisha, and ranked among the slowest growing regions of the country until recently. High maternal, low life expectancy, high fertility, high unmet need for contraception, low literacy rate, low coverage of child immunization and high child malnutrition

(ORGI, 2012; IIPS and ORC Macro, 2007) are the main demographic characteristics of Bihar. Among the empowered action group of mentioned above, Bihar is the one that has shown a near stall in fertility decline in the post-1997 period. The low rate of contraceptive use and high level of fertility in Bihar are of considerable concern to the Indian Government, which has launched innovations in family planning services project intended to increase contraceptive use in the state. According to DLHS–3, in Bihar the total unmet need for contraception either for spacing or limiting is 36 per cent. As mentioned above, 13.2 and 22.6 per cent of currently married women have unmet need for spacing and limiting respectively.

There is also a wide variation in use and unmet need for family planning by region and socio-economic characteristics of population. The Scheduled Caste and Scheduled Tribe population are socially and economically a backward class in social hierarchy and constitutes about 24.4 per cent of the country's total population (Registrar General India, 2004). The SC/ST population in Bihar constitutes 17.2 per cent of total population of Bihar, including 15.9 per cent schedule caste and 1.3 per cent schedule tribe population as per census 2011. The study on use of contraception and unmet need among SC/ST and general population in Bihar will be very useful for policy implication. It will be interesting to know the use and unmet need of family planning among this group and whether and to what extent their behaviour differs from the other caste group. Therefore, an attempt has been made in this study to know the differential and correlates of current use of family planning and unmet need for family planning among Schedule Caste and Scheduled Tribe (SC/ST) and non-SC/ST population at state and district level in Bihar.

Objectives

The specific objectives of the present study are as follows:

1. To study the district-wise variation in contraceptive use and unmet need among scheduled and non-scheduled women in Bihar.
2. To assess the quality of family planning services among scheduled and non-scheduled women in Bihar.
3. To understand the differential and to find out the determinants of contraceptive use and unmet need in family planning among scheduled and non-scheduled women in Bihar.

Data Sources and Methodology

The study utilized data from District Level Household and Facility Survey, 2007–2008 (DLHS–3). The DLHS–3 was the national level household and facility survey conducted by International Institute for Population Sciences, Mumbai and sponsored by Ministry of Health and Family Welfare, Government of India. The total number of households and ever married women covered under DLHS–3 for state of Bihar was 47,137 and 46,840 respectively. The bivariate analysis techniques have been used to understand the problems at first stage. Further, multivariate techniques have been used to analyse the data.

Results and Findings

District-wise Variation in Contraceptive use and Unmet Need

District-wise variation in use of any modern method among non-SC/ST and SC/ST is depicted spatially in Table 1. Contraceptive Prevalence Rate (CPR) for any modern method among non-SC/ST is below 25 per cent in Gopalganj, Siwan, Katihar and Kishanganj, while CPR is in the range of 25.1 to 40 per cent in the districts of Sheikhpura, Jehanabad, Saran, Begusarai, Purnia, Kaimur (Bhabua), Nalanda, Gaya, Khagaria, Buxar, Pashchim Champaran, Samastipur, Lakhisarai, Araria, Madhubani, Darbhanga, Saharsa, Bhojpur, Madhepura, Aurangabad, Muzaffarpur, Munger, Rohtas and Bhagalpur. In the remaining three districts of Bihar namely Vaishali, Patna and Supaul the CPR for any modern method is above 40 per cent. There are 19 districts in Bihar where the prevalence of modern method among non-SC/ST is below the state average (31.7%).

Contraceptive Prevalence Rate (CPR) for any modern method among SC/ST is below 15 per cent in Purba Champaran, Sheohar, Buxar, Sheikhpura, Jamui and Khagaria, while CPR is in the range of 15–30 per cent in the districts of Gopalgunj, Siwan, Kaithar, Banka, Sitamarhi, Jehanabad, Saran, Begusarai, Purnia, Kaimur (Bhabua), Nalanda, Gaya, Samastipur, Lakhisarai, Madhubani, Darbhanga, Saharsa, Bhojpur, Madhepura, Aurangabad, Muzaffarpur, Munger, Rohtas and Bhagalpur. In the remaining districts of Bihar namely Kishanganj, Araria, Vaishali, Patna and Supaul the CPR for any modern method is above 30 per cent. There are 22 districts in Bihar where the prevalence of modern method among SC/ST is below the state average (21.5%).

Table 1

Percentage of Currently Married Scheduled and Non-scheduled Women Aged 15–49 Years who are Currently using any Method and any Modern Method by Districts, Bihar, 2007–08

District	*Current use Any Methods*		*Current use Modern Method*		*No. of Women**
	SC/ST	*Non SC/ST*	*SC/ST*	*Non SC/ST*	
Pashchim Champaran	30.7	35.7	27.7	30.1	1,030
Purba Champaran	18.1	31.2	13.2	27.4	1,368
Sheohar	17	32.5	13.8	26	1,202
Sitamarhi	23.6	27.5	21.3	26.3	1,274
Madhubani	33.4	36	28.7	31.6	1,507
Supaul	34.3	46.2	32.4	45.3	1,424
Araria	35.6	35.7	33.8	33.9	1,360
Kishanganj	42	28.2	40	24	1,322
Purnia	20.7	30.9	18.4	29.5	1,210
Katihar	27.8	27.6	22.4	21.9	1,086
Madhepura	25.4	39.7	20.2	35.6	1,345
Saharsa	23.8	38.8	19.3	36.4	1,122
Darbhanga	29.6	31.8	28.8	30.3	1,087
Muzaffarpur	30	36.5	29.1	35.5	996
Gopalganj	16.5	23.7	16.5	21.7	908
Siwan	23.2	24.4	19	20.7	958
Saran	20.7	33	17.2	29	1,250
Vaishali	40.3	47.1	34.6	43.8	1,277
Samastipur	30.8	37.8	26.3	31.8	1,287
Begusarai	23.1	33.2	21.7	30.1	1,321
Khagaria	15.8	36.5	13.8	32.5	1,329
Bhagalpur	32	44.6	26	39.5	866
Banka	18.6	28.6	17.5	26.2	983
Munger	23.8	46	19	38.3	985
Lakhisarai	22.8	36.5	19.7	33.3	1,302
Sheikhpura	19.5	31.8	14	28.6	1,219
Nalanda	21.2	34.8	19.9	30.6	1,263
Patna	36.9	51.8	32.1	47.6	896
Bhojpur	25.6	38.9	19.8	34	1,177
Buxar	20.9	36.7	15	32.1	1,276
Kaimur bhabua	24.7	37.2	17.7	32.2	1,375
Rohtas	33	44.8	25.6	38.5	1,104
Jehanabad	19	33.9	16	29.6	1,388

Cont'd...

...Cont'd

Aurangabad	26.2	39	21.5	35.5	1,107
Gaya	22.5	39.7	19	34.9	1,234
Nawada	18.1	31.5	15.1	28.9	1,229
Jamui	21.8	31.9	13.6	25.4	1,272
Total	25.4	35.6	21.5	31.7	44,332

Note: Investigated cases.

Table 2

Percentage of Currently Married Scheduled and Non-scheduled Women Aged 15–49 Years by Unmet Need of Family Planning in Districts, Bihar, 2007–08

Districts	*Unmet need for Spacing*		*Unmet need for Limiting*		*No. of Woman**
	SC/ST	*Non SC/ST*	*SC/ST*	*Non SC/ST*	
Pashchim Champaran	17.2	12.8	21.6	21.9	1,030
Purba Champaran	11.5	12	24.2	21.8	1,368
Sheohar	14.9	13.2	28.7	25.2	1,202
Sitamarhi	16	10.8	26.2	24.1	1,274
Madhubani	19.5	16.4	21.6	21.1	1,507
Supaul	13.2	11.8	18.6	14.2	1,424
Araria	16.2	11.6	18.1	20.2	1,360
Kishanganj	14	14.5	14	24.2	1,322
Purnia	16.2	16.8	28.8	23.2	1,210
Katihar	17.5	18.1	21.5	27	1,086
Madhepura	10.3	10.3	25.1	20.9	1,345
Saharsa	15.3	14.5	28.2	19.3	1,122
Darbhanga	13.3	14.3	20.8	22.9	1,087
Muzaffarpur	9.3	10.4	29.5	25.5	996
Gopalganj	5.7	9.6	36.7	29.9	908
Siwan	7.7	10.2	33.1	30.1	958
Saran	15.2	11.8	31.3	27	1,250
Vaishali	11.3	11.5	17	16	1,277
Samastipur	15.4	12.9	21.5	21.2	1,287
Begusarai	19.7	14.6	27.4	20	1,321
Khagaria	18.8	14.6	27.9	18.8	1,329
Bhagalpur	10.7	11.9	28.7	20.1	866
Banka	14.7	15.5	26.6	24.1	983
Munger	18.5	13.7	22.6	16.3	985
Lakhisarai	15	14.5	31.3	21	1,302

Cont'd...

...Cont'd

Sheikhpura	17.9	14.5	24.4	22.6	1,219
Nalanda	16	12.8	26.7	21.7	1,263
Patna	13.4	6.9	18.7	16.5	896
Bhojpur	14	13.2	25.2	19.3	1,177
Buxar	13	10.1	29.1	22.4	1,276
Kaimur (Bhabua)	14.8	11.4	22	22.1	1,375
Rohtas	14.5	11.2	20.2	15.6	1,104
Jehanabad	16.9	12.4	22.2	22.4	1,388
Aurangabad	15.8	10.6	24.7	22.8	1,107
Gaya	16	9.5	23	19.5	1,234
Nawada	14.3	11.6	34.2	26.2	1,229
Jamui	13	18.2	30.2	23.5	1,272
Total	14.8	12.8	25.1	21.8	44,332

Note: Investigated cases.

District wise variation in unmet need for spacing and limiting method of contraception among non-SC/ST and SC/ST is depicted spatially in Table 2. It is evident that unmet need for limiting method of contraception among non-SC/ST is below 15 per cent in Supaul while unmet need in the range of 15–30 per cent in the districts of Purba Champaran, Sheohar, Buxar, Sheikhpura, Jamui, Khagaria, Gopalgunj, Kaithar, Banka, Sitamarhi, Jehanabad, Saran, Begusarai, Purnia, Kaimur (Bhabua), Nalanda, Gaya, Samastipur, Lakhisarai, Madhubani, Darbhanga, Saharsa, Bhojpur, Madhepura, Aurangabad, Muzaffarpur, Munger, Rohtas, Bhagalpur, Kishanganj, Araria, Nawada, Vaishali and Patna. Only one remaining district of Bihar, namely, Siwan the unmet need for limiting method of contraception is above 30 per cent. There are 17 districts in Bihar where the prevalence of unmet need for limiting method of contraception among Non SC/ST is below the state average (21.8%).

Unmet need for limiting method of contraception among SC/ST is below 15 per cent in Kishanganj district while unmet need in the range of 15–30 per cent in the districts of Purba Champaran, Sheohar, Buxar, Sheikhpura, Khagaria, Kaithar, Banka, Sitamarhi, Jehanabad, Begusarai, Purnia, Kaimur (Bhabua), Nalanda, Gaya, Samastipur, Madhubani, Darbhanga, Saharsa, Bhojpur, Madhepura, Aurangabad, Muzaffarpur, Munger, Rohtas, Bhagalpur, Araria, Vaishali and Patna. Only in remaining districts of Bihar, namely Gopalgunj, Siwan, Saran, Nawada, Lakhisarai and Jamui the unmet need for limiting method of contraception is above 30 per cent. There are 18 districts in Bihar where the prevalence of unmet need for limiting method of contraception among SC/ST is below the state average (25.1%).

Unmet need for spacing method of contraception among non-SC/ST is below 10 per cent in Gopalganj, Patna and Gaya districts while unmet need is in the range of 10 to16 per cent in the districts of Purba Champaran, Sheohar, Buxar, Sheikhpura, Khagaria, Banka, Sitamarhi, Jehanabad, Begusarai, Kaimur (Bhabua), Nalanda, Samastipur, Darbhanga, Saharsa, Bhojpur, Madhepura, Aurangabad, Muzaffarpur, Munger, Rohtas, Bhagalpur, Araria, Vaishali, Siwan, Saran, Nawada, Lakhisarai and Kishanganj. In remaining districts of Bihar namely Madhubani, Purnia, Kaithar and Jamui the unmet need for spacing method of contraception is above 16 per cent. There are 19 districts in Bihar where the prevalence of unmet need for spacing method of contraception among non-SC/ST is below the state average (12.8%).

Unmet need for spacing method of contraception among SC/ST is below 10 per cent in Gopalganj, Siwan, Muzzaffarpur districts while unmet need is in the range of 10–16 per cent in the districts of Purba Champaran, Sheohar, Buxar, Banka, Sitamarhi, Kaimur (Bhabua), Nalanda, Samastipur, Darbhanga, Saharsa, Bhojpur, Madhepura, Aurangabad, Rohtas, Bhagalpur, Vaishali, Saran, Nawada, Jamui, Lakhisarai, Kishanganj, Patna and Gaya. Only in remaining districts of Bihar namely Paschim Champaran, Madhubani, Araria, Purnia, Kaithar Khagaria, Begusarai, Sheikhpura, Munger, and Jehanabad the unmet need for spacing method of contraception is above 16 per cent. There are 17 districts in Bihar where the prevalence of unmet need for spacing method of contraception among SC/ST is below the state average (14.8%).

Quality of Family Planning Services in Bihar

Under this section, quality of family planning services either from health professionals' side or from client's side has been discussed. The literatures suggest that considerable responsibility lies on doctors and health workers since a very large proportion of users (and potential users) depend on the information provided by these health professionals while selecting a family planning method. For analysing the quality of family planning services provided from health personals, the indicators like users who are sterilized and received cash benefits, those who received advice before, adapting the method and were told about side effects. While from users side indicators which show their perception regarding quality of family planning services were utilized viz. rating about services provided and satisfaction with the method currently in use.

Table 3 reveals that a very less proportion of women received cash benefits after sterilization, which is about 43 per cent among SC/ST category and 39 per cent among non-SC/ST. The same figure at state level is around 40 per cent. Among SC/ST category, the women who are sterilized and received cash benefits decreases with increase in education. The proportion of non-literate sterilized SC/ST women who received cash benefit is 46 per cent, whereas it decreases with increase in education with only 28 per cent among women with 10 or more years of education. Similar kind of situation has been observed among non-SC/ST women in Bihar.

Table 3

Percentage of Currently Married SC/ST and Non-SC/ST Women Aged 15–49 Years who are Currently Sterilized and received Cash Benefits After Sterilization According to Socio-economic Characteristics, Bihar, 2007–08

Socio-economic Characteristics	*SC/ST*	*Non-SC/ST*	*Total*
Age			
Below 25	52.8	32.6	36.6
25–34	36.2	28.6	29.9
35+	49.0	49.0	49.0
Education			
Non-literate	45.6	41.6	42.5
less than 5	40.9	41.4	41.3
5–9 years	38.2	40.4	40.2
10 or more years	27.6	27.9	27.9
Residence			
Rural	43.6	39.9	43.5
Urban	42.1	36.7	39.5
Number of Children			
One	22.7	34.8	32.4
Two	38.8	33.2	33.7
Three	48.4	40.1	41.2
Four plus	42.5	41.1	41.4
Religion			
Hindu	43.8	40.0	40.6

Cont'd...

...Cont'd

Muslim	33.3	30.3	30.4
Christian	22.2	50.0	33.3
Others	42.9	25.0	36.4
Wealth Quintile			
Poorest	48.6	41.3	43.2
Second	43.1	41.2	41.6
Middle	39.1	40.5	40.3
Fourth	38.3	37.3	37.4
Richest	27.9	31.0	30.7
Total	42.9	38.6	40.2

A very interesting picture has been observed with number of children that is, the proportion of women receiving cash benefits increases with number of children. The proportion of SC/ST women with one child receiving cash benefit is 23 per cent while that for 4 plus children are 43 per cent. The proportion of non-SC/ST women with one child receiving cash benefit is 35 per cent while that for 4 plus children are 42 per cent. When the wealth status of sterilized women was observed it came into light that the proportion of women receiving cash benefit decreases as the wealth status of women improves and the case was same for SC/ST women as well as non-SC/ST women.

Table 4 shows that currently married women among SC/ST and non-SC/ST who received advice before using the current method, percentage of currently married women who were using contraception and were informed about side effects of the current method and proportion of currently married women using contraception who were satisfied with the current method. For Bihar state as a whole only 15 per cent currently married women who are currently using family planning received advice. These figures are more or less same for SC/ST and non-SC/ST women. The proportion of women who received advice is high for women having 10 or more years of education for SC/ST category (26%) than non-SC/ST category (18%). Even the wealth status of women shows positive relation with the women who receive advice. Eighteen per cent women in urban area were advised about current method as compared to only 15 per cent in rural area in Bihar.

The Table also reveals that only 18 per cent SC/ST women and 18.6 per cent non-SC/ST women were informed about side effects of the use of methods. The use of contraception for women who were told about side effects of current method is high among rural areas (18%) than urban areas (13%) among SC/ST, whereas among non-SC/ST the situation is same with 19 per cent in rural area and 13 per cent in urban area. The proportion of women who were told about the side effects due to use of current method decreases very quickly when parity of women increases, that is, the women with less number of children were more informed about side effects than women with more number of children. For instance, the proportion of women who were informed about side effects due to use of current method with one child is 32 per cent as compared to 18 per cent of women with four plus children among SC/ST.

Table 4

Percentage of Currently Married SC/ST and non-SC/ST Women Aged 15–49 Years who are Currently using Contraceptive Methods Received Advice, Informed about side effects before Adopting Current Method and told that Satisfied with Current Method According to Socio-economic Characteristics, Bihar, 2007–08

Socio-economic Characteristics	*Received Advice*		*Informed about side effects*		*Satisfied with Current Method*	
	SC/ST	*Non SC/ST*	*SC/ST*	*Non SC/ST*	*SC/ST*	*Non SC/ST*
Age						
Below 25	14.3	18.3	19.0	18.5	71.8	78.7
25–34	17.3	14.3	19.2	18.7	78.2	79.2
35+	13.8	15.5	16.7	18.5	74.1	79.9
Education						
Non-literate	13.4	13.1	16.8	18.9	72.9	75.1
less than 5	19.1	18.1	25.0	20.3	75.0	75.5
5–9 years	21.6	17.4	20.7	18.6	80.8	77.3
10 or more years	26.0	18.5	20.2	16.3	79.5	86.6
Residence						
Rural	14.2	15.0	18.4	19.3	74.3	77.9
Urban	28.0	16.2	13.2	13.3	82.0	85.0
Number of Children						
One	4.5	14.1	31.8	23.5	74.2	83.2
Two	18.5	16.6	16.4	17.9	77.1	83.2
Three	14.5	15.7	18.1	19.2	74.1	77.2
Four plus	15.6	14.4	17.9	18.3	75.1	76.3

Cont'd...

...Cont'd

Religion						
Hindu	15.4	15.1	18.1	18.7	75.5	79.8
Muslim	16.7	16.7	16.7	16.9	66.7	76.6
Christian	11.1	16.7	11.1	33.3	63.6	0.0
Others	0.0	0.0	0.0	66.7	0.0	100.0
Wealth Quintile						
Poorest	12.3	12.3	16.6	18.9	73.3	73.5
Second	16.2	14.5	19.4	19.6	75.2	75.7
Middle	16.1	15.0	18.4	19.1	72.3	78.8
Fourth	20.1	18.3	19.3	18.1	82.5	81.6
Richest	25.4	18.3	10.3	14.1	76.9	88.1
Total	16.1	15.2	18.0	18.6	75.0	79.3

From Table 4 it is clear that quite a high number, i.e. 75 per cent among SC/ST and 80 per cent among non-SC/ST women are satisfied with the current method. It was found that the proportion of women satisfied with current method was high among urban areas (82% in SC/ST and 85% in non-SC/ST) than rural areas (74% in SC/ST and 78% in non-SC/ST). The proportion of women satisfied with the use of current method which they were using increases with the increase in level of education. It was seen that among non-SC/ST women, having no education, this proportion was 75 per cent and it increases with 76 per cent for women less than 5 years of education, 77 per cent for 5–9 years of education and 87 per cent for 10 or more years of education.

Table 5

Per cent of Currently Married SC/ST and non-SC/ST Women using Family Planning Method who have Rated the Services received and Visited by Health Personnel and Advice Received, Bihar, 2007–08

Rating/Follow up Visit	*SC/ST*	*Non-SC/ST*	*Total*
Rating the care for sterilization/IUD			
Very good	77.8	61.7	63.7
Somewhat good	22.2	33.7	32.1
Follow up within 48 hours after adopting the method			
health personal visited	33.3	31.8	31.9
self/husband visited health facility	16.7	25.3	24.5
not visited at all	50.0	42.9	43.6
Advice given by health worker to the user of traditional methods	7.2	10.2	9.5

Table 5 reveals that about 78 per cent of SC/ST and 62 per cent of non-SC/ST women rated the care for sterilization/IUD as very good. Thirty-three per cent of SC/ST and 32 per cent of non-SC/ST women reported that health personnel visited them for follow up services within 48 hours after adopting the method and 17 per cent of SC/ST women and 25 per cent of non-SC/ST women said that either their husband or they themselves visited the health facility for follow up. A very large proportion (50% among SC/ST and 43% among non-SC/ST) of women said that neither health personnel nor they visited for the follow up of the method adopted.

Differentials and Determinants of Contraceptive Use and Unmet Need

As we are aware that one of the aims of NRHM programme in India is to achieve population stabilization and promote healthy married life, the NRHM programme promotes the use of contraception. Table 6 shows the status of contraceptive use among SC/ST and non-SC/ST by any method and any modern methods. The use of any method of family planning is very low in Bihar, only thirty-three per cent currently married women are using family planning. Similarly, figures for SC/ST and non-SC/ST women are 25.4 per cent and 36.0 per cent respectively, which reflects the variation in use of any method of family planning between SC/ST and non-SC/ST women. The use of modern methods of family planning among all women in Bihar is only 29.4 per cent. The use of modern methods among SC/ST women is lower (22.5%) as compared to non-SC/ST women (32.0%).

Table 6

Percentage of Currently Married SC/ST and Non-SC/ST Women who are Currently using any Method and any Modern Methods, Bihar, 2007–08

Type of Family Planning Method Used	*SC/ST*	*Non SC/ST*	*Total*
Any Method	25.4	35.6	33.3
Any Modern Method	21.5	31.7	29.4
Male Sterilization	0.7	0.4	0.3
Female sterilization	18.3	26.6	24.7
IUD	0.2	0.5	0.4
Pill	0.7	1.1	1.0
Condom/Nirodh	0.8	1.3	1.2
Rhythm Method	2.5	2.4	2.4
Withdrawal Method	0.7	0.9	0.9
Other	0.9	1.8	1.8
No. of women (15–49)	9,986	34,307	44,293

Table 6 is showing the percentage of currently married women aged 15–49 years, who are currently using specific contraceptive method according to SC/ST and non-SC/ST. The Table reveals that about 9,986 of SC/ST and 34,307 of non-SC/ST women are currently using contraception out of 44,293 total women in Bihar. The female sterilization method is a popular method as it is being used by around 25 per cent currently married women in Bihar, where contraceptive prevalence rate is only 33 per cent. The female sterilization method is the predominant limiting method being used by 18 per cent of currently married SC/ST women and 27 per cent of currently married non-SC/ST women in 15–49 years age group, and popular male-oriented spacing or temporary method of condom/nirodh is being used by 1 per cent of husbands of currently married women in Bihar. The use of oral pills and IUD are being mainly used by 1.2 per cent of women (0.7% of SC/ST women and 1.1% of non-SC/ST women) and 0.4 per cent of women (0.2% of SC/ST women and 0.5% of non-SC/ST women) respectively. Among the currently married women, the proportion of traditional method is also seen to be significant with 2.4 per cent (2.5% among SC/ST and 2.4% among non-SC/ST) using Rhythm method.

Table 7

Percentage of Currently Married SC/ST and non-SC/ST Women Aged 15–49 Years who are Currently using any Method according to Socio-economic Characteristics, Bihar, 2007–08

Socio-economic Characteristics	*SC/ST*	*Non-SC/ST*	*Total*
Age			
Below 25	8.3	10.8	10.2
25–34	30.6	42.2	39.6
35+	38.9	50.5	48.1
Education			
Non-literate	23.7	31.1	29.12
Less than 5	27.6	37.2	35.3
5–9 years	30.9	40.3	39.1
10 or more years	40.4	49.7	48.8
Residence			
Rural	24.6	34.1	31.96
Urban	37.2	49.4	47.5
Number of Children			

Cont'd...

...Cont'd

One	6.3	9.6	8.8
Two	17.1	34.8	31.3
Three	35.8	52.2	49.0
Four and above	37.9	46.7	44.6
Religion			
Hindu	25.7	39.5	36.0
Muslim	12.4	15.0	14.8
Christian	39.2	83.3	43.9
Others	21.6	53.8	30.0
Wealth Quintile			
Poorest	20.0	26.6	24.4
Second	25.9	31.7	30.3
Middle	34.0	38.3	37.7
Fourth	46.0	47.8	47.6
Richest	49.7	59.4	58.7
Total	25.4	35.6	33.3

Table 7 shows the level of contraceptive use among SC/ST and non-SC/ST women with their socio-economic characteristics. It is observed that there is a high prevalence of contraceptive use among non-SC/ST (35.6%) women than SC/ST (25.4%) women in Bihar. It is found that there is a high prevalence of use of contraception in older women than younger women among both the categories. That is about 39 per cent of SC/ST women and 51 per cent of non-SC/ST women of age-group 35–49 respectively are using any method of contraception while only 8 per cent of SC/ST women and 11 per cent of non-SC/ST women of age-group 15–24 are using any method of contraception.

There is a high prevalence of contraceptive use among women with 10 or more years of education, which is about 40 per cent among SC/ST women and 50 per cent among non-SC/ST women. Same is the case with place of residence; there is a high prevalence among women residing in urban area than women residing in rural areas. The prevalence of contraception also increases with increase in number of living children. That is women with one child are less prone to use contraception than those who have more than two children among both SC/ST and non-SC/ST women in Bihar. It is also evident that prevalence of contraceptive use increases with wealth quintile. The differentials for sources of limiting method among SC/ST and non SC/ST women who are currently using limiting method by socio-economic category have been shown in Table 8.

Table 8

Percentage of Currently Married SC/ST and non-SC/ST Women aged 15–49 Years who are Currently using Limiting Methods by Source and Socio-economic Characteristics, Bihar 2007–08

Socio-economic Characteristics	*SC/ST*			*Non SC/ST*		
	Government	*Private*	*Other*	*Government*	*Private*	*Other*
Age						
Below 25	63.0	33.9	3.1	48.5	49.8	1.7
25–34	57.5	41.0	1.6	51.0	47.4	1.6
35+	72.7	26.5	0.7	68.9	29.9	1.3
Education						
Non literate	68.7	29.9	1.4	63.9	34.7	1.4
Less than 5	55.5	43.1	1.5	60.9	36.8	2.3
5–9 years	57.6	41.9	0.5	59.8	39.1	1.2
10 or more years	45.7	53.3	1.0	45.0	53.8	1.2
Residence						
Rural	65.7	33.0	1.3	60.9	37.6	1.4
Urban	61.2	38.2	0.6	54.9	43.6	1.4
Number of Children						
One	36.4	59.1	4.5	54.5	44.3	1.1
Two	54.1	43.2	2.7	50.9	47.3	1.8
Three	66.7	31.9	1.4	60.5	37.8	1.7
Four and above	66.5	32.5	1.0	63.0	35.9	1.1
Religion						
Hindu	65.5	33.3	1.2	60.9	37.7	1.4
Muslim	50.0	50.0	0.0	46.8	51.4	1.7
Christian	55.6	33.3	11.1	66.7	33.3	0.0
Others	71.4	28.6	0.0	25.0	75.0	0.0
Wealth Quintile						
Poorest	70.4	28.2	1.3	64.8	33.5	1.6
Second	66.1	32.4	1.5	63.1	35.2	1.7
Middle	58.3	40.4	1.3	61.4	37.7	0.8
Fourth	57.1	42.9	0.0	55.1	43.7	1.2
Richest	50.0	50.0	0.0	46.0	52.2	1.7
Total	65.3	33.5	1.3	60.2	38.3	1.4

Table 8 reveals that a high proportion (65%) of SC/ST women is availing limiting methods from government health facilities which is higher than non-SC/ST women (60%). Whereas, the situation is vice-versa for private health facilities, i.e. only 33 per cent of SC/ST women are availing their limiting methods from private facilities while this per cent is a little high (38%) for non-SC/ST women. The currently married women, both among SC/ST and non-SC/ST, the women in higher age group, non-literate women, women living in rural areas, women with at least four children and women in the poorest quintile are more availing limiting methods from government sources.

Unmet Need of Family Planning

Unmet need refers to fecund women who either wish to postpone the next birth (spacers) or who wish to stop childbearing (limiters) but are not using a contraceptive method. This concept clearly indicates a gap between a woman's reproductive intention and contraceptive behaviour. An estimated 150 million women worldwide want to delay or avoid pregnancy but are not using family planning methods. Most of the married women want to use the contraceptive methods but are unable to use them because of lack of knowledge, economical problem, fear of side effects, religious cause, insufficiency of family planning worker, uncooperative husband and limited supply and high cost. Unmet need is a valuable indicator for national family planning programmes because it shows how well they are achieving the key mission of meeting the population's felt need for family planning.

Unmet Need of Family Planning by Method and Socio-economic Characteristics

This section particularly describes the level and socio-economic correlates of unmet need (spacing, limiting) for family planning by background characteristics among SC/ST and non-SC/ST. It can be seen from Table 9 that the level of unmet need among SC/ST women for limiting is relatively high (25%) as compared to non-SC/ST women (22.0%). Similarly, the level of unmet need among SC/ST women for spacing is relatively high (15.0%) as compared to non-SC/ST women (12.8%). It was found that unmet need for spacing method decreases with increase in age among both SC/ST and non-SC/ST group, whereas unmet need for limiting method increases with increase in age of women among both the groups. For instance, among SC/ST women in the age 25 years the unmet need for spacing method was 30 per cent and it decreases as 11 per cent for age group 25–34 and 1 per cent for age group 35 years and above women respectively. The women residing in rural areas have more unmet need among both SC/ST and non-SC/ST women.

Table 9

Percentage of Woman having Unmet need, according to Socio-economic Characteristics among SC/ST and non-SC/ST Women, Bihar 2007–08

Background Variables	*Spacing*		*Limiting*	
	SC/ST	*Non-SC/ST*	*SC/ST*	*Non-SC/ST*
Age				
Below 25	30.5	30.6	9.2	10.1
25–34	11.4	9.3	31.9	26.6
35+	0.8	0.7	35.1	27.1
Education				
Non-literate	13.9	12.3	27.1	25.1
less than 5	19.1	13.7	20.2	18.3
5–9 years	17.4	14.2	15.6	17.1
10 or more years	17.3	12.8	16.2	14.9
Residence				
Rural	14.9	13.1	25.4	22.2
Urban	13.3	9.7	19.6	18.1
Number of children				
No child	12.7	14.4	0.6	0.4
One	40.2	40.4	2.5	4.7
Two	27.5	18.7	17.8	20.6
Three	12.1	7.4	29.2	24.6
Four plus	3.2	2.5	41.2	33.8
Religion				
Hindu	14.8	12.4	24.7	19.7
Muslim	13.8	15.1	35.5	33.2
Christian	13.7	0.0	25.5	0.0
Others	10.8	23.1	27.0	7.7
Wealth quintile				
Poorest	14.6	13.3	28.9	27.8
Second	15.5	14.0	23.2	22.4
Middle	15.4	12.8	20.0	19.3
Fourth	10.0	11.2	18.2	16.7
Richest	11.0	7.6	14.5	13.6
Total	14.8	12.8	25.1	21.8

Results of Logistic Regression Analysis

This section presents the odds ratios from logistic regression analysis. To study the net effect of different background variables on the contraceptive practice and unmet need among currently married women aged 15–49, logistic regression analysis has been carried out. The authors used a range of socio-demographic variables in the analysis that have been found to be significantly associated with contraceptive use and unmet need for family planning in India and elsewhere. These variables are respondent's age (five years of age-interval), place of residence, religion, (Hindu; Muslim; others), number of living children (none; one; two; three; four or more), wealth quintile (poorest, second, middle, fourth) and woman's education (illiterate; less than 5; 5–9 years; 10 or more years).

Table 10

Odds Ratio Showing the effect of Background Variables on the use of any Modern Contraceptive Method and Unmet need among Women Aged 15–49 Years, Bihar, 2007–08: Results of Logistic Regression Analysis

Independent Variables	*Contraceptive Use*	*Unmet Need*
Age		
Below 25		
25–34	2.495***	0.435***
35+	3.830**	0.565***
Education		
non literate		
less than 5	0.561***	0.956**
5–9 years	0.820***	0.588***
10 or more years	0.878***	0.520***
Residence		
Rural ®		
Urban	1.878***	0.877*
Number of Children		
No children ®		
One	4.513***	3.090***
Two	7.907***	1.687***
Three	0.965	1.383***
Caste		
SC/ST®		
Non SC/ST	1.691***	0.816***
Religion		
Hindu ®		
Muslim	1.471**	0.998
Other	1.361*	1.083**

Cont'd...

...Cont'd

Wealth Quintile		
poorest ®		
Second	1.645	1.066
Middle	5.350	1.041
Fourth	4.619	1.012
Richest	5.218	1.215
Constant	1.300	8.634***

Note: ®: Reference Category; *, **, *** shows 10 per cent, 5 per cent and 1 per cent level of significance respectively.

Table 10 explains that age has highly significant relation with use of modern method. As age increases the women are more likely to use contraception. Educational level of women makes a significant difference in the use of contraception in all categories of education, that is 44 per cent of women with less than 5 years of education are more likely to use contraception than those with no education and this percentage increases as we move towards the higher categories of education. The prevalence of contraception depends to a large extent on the type of the place of residence. Women residing in urban areas are 0.878 times more likely to use contraception than their counterparts residing in rural areas. Again, the number of living children influences the use of contraception. Women with 1 child are 4.51 times more likely to use contraceptives than women without any child and women with 2 children are 7.90 times more likely to use contraceptives than women without child and so on. The analysis also indicates that religion and wealth index of women are playing insignificant role in contraceptive use. Hence the variables age, education, place of residence and number of living children are affecting the contraceptive use mostly and have some significant impact.

The Table also shows the odds ratios from logistic regression analysis for unmet need for family planning. Age of women, number of children, and religion are highly significant factors influencing the unmet need for spacing. With increase in age, the unmet need for spacing increased significantly. Among currently married rural young (<25) women, Muslim women of Bihar, unmet need increased significantly by 8 per cent compared to Hindu women. As the number of children increases, the unmet need reduced, i.e. the women with one child is 3.090 times more likely to have unmet need of contraception, women with two children are 1.69 times more likely to have unmet need and women with 3 children are 1.38 times more likely to have unmet need of contraception than women with no children.

Conclusion

From the analysis it has been found that use of contraception in Bihar is low. Only 33 per cent and 29 per cent currently married women are using any method and any modern method of contraception respectively, in Bihar. Also there are considerable differences in use of contraception between currently married women of SC/ST and non-SC/ST in Bihar. The use of any modern methods among SC/ST women is low (22%) as compared to non-SC/ST women (32%) in Bihar. Like other states in India, the use of female sterilization method in Bihar is popular. Around 25 per cent of currently married women belonging to SC/ST are currently using female sterilization method. It has been found from regression analysis that age, education, residence and number of children of currently married women is positively associated with the use of any modern method of contraception in Bihar.

There is considerable variation in use of contraception by districts in Bihar. The quality of family planning services has been assessed with available few indicators. Eighteen per cent and 19 per cent currently married women among SC/ST and non-SC/ST respectively were informed about side effects of family planning in Bihar. Seventy per cent SC/ST women and 62 per cent non-SC/ST women respectively, rated the care for sterilization/IUD as very good. The unmet need for family planning is high among SC/ST as compared to non-SC/ST women in Bihar. For example, unmet need for spacing is 15 per cent among SC/ST women as compared to 13 per cent among non-SC/ST women. Similarly, unmet need for limiting method is 25 per cent among SC/ST women as compared to only 22 per cent among non-SC/ST women. The results of regression analysis show that age and number of children of currently married women are positively associated with unmet need of family planning in Bihar.

References

Bhattacharya, S.K., R. Ram, D.N. Goswami, U.D. Gupta, K. Bhattacharya and S. Ray. 2006. 'Study of Unmet Need for Family Planning among Women of Reproductive Age Group Attending Immunization Clinic in a Medical College in Kolkata', *Indian Journal of Community Medicine*, 31(2): 73–75.

Bongaarts, J. 1978. 'A Framework for Analysing the Proximate Determinants of Fertility', *Population and Development Review*, 4(1): 105–132.

Bongaarts, J. and J. Bruce. 1995. 'The Causes of Unmet Need for Contraception and the Social Content of Services', *Studies in Family Planning*, 26(2): 57–75.

Curtis, S.L. and C.F. Westoff. 1996. 'Intention to Use Contraceptives and Subsequent Contraceptive Behaviour in Morocco', *Studies in Family Planning*, 27(5): 239–250.

Devi, Radha D., S.R. Rastogi and R.D. Rutherford. 1996. Unmet Need for Family Planning in Uttar Pradesh. National Family Health Survey Subject Report No. 1, 1–27.

Dwivedi, S.N. 1992. 'Contribution of Some Socio-economic Variables Towards Explaining the Level of Adoption of Various Family Planning Devices in India During 1987', *Demography India*, 21(2): 239–245.

Fathonah, Siti. 1996. Contraceptive Use Dynamics in Indonesia. DHS Working Papers, Number 20, Macro International Inc., Calverton, Maryland, USA.

Gulati, S.C. 1996. 'Contraceptive Method's Use and Choice in Kerala and Uttar Pradesh: Multinomial Logit Analysis of NFHS Data', *Demography India*, 25(2): 205–220.

International Institute for Population Sciences (IIPS) and ORC Macro. 2007. *National Family Health Survey (NFHS), 2005–06, Uttar Pradesh*. Mumbai: IIPS.

International Institute for Populatin Sciences (IIPS) and Population Research Centre (PRC). 1985. Baseline Survey on Fertility, Mortality and Related Facts and in Rural Gujarat, IIPS, Bombay and PRC, Baroda.

Islam, Jahirul and Shahin Reza. 2013. 'Determinants of Current Contraception Use among the Ever-married Females in Rajshahi District of Bangladesh', *Middle East Journal of Nursing*, 7(2): 191–195.

Jain, A. 1997. 'Consistency between Contraceptive Use and Fertility in India', *Demography India*, 26(1): 19–36.

Jain, Anrudh K. and Aparna Jain. 1995. *Family Planning in Asia and the Pacific: Addressing the Challenges*. UNFPA.

Kanitkar, Tara and B. Murthy. 1983. *Factor Associated with Contraception in Bihar and Rajasthan: Findings from Recent Sample Surveys, Dynamics of Population and Family Welfare*. Delhi: Himalaya Publishing House.

Kishore, J. 2007. *National Health Programs of India*, 7th edition. New Delhi: Century Publications.

Laya, K.S. 2012. 'Prevalence and Determinants of Unmet Need for Family Planning among Women in India', *Research and Social Practices in Social Sciences*, 7(2): 59–70.

Mehmood, Arshad and Syeda Saman Naz. 2008–09. *Contraceptive Use: Dynamics in Pakistan*. Islamabad: Population Council.

Ministry of Health and Family Welfare. 2009. *Family Welfare Programme in India: Year Book 2008*. Department of Family Welfare, New Delhi.

Office of Registrar General, India (ORGI). 2012. Sample Registration System, Ministry of Home Affairs, Government of India, New Delhi.

Okech, Timothy C., Nelson W. Wawire and Tom K. Mburu. 2011. 'Contraceptive Use among Women of Reproductive Age in Kenya's City Slums', *International Journal of Business and Science*, 2(1): 22–43.

Raju, K.N.M. and T.N. Bhat. 1995. 'Sex Composition of Living Children Against Socio-economic Variables with Accepting Family Planning Methods', *Demography India*, 24: 87–99.

Ramesh, B.M., S.C. Gulati and D. Rutherford. 1996. Contraceptive Use in India 1992–93. NFHS Subject Report No. 2, Mumbai: International Institute for Population Sciences and Honolulu: East West Centre.

Registrar General, India, 2004. 'Census of India 2001, Population Probiles: (India, States and UTs): Total Population and Scheduled Castes and Scheduled Tribes'. New Delhi: Registrar General of India.

Roy, K.P., P. Haldar, S. Bisoi, R.T. Guha, R. Chowdhury and T.K. Sarkar et al. 2011. 'Bridging the Unmet Need in Contraceptive Practice with Natural Methods: A Study from Kolkata, India', *The Health*, 2(3): 78–81.

Roy, T.K., D.R. Devi, R.K. Verma, S. Parsuraman and B. Paswan. 1991. Health Services and Family Planning in Rural Maharashtra (Baseline Survey in Bhandana, Chandrapur, Dhule and Nagpur District), IIPS, Bombay.

Sahoo, H. 2007. 'Determinants of Contraceptive Use in Orissa: An Analysis of National Family Health Survey III', *Health and Population: Perspectives and Issues*, 30(3): 208–221.

Srivastava, D.K., P. Goutam, R. Goutam, N. Gour and M. Bansal. 2011. 'A Study to Assess the Unmet Need of Family Planning in Gwalior District and to Study the Factors that Helps in Determining it', *National Journal of Community Medicine*, 2(1): 28–31.

Visaria, Leela. 2002. The Proximate Determinants of Fertility in India. India Project, Working Paper, Department of Social Policy, London School of Economics.

7

Adolescent Fertility Behaviour in Bihar

Evidence from NFHS–3 Data

P.K. SARANGI

The term adolescence is a relatively new concept, especially in rational thinking. Adolescence is a developmental transition between childhood and adulthood. It is generally considered to begin at about the age of thirteen and to end in the late teens. This is the period where maximum changes can be observed in an individual as compared to the other phases of life. Adolescence is a distinct group with their own unique needs and concerns. The increase in attention towards adolescents is due to the recognition of this group as a significant proportion of the total population, and also as the future guardians of the nation's development.

Adolescence is a crucial period for emotional life, because of experimentation in sexual relationship. Understanding the various factors affecting overall development of adolescent is as important as understanding the significance of studying adolescents. Adolescents' reproductive behaviour has been a concern, especially, during the recent decades. The adverse socio-economic and personal repercussions of adolescent childbearing are inversely related to teenage mothers. The young mother invariably drops out of school and becomes overly dependent on her family for economic support. They lose educational opportunities and their lifetime opportunities for self-advancement are seriously damaged. The fertility pattern and contraceptive use among adolescents help us to understand the implications for adolescent reproductive health in a society. It also gives insight to the future reproductive health situation, as this group traverses through the reproductive span. International Conference on

Population and Development held in 1994 has identified the adolescents as a distinct target group in need of ad hoc reproductive health programmes and services. In developed countries, it has taken on a different dimension and various steps have been taken in terms of policy orientation to control and reduce adolescent pregnancy. In developing countries, even though, adolescent pregnancy has been identified as a pressing social issue, this perception is hardly translated into policies and programmes, intended for the adolescents.

The status of the country's reproductive health reflects the socio-economic diversity of its states. For example, the average number of children women have over their lifetime, one of the primary indicators of their reproductive health, is comfortably below the replacement level of fertility in several states of India (Andhra Pradesh, Kerala and Tamil Nadu in the South; Goa in the West; and Himachal Pradesh in the North). Yet the fertility rate remains at nearly four children per woman in the first and third most populous states, Uttar Pradesh and Bihar, respectively. Taking this view into consideration, studying reproductive behaviour of adolescent girls from the social perspective is very much important.

Jejeebhoy documented the existing information on sexual and reproductive behaviour, as well as knowledge and attitudes among the adolescents in India. The review argues, despite the fact that adolescents represent a quarter of the population till recent years, they have not been considered a distinct group, and little information is available regarding their reproductive health behaviour. Some of the established findings are: adolescent marriage and fertility rates are disturbingly high and adolescents face a variety of reproductive health problems. The review also suggests more community-based and behavioural research to be done alongside biomedical studies, giving the following recommendations: (i) investigate reproductive health needs and decision-making authority among married adolescent girls; (ii) investigate premarital sexual behaviour, awareness, and attitudes among adolescent boys and girls; (iii) describe the levels, patterns, and context of abortion among both unmarried and married adolescent girls, and awareness of its legal status.

Pathak and Ram (1993) highlighted the effects on child survival and maternal mortality in context of adolescent marriages and motherhood in India. Insight is provided into the prevailing cultural norms in India that see early motherhood and large family size as old-age security. A study by Aggarwal and Kumar (1997), evaluated the existing level of knowledge and awareness about AIDS from rural and urban areas. The adolescents feel neglected as they are neither recognized as children nor as adults.

Pandey et al. (1999), in a handbook on Indian adolescents raises crucial issues concerning literacy rates, reproductive health behaviour, drug-abuse, gender issues, and rising crime rates. A need for educational intervention to provide accurate knowledge has been cited as the rationale behind the package.

In this paper, a broad descriptive overview of the current status and recent changes in indicators of early marriage and child-bearing in Bihar is presented. It may help policymakers and programme planners by assessing the needs of adolescents for information and services, and the extent to which those needs are being met. The analysis is made using data from National Family Health Survey (NFHS-3) conducted during 2005–06. When needed, projections from the census and published studies are used to supplement these data.

Objectives of the Study

The main objectives of this study are:

1. To examine magnitude of adolescent fertility in Bihar.
2. To find out the factors of teenage motherhood, child loss and their pregnancy wastage in Bihar.

Data Source and Methodology

The analysis focuses primarily on adolescent women. The data for the study are taken from NFHS–3, which is the most recent major survey on health and demography in India. The survey was designed to collect quality data on population and health through indicators of fertility, family planning, maternal and child health, nutrition, HIV/AIDS and socio-economic conditions (International Institute for Population Sciences and Macro International, 2007). In addition, census and published studies are used to supplement these data. The study analyses the importance of socio-economic and demographic factors, affecting adolescent's fertility in the state of Bihar using Logistic Regression Analysis.

Adolescent Women in India

Adolescent women comprise a sizable proportion of India's total population. The characteristics that influence the likelihood of becoming a mother at a young age, their family's values and socio-economic status and their goals and expectations, are mainly shaped by their place of residence, their educational attainment and the extent of their exposure to the mass media, which also vary substantially.

According to NFHS–1 (1992–93), India had 38 million adolescent women (International Institute for Population Sciences, 1995) and by 2005–06 that number increased to 50.5 million. The three states with the largest female adolescent population are Andhra Pradesh, Maharashtra and Uttar Pradesh, together account for one-third of all adolescent women in the country, with nearly 16 per cent of the total living in Uttar Pradesh alone. In many states including Bihar, 15–19 year-old women make up at least 10 per cent of the state's population. A general decline in fertility is evident in the three low fertility states of Himachal Pradesh, Goa and Kerala as adolescent women account for a smaller proportion of the total state population (8–9%) than they do elsewhere (10–13%). Adolescence is a time of gradual transition from childhood to adulthood. For a high proportion of Indian girls, this stage of their lives is very short, since many transcend directly from childhood to motherhood. Because the social status of women is intricately linked with their marital and reproductive behaviour, understanding how and when girls marry and begin their families is essential to study for change.

Early Marriage

Marriage identifies the onset of exposure to the risk of socially sanctioned childbearing in all the societies, and is considered as the principal determinants of fertility. The practice of early marriage of girls is still widely followed in India. At the national level, it has decreased to 28 per cent (46% in Bihar) in 2005–06 from 39 per cent (51% in Bihar) in the year 1992. Still, the proportion is significant as more than a quarter of the females are married in their teens. For some states like Himachal Pradesh, the proportion is as low as 6 per cent, whereas in Bihar; the proportion is as high as 46 per cent. Undoubtedly, there has been a decline in the number of child marriages, but adolescents are still marrying at almost the same rate. It seems, the Marriage Act, 1978 has no impact on marriage behaviour. Therefore, in order to bring about a rise in age at marriage, we need to bring about congenial social change, wherein the parents are able to accommodate modern ideas by engaging their adolescent daughters in school.

Early Motherhood

In Indian cultural context, teenage pregnancy is socially accepted, gives identity, is a source of status, and reaffirms entry into adulthood. The expectation in the Indian socio-cultural milieu that after marriage a woman will become pregnant as soon as possible encourages early onset of maternity and higher adolescent fertility. Having children early in life exposes adolescent girls to unnecessary risks. Their chance of dying is twice as high as that of a woman who waits until her 20s to begin childbearing. In addition, early childbearing greatly reduces the likelihood of a girl advancing her education and limits her opportunities for training and employment. The trend has certainly been downward, but there are very sharp differences in levels and trends across regions.

At the national level, the proportion of adolescent mothers has decreased to 0.16 in 2005 from 0.70 in the year 1961. Still the proportion is significant as one-sixth of the mothers are in their teens. For some states like Himachal Pradesh, the proportion is as low as 0.03, whereas in Bihar the proportion is as high as 0.25. An analysis of age-specific fertility rate (ASFR) for married Indian women 15–19 years reveals that nationally it ranges between 0.08 to 0.09. ASFR is highest for the state of Bihar (0.13) and lowest for the state of Goa (0.03). It is also relatively low for the states of Himachal Pradesh, Kerala, J&K and Punjab, implying that the rate at which married adolescents are becoming mothers are directly proportional to the proportion married.

Contraceptive Use

Delaying the first birth, subsequent births and preventing infection is a complicated issue for married girls. They are under pressure to prove their fertility in their marital home (Santhya and Jejeebhoy, 2003). Contraceptive Prevalence Rate (CPR) is very low in all the states which ranges from 1.9 per cent (Bihar) to 18 per cent (Delhi), implying that the fertility inhibiting effect of contraception is almost insignificant in this age group. The main reason may be that women want children, which is obvious in the newly wedded status of marriage.

Unmet Need for Contraception

Adolescents' ability to prevent unwanted pregnancy may be assessed by examining the extent to which they can act on their reproductive desires. Though, majority of married adolescent women (52%–74%) do not want a child during first two years of marriage, the proportion using a modern method to achieve the goal is far lower. At the national level, the unmet need among adolescents is around 43 per cent. Substantial variations are found across states and regions with respect to unmet need. Assam, West Bengal, Uttar Pradesh and Bihar are the states having unmet need of 54 per cent, 51 per cent, 50 per cent and 49 per cent, respectively, while Andhra Pradesh shows low per cent of unmet need (23%) among adolescents.

Female Education

Female education is accepted as the most promising agent of change in woman's access to power and control over resources, as well as demographic conditions. It enhances women's ability to interpret and act on those messages. Throughout the world, higher levels of educational attainment are consistently associated with higher status for women, related delays in marriage and desire for and achievement of smaller families. Over the past decade and a half, Indian women have achieved substantial educational gains. Nationally, 63 per cent of 15–19 year-old women had at least six years of education in 2006, compared with just 45 per cent in 1993. Data reveals that there are wide variations among adolescents of different states and the prevalence of illiteracy is quite high in many states. State-wise; Kerala and Himachal Pradesh have very high proportion of educated girls, 98 per cent and 93 per cent, compared to Bihar with 39 per cent. The increase was proportionately greater in rural areas, where the starting point was far lower.

Across regions, it is found that adolescent marriage has decreased with increasing years of schooling. Although the empirical evidence in support of this relationship is ambiguous, still, education has been proven to have the undisputed effect of delaying the age at marriage, and higher levels of education shows, the incidence of adolescent pregnancy decreasing. Also, there is a close association between educational attainment with age at marriage and fertility regulation.

Female Autonomy

Women's autonomy constitutes a key element of her social status. Amin et al. (2002) found in Bangladesh that married adolescent girls had less autonomy than their aged counterparts. NFHS–3 revealed that more adolescent women are involved in household decision-making in Tamil Nadu, followed by Gujarat with UP and Rajasthan at the bottom. In India, 53.9 per cent (46.4% in Bihar) of the adolescent women are involved in household decision-making. The involvement is 96.2 per cent for married women of age 45–49 years, which shows, that age plays an important role in autonomy of women.

Place of Residence

Young women's marital and reproductive behaviours are conditioned by place of residence, and most adolescents still live in rural areas. Fewer than three in 10 women aged 15–19 currently reside in urban areas. That proportion has increased for the country as a whole, by an annual rate of about 1 per cent (i.e. the percentage residing in urban areas rose from 25% in 1992 to 28% in 2005). However, the pace of urbanization has varied from state to state and is as low as 16 per cent in Bihar (2005).

Exposure to Mass Media

A woman's exposure to media can link her to modern messages and inherently determine the degree to which she hears or sees public information campaigns. Kishor (2000) found media exposure was positively associated with two dimensions of women's empowerment, namely participation in the modern sector and sharing of roles and decision-making. In the study, it is found that married girls consistently have less exposure to the media and more than one-fourth (28.5%) of the adolescent women are not regularly exposed to any mass media. More married adolescent women are exposed to mass media in southern and western states, compared to their counterparts in the eastern and central states like Bihar, Rajasthan, Odisha and UP. In India, the proportion of ever-married adolescent women who watch television nearly doubled from 23 per cent in 1993 to 40 per cent in 2006. Exposure to television has been significantly associated with factors that enhance women's status, such as lower fertility, reduced preference for sons and increased autonomy. Although the mechanisms of these relationships are difficult to identify and measure, there is enormous potential to convey reproductive health messages through entertainment programmes.

Table 1

Fertility Behaviour among Women age 15–19 Years by Region, India, 2005–2006

Region and States	*% ever Married*	*% started Child Rearing*	*% using Contraceptives*	*% Unmet Need*	*ASFR*
North: (Delhi, Haryana, Himachal Pradesh, J&K, Punjab, Rajasthan and Uttarakhand)	16	8	7.5	34	0.05
Central: (Chhattisgarh, Madhya Pradesh and UP)	27	15	5.6	46	0.1
East: (Bihar, Jharkhand, Odisha and West Bengal)	41	23	7.9	48	0.11
North-East: (Arunachal Pradesh, Assam, Manipur, Meghalaya, Mizoram, Nagaland, Sikkim and Tripura)	20	10	7.7	51	0.06
West: (Goa, Gujarat and Maharashtra)	21	12	9.7	38	0.07
South: (Andhra Pradesh, Karnataka, Kerala and Tamil Nadu)	23	14	6.6	32	0.08
Bihar	46	25	1.9	49	0.13
India	28	16	6.9	43	0.12

Sources: Computed from National Family Health Surveys, 2005–2006.

Table 2

Selected Socio-demographic Characteristics among Adolescent Women by Region, India, 2005–2006

Region and States	*% having more than 6 years of Education*	*% with TV exposure at least once a week*	*% staying in Urban Area*	*Among 20–24 Years, % Marrying before Age 18 Years*
North: (Delhi, Haryana, Himachal Pradesh, J&K, Punjab, Rajasthan and Uttarakhand)	73	52	37	26.8
Central: (Chhattisgarh, Madhya Pradesh and UP)	55	36	27	52.9

Cont'd…

...Cont'd

East: (Bihar, Jharkhand, Odisha and West Bengal)	53	23	21	51.8
Northeast: (Arunachal Pradesh, Assam, Manipur, Meghalaya, Mizoram, Nagaland, Sikkim and Tripura)	66	42	23	26.6
West: (Goa, Gujarat and Maharashtra)	82	56	42	32.4
South: (Andhra Pradesh, Karnataka, Kerala and Tamil Nadu)	83	63	35	37.1
Bihar	39	16	17	60.0
India	63	40	28	45

Source: Computed from National Family Health Surveys, 2005–2006.

Bihar: A Snap Shot

Bihar is India's third most populous state after UP and Maharashtra. According to 2011 population census, the population of Bihar is 103 million, which is about 8.58 per cent of the total population of the country. Over the last decade, the state has witnessed a 25 per cent growth in its population, which is among the highest in India and with a fertility rate of 3.9 (2005), it is only going to increase further. Bihar's performance on HDI such as health, education and sanitation is below the national average. The state has the lowest literacy rate at 63.82 per cent and 50 per cent of the population above 15 years of age are illiterate.

Table 3

Socio-Demographic Indicators of Bihar and India

Indicator	*Bihar*	*India*
Total population (In Crore) (Census 2011)	10.38	121.01
Decadal Growth (%) (Census 2011)	25.07	17.64
Crude Birth Rate (SRS 2011)	27.7	21.8
Crude Death Rate (SRS 2011)	6.7	7.1
Natural Growth Rate (SRS 2011)	21	14.7
Infant Mortality Rate (SRS 2011)	44	44
Maternal Mortality Rate (SRS 2007–09)	261	212

Cont'd...

...Cont'd

Total Fertility Rate (SRS 2011)	3.6	2.4
Sex Ratio (Census 2011)	916	940
Child Sex Ratio (Census 2011)	933	914
Total Literacy Rate (%) (Census 2011)	63.82	74.04
Male Literacy Rate (%) (Census 2011)	73.39	82.14
Female Literacy Rate (%) (Census 2011)	53.33	65.46

Source: RHS Bulletin, March 2012, M/O Health & F.W., GOI

Girls in Bihar have traditionally been married young; face extreme social and economic inequality; and are pressed by parents, in-laws and the community to prove their fertility soon after marriage. The results:

- Nearly all women in Bihar (80%) are married before their 20th birthday.
- Twenty-five per cent of young women aged 15–19 in Bihar have already begun childbearing compared to only 16 per cent of young women in India.
- By age 19, more than half (58%) of young women in Bihar are pregnant or already have children.
- Repeated childbearing with short birth intervals is a common risk factor.
- These patterns of marrying early, giving births in their teens and too short birth intervals adversely affect the health and lives of women, as well as the survival and development of their children and their entire communities.

Logistic Regression Analysis and Findings

Determinants of Adolescent Fertility

To understand the influence of each predictor variable on the response variable (children ever-born), the technique of logistic regression analysis has been used and the summary results are presented in Table 4. The findings outline that women educated up to middle school and those up to high school & above were found less likely to be mothers in teenage as compared to the illiterate women. Obviously, education of at least up to the standard of middle school and high school level influences the teenage motherhood, through knowledge and awareness about the planned family and hazards behind early motherhood. An examination into the age at marriage showed that women marrying after the legal age are less likely to attain motherhood at teenage. Other factors, use of contraception and exposure to mass media, affect the adolescent fertility most significantly.

Determinants of Child Loss

Survival of children in the context of teenage motherhood is always at an elevated risk. To find out the determinants of child loss to teenage mothers, a logistic regression analysis is carried out. Table 4 shows that the teenage women educated up to middle school and above are less likely to have child loss as compared to the illiterate women. Implicitly, education influences the child survival within teenage motherhood through knowledge and awareness about childcare. It may be affecting the child loss indirectly through factors like birth interval, maternal age at childbirth and prenatal health care. The odds of the child loss to women were found to be higher in case of the women living in rural areas in comparison to those living in urban areas. The difference is also found to be statistically significant. In addition, media exposure also explains significant influence on the child loss to the teenage women.

Table 4

Determinants of Teenage Motherhood, their Child Loss and Pregnancy Wastage in Bihar: Results from Logistic Regression Analysis

Predictor Variables	*Teenage Motherhood*		*Child loss to the Teenage Mothers*		*Pregnancy Wastage to Teenage Mothers*	
	B	*EXP(B)*	*B*	*EXP(B)*	*B*	*EXP(B)*
Age at Marriage						
18–19 Years®						
15–17 Years	0.894***	2.455	0.154	1.167	.511**	1.612
Use of Contraception						
Using ®						
Not using	0.501**	1.65	0.035	1.036	–	–
Exposure to Mass media						
Exposed ®						
Not Exposed	0.221*	1.247	0.550**	1.734	.367**	1.443
Women's Autonomy						
Autonomy ®						

Cont'd...

...Cont'd

No Autonomy	–0.033	0.968	0.55	1.734	0.035	1.036
Woman's Education						
Illiterate ®						
Up to Middle School complete	–.471**	0.624	–.503**	0.605	–.5334**	0.5866
High School Complete and above	–.533**	0.587	–.963**	0.382	–.963**	0.382
Residence						
Urban ®						
Rural	–0.145	0.867	.369*	1.446	–.1445*	0.8665
Delivery Complication						
Not Experiencing						
Experiencing complication	–	–	0.331**	1.565	–	–

Note: ®: Reference Category; *P < 0 .05, **P <0.01, ***P <0.001.

Determinants of Pregnancy Wastage

The fate of pregnancy outcomes particularly, still births and abortions (pregnancy wastage) has lot more importance in case of teenage mothers. From the summary result of logistic regression analysis in Table 4, it is found that women having education up to high school and above and marrying late are less likely to have pregnancy wastage. A small contradiction is observed when higher odd values are found for women with urban residence and who do have exposure to mass media. The reason may be attributable to health facility in urban areas and exposure to health bulletins (through mass media) that helped them to get rid of unwanted pregnancies and resume safe birth.

Govt. Policies to Promote Adolescents' Reproductive Health

The Government of India and the state government have adopted several policies that have the potential to advance the reproductive health of adolescents, both directly and indirectly.

- The National Population Policy, 2000 specifies the goals of educating adolescents about the risks of unprotected sex and mentions the special requirements for accessible and affordable contraceptive services in rural areas. The policy calls for stricter enforcement of the minimum age at marriage and also recommends financial incentives to induce both postponing first births and having fewer births.

- The 2001 National Policy for the Empowerment of Women explicitly defines child marriage as a form of 'discrimination against the girl child' and calls for compulsory registration of marriages and of births. It predicted that by 2010, child marriages will be eliminated through consistent improvements in education, better marriage registration and increased use of incentives. Though the goal has been achieved to a large extent, child marriage is still taking place at a slow pace.
- The 2003 National Youth Policy identifies adolescents and females in particular, as a priority target group and acknowledges their needs for separate general health clinics. It includes text on sensitizing adolescents on the correct age to marry and begin a family.
- The country's National Plan of Action for Children of 2005 asserts that all adolescents with no mention of marital status—receive sexual and reproductive health information, including information on HIV/AIDS, in school curricula.
- The country's Eleventh Five-Year Plan, for the years 2007–2012, insists on the compulsory registration of marriage and on verification of age at the time of marriage.

Conclusion

This paper introspects to identify the lead factors responsible for teenage motherhood and the consequences to the pregnancy outcomes within the prevailing societal framework of teenage marriage in the state of Bihar. The results show that most of the households who follow adolescent fertility norms come from the rural section of the society with a low literacy rate. Age at marriage sharply varies across the states in India. Except a few states, more than 25 per cent of the girls get married in their adolescence which is as high as 46 per cent in Bihar. This study also attempted to highlight the magnitude of adolescent marriage and levels of adolescent fertility in terms of proximate determinants. From the logistic regression analysis (Table 4), it is found that age at marriage, use of contraception, exposure to mass media and woman's education affect the adolescent fertility most significantly. The fate of pregnancy outcomes, particularly still births and abortions (pregnancy wastage) bear importance to teenage mothers. Women having a higher level of education are much less likely to have pregnancy wastage than illiterate women and the difference is found to be statistically significant. The other factors having significant effects are early marriage, exposure to mass media and urban residence. A small contradiction is observed when higher odds values are found for women with urban residence and who have exposure to mass media than those who have not.

For achieving both these objectives – delaying marriage and supporting married girls—we need a mix of social, economic, and health interventions. Increased enforcement of existing policies is crucial for prevention of child marriage, as future policy formulation, suitable cultural opportunities are required to provide them for late marriage. This is possible by raising awareness among girls through their parents, school and communities about the harmful health consequences of early pregnancy. There is also a need to educate adolescents about puberty, menstruation, contraception and infections and help them acquire good health. Support and access to improved family welfare programmes are urgently needed for teenaged married women, their husbands, and their families to reduce the high fertility.

Adolescent-specific reproductive health services continue to be scarce and inadequate, and targeted mainly towards married adolescents. Service providers must treat pregnant adolescents as high-risk group and closely monitor the service needs of adolescents. The adolescent marriages can be rooted out if we have a literate society, wherein the parents are able to provide a congenial environment to their adolescent daughters by engaging them in schools, colleges etc. Programmes to keep girls in schools hold promise for decreasing early marriages. Since childbearing outside marriage is rare, delay in marriage will go a long way towards reducing adolescent fertility. There is also a need to provide them with suitable culturally sensitive opportunities for economic activities to delay marriage. If married adolescent girls can be better educated about family planning methods and can be motivated to adopt the small family norm by postponing the birth of the first child and properly spacing birth, both infant and maternal mortality rates can be significantly reduced.

References

Aggarwal, A.K. and R. Kumar. 1997. 'Awareness of AIDS among School Children in Haryana', in O.P. Aggarwal et al. (eds), *HIV/AIDS Research in India*. New Delhi: NACO, Ministry of Health and Family Welfare, Government of India, 176–189.

Amin, Sajeda et al. 2002. Baseline Survey Report on Rural Adolescents in Bangladesh. Dhaka: Ministry of Women's Affairs, Government of Bangladesh.

International Institute for Population Sciences (IIPS) and Macro International. 2007. *National Family Health Survey (NHFS–3), 2005–06, India*. Mumbai: IIPS.

International Institute for Population Sciences (IIPS). 1995. *National Family Health Survey (MCH and Family Planning), India, 1992–93*. Mumbai: IIPS.

Jejeebhoy, S. 1996. 'Adolescent Sexuality and Fertility', *Seminar*, 447: 16–23.

Kishor, Sunita. 2000. 'Empowerment of Women in Egypt and Links to the Survival and Health of Their Infants', in Harriet Presser and Gita Sen (eds), *Women's Empowerment and Demographic Processes: Moving Beyond Cairo*. Oxford: Oxford University Press, 119–156.

Pandey, J. et al. 1999. *Adolescence Education in Schools: A Package of Basic Materials*. New Delhi: NCERT.

Pathak, K.B. and F. Ram. 1993. 'Adolescent Motherhood: Problems and Consequences', *The Journal of Family Welfare*, 39(1): 17–23.

Santhya, K.G. and Shireen Jejeebhoy. 2003. 'Sexual and Reproductive Health Needs of Married Adolescent Girls', *Economic and Political Weekly*, 38(41): 4370–4377.

8

Demographic Outcomes and RCH Services Utilization in Bihar

Where is the Gap?

RAJESH RAUSHAN, MUKESH RAVI RAUSHAN AND SHANTI BHUSHAN KUMARI

India was the first country in the world to implement a population control policy in early 50s for control over fertility and providing a healthy nation with healthy families. Even the pre-independence, Bhore committee (1946) had been recommended to improve the public health with cantering on control over various infectious diseases, high maternal and infant & child mortality and gross malnutrition across the country. The major paradigm shifts in India's population policies have occurred since ICPD (1994).[1] The population control policies shifted from earlier method-mix target oriented approach to client-oriented and demand driven community-needs assessment approach, subsequently renamed as reproductive and child health (RCH) services in 1996–97. The same RCH approach predominantly got reflected in the National Population Policy, 2000; and finally in National Rural Health Mission, 2005, implemented in 2006 (now under National Health Mission). Subsequently, a new strategic approach 'Reproductive, Maternal, Newborn, Child Plus Adolescent Health (RMNCH+A)[2] is initiated for second phase of NRHM (2012–17) to improve the quality of health and reduce the maternal and child mortality in the line of Millennium Development Goals 4 and 5 and also to reduce the fertility to replacement level to accelerate the goal of population stabilization till 2045, by enhancing the maternal and child health (MCH) care components. Undoubtedly, country has progressed much on demographic and health outcomes with decline in fertility but with much faster rate in mortality for mothers and children. But, globally we are lagging behind and despite much progress, India is amongst the top five countries in terms of absolute numbers of maternal and child deaths (MoHFW, 2013). Higher wanted as well as unwanted fertility in many states of India, still substantially higher levels of unmet need for contraception and lack of quality health care services as well as reproductive and child health (RCH) services are haunting India's development planners.

Theoretical and empirical findings depicts that utilization of RCH services and their linkages with basic demographic parameters and socio-economic developmental factors have often been found significantly in abundant studies across the world and in case of India (Satia and Jejeebhoy, 1991; Bose, 1996; Visaria et al., 1999; Gulati, 2005; IIPS and Macro International, 2007; Rutherford et al., 2009; Gulati et al., 2010; Dyson, 2011; Kumar, et al., 2012; MoHFW, 2013). Furthermore, various policies and programme implementation strategies have also affirmed the provision of quality RCH services to come forward with better demographic outcomes (IIPS and Macro International, 2007; Gulati et al., 2010; MoHFW, 2013). But, there is wide variation in inter-state vis-a-vis intra-state variation in demographic outcomes, RCH services utilization, and it can be said that there is a clear north-south divide (Bose, 1996; Viasria et al., 1999) on one hand, and more complexity and variation in north India as compared to the south India on the other hand. In north India, Empowered Action Group (EAG) sates are performing the worst on those indicators making it a ridiculous task to achieving population stabilization. The highest fertility rate persisting in Bihar further raises the issue to deepen it to micro level to understand intra-state complexity of RCH services utilization and demographic outcomes in this regard.

Why Bihar Matters?

In India, at regional as well on state level, there is huge variation on demographic outcomes and RCH services utilization needs more attention in the states of poor RCH components utilization and adverse demographic outcomes. As per the nationwide reports from national family health survey and latest sample registration system, it is evident that most of the south Indian states have reached near to replacement level fertility, or near to it, but the major problem is with north Indian states (IIPS and Macro International, 2007; MoHFW, 2013). Plethora of studies and evidences supports that is

EAG sates are performing worst on those indicators making ridiculous task to achieving population stabilization. Most of the southern states viz. Kerala, Tamil Nadu, Andhra Pradesh; and other states like Karnataka, Maharashtra, Punjab and West Bengal had already achieved below replacement fertility i.e. TFR <2.1, by 2009. Currently, twenty-one states/union territories have already achieved the replacement level of fertility (i.e. 2.1) or less, while seven more states are on the verge of achieving replacement level fertility. The states with TFR>3.0 amongst larger states are Bihar Jharkhand, Madhya Pradesh, and Uttar Pradesh and among them Bihar is having highest fertility (3.6 per woman) not only at regional level but at country level which is of major concern and constraint for population stabilization.

At present, Bihar is the state having highest of TFR in the country performing poorly on other demographic and RCH indicators and needs more attention in this regard. Even within the state there is wide variation across the district on those parameters of demographic components and RCH services utilization. Like TFR ranges from lowest of 2.7 to 4.6 per woman, IMR varies from a lowest of 37 to maximum of 68 per 1,000 live births, full antenatal care (ANC) ranges from minimum of 2 per cent to 14 per cent, contraceptive use from 27 per cent to 52 per cent and child full immunization from 26 per cent to 86 per cent (GoI, 2013). Thus, the district being the basic planning unit under decentralized planning strategy in the country and for the state, there is a need to investigate the underlying relationship of demographic behaviour and RCH services utilization for the state of Bihar to facilitate district-based demographic and health policy and planning to achieve population stabilization goal at country level in wider context.

In the backdrop, rest of the paper is organized as follows: Third section delineates method and materials with details of data source, variables under consideration and statistical techniques. Section four explains about the current situation of demographic parameters and RCH services utilization comparing with country and among the Annual Health Survey (AHS) states. Section five explores the underneath structural relationship of adverse outcomes with poor RCH services utilization across the districts of Bihar and performance of districts on composite score of demographic outcomes and RCH services utilization is also depicted in this section. Last section covers discussion and ends with conclusion.

Methods and Materials

Data Source

The study is focused on examining mismatch between demographic outcomes and RCH services utilization at district level in the state of Bihar, and used latest available Annual Health Survey (AHS)[3] data for 2011–12 and 2012–13. Apart from AHS data, other key source of demographic and RCH data like Census, sample registration system (SRS) data, national family health survey (NFHS) data, district level household and facility survey (DLHS) data and family welfare statistics–2012 of Government of India has been utilized wherever it is applicable.

Selection of Variables Under Study

Variable is selected in the way that reflects the outcomes on the demographic front on one hand, and utilization of maternal and child health care services on the other hand. These two components of demographic & health outcomes and health care behaviours have been found to be dependent on each other.

Demographic Parameters

Demographic indicators selected for the study covers two variables of fertility: Total fertility rate (TFR), Birth order 3 & above and three variables of mortality: Infant mortality rate (IMR), Under–5 mortality and Maternal mortality ratio (MMR). High value of these parameters will reflect into high burden of demographic outcome at district level.

RCH Parameters

Under the umbrella of reproductive and child health services, to understand the utilization of RCH services, four indicators of maternal health care, namely full antenatal care (ANC), delivery at institutions (both govt. & private), postnatal care (PNC) within 7 days of delivery, and use of any family planning (FP) methods are included. Further, three indicators of child health care namely; full immunization (within 12–23 months), treatment for diarrhoea and acute respiratory infection (ARI).

Methodology and Analytical Framework

Analysis has been done at district level to understand the micro-level picture of district level variation in demographic outcomes and their linkages with use of the RCH services in the state of Bihar. Descriptive statistics provide state level comparison among EAG plus Assam states (hereafter, AHS states) for the base year of 2011–12. Further, progress within one year is observed on selected demographic and RCH indicators for the state of Bihar comparing it with base year. Then, after considering multivariate techniques, factor analysis method is employed to establish structural relationship of demographic outcomes and RCH services utilization at district level. Factor analysis is a method that simplifies complex and diverse relationships that exists among a set of observed variables by uncovering common dimensions or factors that link together the seemingly unrelated variables, (and) consequently provides insight into the underlying structure of the data (Dillon and Goldstein, 1984). Here, factor analysis is undertaken using the principal component method of extraction with Varimax rotation criterion. The principal factor method extracts factors in such a way that each factor accounts for the maximum possible amount of the variance contained in the set of variable being factored. Here, number of factors is restricted to the Kaiser's criterion of the Eigen (E-value) values greater than unity.

Finally, based on factor scores of different variables used under the study, a district-wise composite index score for demographic outcomes and RCH services utilization has been elicited separately. It has assumed that high level of RCH services achievements will be reflected into low burden of demographic outcomes and vice versa, with some limitations. As socio-economic development of a district also plays a major role in shaping the supply and demand for RCH services and regulates demographic behaviour of population within the space on given point of time is considered here. Then, aggregate composite index scores of RCH services utilization and demographic outcomes is categorized into poorest, moderate, high and very high performance separately, and the district having specific value is put in the specified category for both the dimensions of the study.

Results

Demographic Outcomes and RCH Services Utilization: Insight from India and Bihar

It is a notable fact that 17 major states comprises around 94 per cent of country's population and major chunk are Uttar Pradesh, Bihar, Chhattisgarh, Jharkhand, Rajasthan and Madhya Pradesh (GoI,

2011). It is not surprising that in 2011 census, Bihar had contributed maximum decennial growth rate among the major states in the country. Delineating Table 1, it is very clear that Bihar is still performing poorly on demographic outcomes and RCH services utilization within the country. Bihar is having the highest TFR of 3.6 and around three-fifths of the women are having birth order of three and above. On the mortality indicators, Bihar is having IMR 43/1000 live birth to under-5 mortality 57/1000 live birth (SRS, 2012) with maternal mortality ratio as high as 261/1,00,000 live births. Demographically, early age at marriage which clearly substantiates into higher levels of adolescent fertility and it can easily be observed that 45.9 per cent girls had married at below age of 18 in 2007–8 and 25 per cent women in 15–19 years were having babies or were pregnant at the time in 2005–06 in Bihar.

Table 1

Performance of Selected Demographic and RCH Indicators in India and Bihar

Indicators	*India*	*Bihar*
Total Persons	1,21,05,69,573	10,40,99,452
Decadal Growth Rate 2001–11	17.7	25.4
Total Fertility Rate	2.4	3.6
Motherhood at 15–19 years	16.0	25.0
Birth Order 3 & Above	44.8	61.1
Crude Birth Rate	21.6	28.4
Crude Death Rate	7.0	6.6
Infant Mortality Rate	42	43
Neonatal Mortality Rate	29	28
Post Neonatal Mortality Rate	13	16
Early Neonatal Mortality Rate	23	23
Under-5 Mortality Rate	52	57
Maternal Mortality Ratio	212	261
Mean Age at Effective Marriage	20.7	20.1
% Marriage below Age 18	6.5	9.3
Institutional Delivery	38.7	19.9
Full Antenatal Care	15.0	5.8
Postnatal Care	41.2	17.8
Current Users	56.3	34.1
Couple Protection Rate*	40.4	16.5

Cont'd...

...Cont'd

Unmet Need	12.8	22.8
Exclusive Breastfeeding	46.3	27.9
Full Immunization	43.5	32.8
Diarrhoeal Treatment	59.8	53.9
ICDS Utilization**	28.4	8.8

Note: * Couple protection Rate: % Couple effectively proceeds due to all methods.
** % of Children below 6 years received any service from Aanganwadi Centre (AWC) in past 12 months at the time of survey. AWC services include distribution of supplementary food, growth promotion, immunizations, health checkups, health and nutrition education, and pre-school education.

Source: Various Government Reports. Detailed Descriptions has been provided in Appendix Table A1.

Further, Table 1 also elicits RCH services utilization in the country as well as for Bihar state. Antenatal care (ANC) utilization elicited by NFHS–3 reveals that only 18 per cent of women at country level and only around 6 per cent in Bihar had received full ANC of those who had a live birth in the five years preceding the survey in 2005–06. Delivery of the family planning services has, however, been tagged with the delivery of public health services right from the beginning, 56 per cent in the country and only 34 per cent women in Bihar were current users by any type of FP methods. Surprising fact is that at 2005–06, around 23 per cent of the married couples depicted unmet need[4] for family planning in the state. Moving on child health scenario, only 33 per cent children aged 12–23 months were found to be fully vaccinated[5] and 54 per cent had been treated for diarrhoea and surprisingly, ICDS service utilization rate in the state was only 9 per cent in 2005–06.

Status of Demographic Outcomes RCH Utilization: Reflections from AHS States

Table 2 elicit performance of selected demographic and RCH parameters among AHS states. Among them, Bihar, being the third largest state after Uttar Pradesh and Maharashtra with around 104 million populations is the major concern here. Table 2 unveils fertility characterized by TFR exceeds 3 per woman in four AHS states viz. Bihar, Uttar Pradesh, Madhya Pradesh, and Rajasthan with highest of 3.6 in Bihar. Furthermore, the demographic backwardness of the state compared with other major states gets

Table 2

Selected Demographic Parameters and RCH indicators in AHS States: 2011–12

	Assam	*Bihar*	*Chhat**	*Jharkhand*	*MP*	*Odisha*	*Rajasthan*	*UP*	*Uttar**
TFR	2.4	3.6	2.8	2.9	3.1	2.3	3.1	3.4	2.1
IMR	57	52	50	38	65	59	57	70	41
MMR	347	294	263	267	277	237	264	300	162
Full ANC	13.3	6.1	20.2	14.4	15.3	22.7	9.2	5.0	16.0
Ins Del**	60.8	51.9	40.4	60.8	79.7	77.7	74.4	51.7	54.6
Immu**	76.6	65.5	68.6	69.1	59.7	62.3	69.2	48.1	77.9

Note: *Chhat: Chhattisgarh, Uttar: Uttarakhand. **Ins Del: Institutional Delivery, Immu: Full Immunization.

Source: Annual Health Survey: 2011–12

characterized by most of the demographic parameters, like maternal mortality ratio is much higher of 294 maternal deaths for every lakh live births but comparatively better off on IMR of 52 per 1,000 live births among the AHS states. Moving on RCH indicators, only 6 per cent women had received full ANC and just more than half (52%) have delivered at institutions, whereas around two-thirds of children aged 12–23 months are fully immunized in 2011–12. The scenario is almost the same on other demographic and RCH indicators in the state and raises the interest for further district level analysis to facilitate the underlying structural interlinkages for evocation of policy imperatives in the state of highest fertility in the country.

Demographic Burden and RCH Services Utilization in Bihar

Table 3 depicts district level variation on selected variables under the study. It is very clear that still almost all the districts are having high fertility rate (2.7–4.6 children per women), infant mortality rate (37/1,000–68/1,000) and maternal mortality ratio with minimum of 241 to maximum of 368 per lakh live birth. On the other front, use of RCH services also depicts poor utilization in the state. Like, only around 6 per cent (2.0–13.8%) of women have undergone full ANC and only 54 per cent have delivered in institutions with minimum of 28 per cent. Only 44 per cent were using any contraceptives in the state. It is also very clear that the districts using any contraceptives have low burden of demographic outcomes and vice versa (Figure 1). Here, it has also tried to

Figure 1

District Level Variation on Demographic Outcome and Contraceptive Use in Bihar

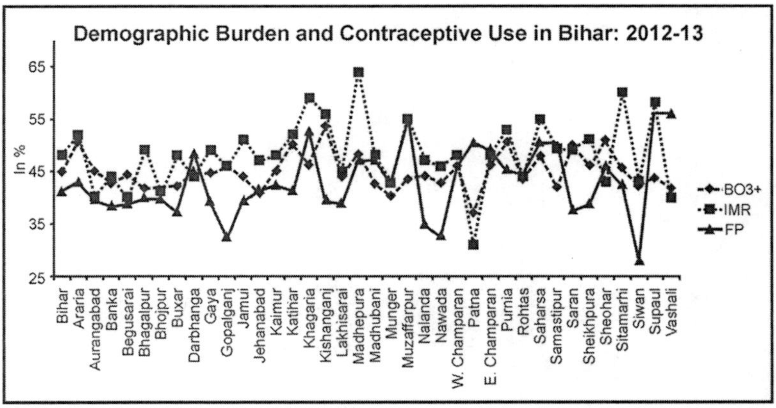

observe the variation in burden of demographic outcomes and RCH services utilization, achievements on RCH indicators reduces the burden of demographic outcomes within the states. Like, on average birth order 3 & above, infant mortality rate, maternal mortality ration has reduced by 2.6, 3.6 and 19 points on one hand, whereas on the other hand, use of RCH services like full ANC, institutional delivery, treatment for acute respiratory infections among children has been increased by 1.6, 3.5, and 1.4 points respectively over 2011–12 within the state (Table 3).

Table 3

Descriptive Statistics of Selected Indicators of Demographic burden and RCH Services in Bihar: 2012–13

	Mean 2013	*Minimum*	*Maximum*	*SD*
Total Fertility rate (Per Woman)	3.5 (–0.1)	2.6 (–0.1)	4.6 (0.0)	0.5 (0.0)
Birth order 3+ among 15–49 years women (%)	44.9 (–2.6)	37.2 (–1.7)	53.6 (–2.2)	3.4 (0.0)
Infant mortality rate (per 1000 live births)	48.3 (–3.7)	31.0 (–6.0)	64.0 (–4.0)	6.5 (0.1)
Under-5 mortality (per 1000 live births)	69.6 (–4.4)	46.0 (–4.0)	97.0 (–4.0)	12.7 (0.0)
Maternal mortality ratio (per 100000 live births)	276.4 (–19)	221.0 (–20.0)	349.0 (–19.0)	38.0 (3.3)
Full ANC (%)	7.3 (1.6)	2.7 (0.7)	15.3 (1.5)	3.1 (0.8)
Institutional Delivery (%)	57.2 (3.5)	29.6 (1.3)	78.0 (2.1)	13.9 (0.8)
Post natal care within 7 Days of delivery (%)	66.1 (1.9)	34.1 (1.4)	90.5 (1.1)	14.6 (0.7)
Full immunization among children 12–23 months (%)	70.2 (4.2)	32.2 (5.6)	87.8 (5.0)	11.1 (–0.4)
Use of any FP methods (%)	43.1 (–1.0)	27.9 (–3.6)	56.3 (–4.5)	6.7 (0.4)
Treatment for Diarrhoea (%)	72.0 (–0.6)	39.7 (2.3)	96.9 (–3.1)	22.7 (–0.1)
Children treated for ARI (%)	99.0 (1.4)	94.2 (22.8)	100.0 (0.0)	1.1 (–4.5)

Value in parentheses shows variation on different indicators over 2011–12 at district level within the states.

Source: Author's calculation based on AHS data: 2012–13 for Bihar.

Relationship of Demographic Outcomes and RCH Services at District Level

The AHS data pertaining to demographic, health and RCH components for 2011–12 has been elicited for 37 districts of the state. The data pertaining to demographic parameters and RCH services utilization has been considered to depict structural linkages of adverse demographic outcomes and poor RCH services utilization at district level in the state on selected indicators. Results from factor analysis using factor loading matrix in Table 4 reveals that most of the variables in the purview of the present analysis have been duly represented in the structure depicted by higher values of communalities of more than 0.75, except for MMR and full immunization. Interestingly, most of the important indicators of demographic outcomes and RCH services utilization are well connected and represented in the factor structure.

Table 4

Varimax Rotation Factor Score of Bihar's District-wise selected Demographic and RCH services Utilization Variables

Parameters	*Component**				*Communality*
	F–I	*F–II*	*F–III*	*F–IV*	
Total Fertility Rate	0.695	–0.377	0.439	0.011	0.817
Birth Order 3 & above	0.501	–0.579	0.273	–0.398	0.819
Full ANC	–0.367	–0.143	0.059	0.792	0.785
Institutional Delivery	–0.366	0.305	–0.742	0.148	0.798
PNC within 7 days of delivery	–0.070	–0.090	–0.945	–0.007	0.904
Full Immunization	0.018	0.746	–0.122	0.035	0.572
Use of any FP Method	0.374	0.466	–0.065	0.671	0.810
Infant Mortality Rate	0.916	–0.077	0.035	–0.134	0.863
Under 5 Mortality Rate	0.886	–0.061	0.301	–0.093	0.886
Maternal Mortality Ratio	0.245	–0.605	0.311	–0.182	0.555
ORS given to Child	0.589	–0.149	0.641	0.272	0.853
Child treated for ARI	–0.162	0.889	0.230	–0.163	0.894
Eigen value	*3.20*	*2.56*	*2.38*	*1.42*	
Variance Explained	*26.7*	*21.3*	*19.8*	*11.8*	
Total Variance Explained = 79.6					

Note: * Using Principal Components Extraction Method, four components with Kaiser's Criterion of Eigen value > 1.

Perusal of Table 4 reveals that the underlying or predominant constituents of the first factor (F–I) are TFR, birth order three and above, IMR and U-5MR. It may be of interest to mention that all the predominant constituents depict consistent linkages such as, fertility and infant and child mortality depict positive linkages implying that districts are having high fertility and high concentration of three and above birth order also having higher infant and child mortality across the districts. On the other hand, the districts having low and very low obstetric care are found negatively associated with higher infant and child mortality in the state. Utilization of obstetric care like antenatal care and institutional delivery imposing negative impact on infant mortality and child immunization are also revealed in the same way. Obviously, obstetric care has often been contended to impact neonatal component of infant mortality and children's immunization is supposed to impact the post-neonatal component of infant mortality (Gulati, 2005). Factor loadings of the predominant constituents of second factor (F–II) clearly depict that infant and child mortality depicts negative association with children's immunization and treatment for ARI. Perusal of factor loadings of third factor (F–III) reveals inverse association of delivery care with infant and child mortality and treatment for diarrhoea. Whereas fourth factor (F–IV) clearly depicts the interdependency of high use of family planning methods with low birth order, three and above and inversely related mortality indicators of child and mothers. It is of interest to point out here that the linkages amongst the main constituents of all the elicited factors turn out to be consistent with general prospect and theoretical and empirical evidences from various studies (Satia and Giridhar, 1991; Bose, 1996; Visaria et al., 1999; Gulati, 2005; IIPS and Macro International, 2007; Kumar, et al. 2012; MoHFW, 2013).

Performance of Districts on Aggregate Scores of Demographic and RCH Parameters

Districts performance on demographic outcomes and RCH services utilization separately into poorest, moderate, high and very high has been done on the basis of value of composite index score for the said districts in Table 5. The ranking of districts into different category has been done on the basis of equal weightage to the composite scores and divided into four equal parts and the subsequently the district falling in the respective category has been ranked on performance scale, accordingly. This has been done separately for demographic parameters as well as for RCH parameters included under the study. Table 5 very clearly shows that the districts performing poorest or moderate on the RCH components are also having poorest or moderate performance on demographic outcomes in the state. Likewise, Kishanganj and neighbouring districts performing worst on demographic outcomes are also found poorest on RCH component in the state. Whereas, the districts having very high performance on RCH components are also performing very high on demographic outcomes likewise, Patna and the neighbouring districts. Further, the districts being moderate in accessing RCH services are also clustered on moderate demographic outcomes and can be very clearly seen in Table 5. It is interesting to mention here that northern Bihar is found to have very poor to poor RCH services utilization resulting into adverse demographic outcomes. More specifically, north-eastern districts are having highest burden of demographic outcomes with lowest utilization of RCH services in the state and are found consistent with other studies (Kumar, et al. 2012).

Table 5

Districts Categorization based on Demographic and RCH Performance in Bihar: 2011–12

Rank	*Districts*
	On Demographic Parameters Performance
Poorest	Sheohar, Saharsa, Katihar, Sitamarhi, Madhepura, Araria, Khagaria, Purnia, Kishanganj
Moderate	Saran, Gaya, Jamui, Darbhanga, Muzaffarpur, Seikhpura, Supaul, W. Champaran, E. Champaran
High	Siwan, Gopalganj, Vaishali, Madhubani, Buxer, Jehanabad, Kaimur (Bhabhua), Nalanda, Bhagalpur, Samastipur
Very High	Patna, Bhojpur, Rohtas, Munger, Aurangabad, Nawada, Begusarai, Banka, Lakhisarai
Moderate	Bihar
	On RCH Services Utilization Performance
Poorest	Kishanganj, E. Champaran, Sitamarhi, Sheohar, Araria, Katihar, Darbhanga, Jamui, Gaya
Moderate	Muzaffarpur, Nawada, Siwan, Purnia, Gopalganj, W. Champaraan, Madhepura, Saran, Saharsa
High	Samastipur, Lakhisarai, Nalanda, Begusarai, Buxar, Supaul, Madhubani, Vaishali, Bhagalpur, Banka
Very High	Aurangabad, Khagaria, Kaimur (Bhabhua), Sheikhpura, Rohtas, Bhojpur, Jehanabad, Munger, Patna
Moderate	Bihar

Discussions and Conclusion

The study tried to examine the relationship for RCH services utilization and fertility as well as mortality pattern at district level in

Bihar. The study delineates that Bihar with highest TFR of 3.6 per women in the country followed by infant mortality and maternal mortality on one hand and low utilization of maternal and child health care services utilization leads the state to very poor condition on human development and other development indicators as well. Plethora of studies have elicited about two-way relationship of fertility and mortality, and their inverse relationship with RCH components in India and their states (Satia and Jejeebhoy, 1991; Hirschman, 1994; Sinha and Sinha, 1994; Mason, 1997; Cleland, 2001) and is also found evident in the study. There is a further, less noticed return from avoiding high fertility: since pregnancy is an absolute requirement for maternal mortality, fewer pregnancies lowers the lifetime risk (Campbell and Graham, 2006) as the districts having high birth order have been found having high maternal mortality also under the study.

Structural relationship between demographic outcomes and RCH services utilization is found consistent with other studies (Gulati, 2005; Kumar et al., 2012) as poor services utilization potentially aggravates the chances of child survival (Rosenfield et al., 2007; Raj et al., 2010) in those districts, whereas improved child survival in the high fertility setting will motivate fertility decline as well (Angeles, 2010). The study has also been strengthened the earlier finding which support that adequate coverage of maternal and child health care interventions can improve child survival at a large (Cleland and Sathar, 1984; Dasgupta, 1990; Haines et al., 2007; Rutherford et al., 2009; Subramanian et al., 2009; UNICEF, 2009; Singh et al., 2012; Ghosh, 2012). A recent study based on AHS states found utilization of family planning and maternity services below the acceptable level. It has been found that less than two in every five currently married women in Uttar Pradesh, Bihar and Jharkhand were using any contraceptive. The situation is more gravelling on utilization of full antenatal care (Kumar et al., 2012).

Overall, there is mismatch in key demographic and RCH utilization and are discerned to be lagging much behind in many districts of Bihar which are the concerned issues. Thus, to begin with the strenuous efforts are necessitated in districts of low utilization to bringing about optimal results in fertility and mortality reduction in the state as a whole and in a district in particular. Despite several policies and programme provisioning, the accessibility, availability and affordability of RCH services remain a challenge to the Indian health care system (Paul et al., 2011). It is also important to evaluate and consistent monitoring of the availability, accessibility and quality of available health care infrastructure and human resources at institutional level under the umbrella of national health mission to strengthen the delivery of RCH services utilization and accessibility of other health care services to reduce the high burden of demographic outcomes. In the decentralized planning era, district based planning and performance to monitor the progress and outcome of various RCH programmes interventions in demographically and socio-economically lagging districts is of urgent need to facilitate faster pace of population stabilization in the state, which will ultimately reflect into faster stabilization of population in the country as a whole. Further, the district based planning would be more focused on block/taluka level to strengthen the strategy of national health mission (NHM). In addition to that, grassroot level PRIs should be made responsible for accountability of the accessibility of the RCH services and this should be monitored and surveillance system may be strengthened in poor socio-economically developed districts. It should be primarily concerned to the vulnerable and deprived section of the district to make them capable to access the services to fill the gap and move forward on better demographic outcomes in the state. This will contribute more to national health mission to speed up the strategy to achieve the goal of a healthy nation with stabilized population.

Notes

1. Cairo's International Conference on Population and Development. India was one of the signatories amongst 179 participating countries.
2. For details go through document on Reproductive, Maternal, New Born, Child and Adolescent Health (RMNCH+A) in India. Ministry of Health and Family Welfare, GoI.
3. The AHS was initiated during 2007–09, to start with for the nine states comprising of eight EAG states viz. Bihar, Jharkhand, Madhya Pradesh, Chhattisgarh, Rajasthan, Uttar Pradesh, Uttarakhand, Odisha and Assam to provide district level estimates on different indicators comprising of core vital indicators, health status and utilization of MCH care and health care services.
4. Unmet need for family planning characterizing per cent couples not wanting to have any more children over coming two years or for all time to come but not using any contraceptive method is termed as unmet need for spacing methods or for limiting methods, respectively.

5. Fully immunized children are those who receive one BCG injection to protect against tuberculosis, three doses each of DPT (diphtheria, pertussis, tetanus) and polio vaccines, and one measles vaccine.

References

Angeles, L. 2010. 'Demographic Transitions: Analyzing the Effects of Mortality on Fertility', *Journal of Population Economics*, 23: 99–120.

Bose, A. 1996. 'Demographic Transition and Demographic Imbalance in India', *Health Transition Review*, 6: 89–99.

Campbell, O.M. and W.J. Graham. 2006. 'Strategies for Reducing Maternal Mortality: Getting on with What Works', *The Lancet*, 368(9573): 1284–1299.

Cleland, J. 2001. 'The Effects of Improved Survival on Fertility: A Reassessment', in Rudolfo A. Bulatao and John B. Casterline (eds), *Global Fertility Transition: Population and Development Review*, Supplement to Vol. 27. New York: Population Council.

Cleland, J.G. and Z.A. Sathar. 1984. 'The Effect of Birth Spacing on Childhood Mortality in Pakistan', *Population Studies*, 38: 401–418.

Dasgupta, M. 1990. 'Death Clustering, Mothers' Education and the Determinants of Child Mortality in Rural Punjab, India', *Population Studies*, 44: 489–505.

Dillon, W.R. and M. Goldstein. 1984. *Multivariate Analysis: Methods and Applications*. New York: John Wiley & Sons.

Dyson, T. 2011. 'India's Demographic Transition and its Consequences for Development in Population', in S.C. Gulati (ed.), *Health and Human Resources in India's Development*. New Delhi: Academic Foundation.

Ghosh, R. 2012. 'Child Mortality in India: A Complex Situation', *World Journal of Pediatrics*, 8(1): 11–18.

Ghosh, R. and A.K. Sharma. 2010. 'Intra- and Inter-household Differences in Antenatal Care, Delivery Practices and Postnatal Care between Last Neonatal Deaths and Last Surviving Children in a Peri-urban Area of India', *Journal of Biosocial Science*, 42: 511–530.

GoI. 2011. Census 2011. New Delhi: Office of the Registrar General and Census Commissioner, Ministry of Home Affairs.

——. 2012. Annual Health Survey: 2010–11. New Delhi: Office of the Registrar General and Census Commissioner and Ministry of Health and Family Welfare.

——. 2013. Annual Health Survey Fact Sheet, Bihar: 2011–12. New Delhi: Office of the Registrar General and Census Commissioner and Ministry of Health and Family Welfare.

Gulati, S.C. 2005. Poverty, RCH-Care Utilization and Fertility in India: A District Level Analysis. Working Paper No. 256, New Delhi: Institute of Economic Growth.

Gulati, S.C., R.M. Singh, R. Raushan and A. Kumari. 2010. Evaluation Study of NRHM in 7 States of India. New Delhi: Planning Commission, GoI.

Haines, A., D. Sanders, U. Lehmann, A.K. Rowe, J.E. Lawn et al. 2007. 'Achieving Child Survival Goals: Potential Contribution of Community Health Workers', *Lancet*, 369: 2121–2131.

Hirschman, C. 1994. 'Why Fertility Changes?', *Annual Review of Sociology*, 20: 203–233.

International Institute for Population Sciences (IIPS) and Macro International. 2007. *National Family Health Survey (NFHS–III), 2005–06.* Mumbai: IIPS.

Kumar, C. Prashant K. Singh and Rajesh K. Rai. 2012. 'Under-five Mortality in High Focus States in India: A District Level Geospatial Analysis', PLOS ONE, 7(5): e37515.

Mason, K.O. 1997. 'Explaining Fertility Transitions', *Demography*, 34(4): 443–454.

MoHFW. 2013. A Strategic Approach to Reproductive, Maternal, Newborn, Child and Adolescent Health (RMNCH+A): For Healthy Mother and Child. New Delhi: Ministry of Health and Family Welfare, GoI.

Paul, V.K., H.S. Sachdev, D. Mavalankar, P. Ramchandran, M.J. Sankar et al. 2011. 'Reproductive Health, and Child Health and Nutrition in India: Meeting the Challenge', *Lancet*, 377: 332–349.

Raj, A., N. Saggurti, M. Winter, A. Labonte, M.R. Decker et al. 2010. 'The Effect of Maternal Child Marriage on Morbidity and Mortality of Children Under Five in India: Cross-sectional Study of a Nationally Representative Sample', *British Medical Journal*, 340: b4258.

Rosenfield, A., C.J. Min and L.P. Freedman. 2007. 'Making Motherhood Safe in Developing Countries', *New England Journal of Medicine*, 356: 1395–1397.

Rutherford, M.E., J.D. Dockerty, M. Jasseh, S.R.C. Howie, P. Herbison et al. 2009. 'Access to Health Care and Mortality of Children Under 5 Years of Age in the Gambia: A Case-control Study', *Bulletin of the World Health Organization*, 87: 216–224.

Satia, J.K. and G. Giridhar. 1991. 'Supply Aspects of Meeting Demand for Family Planning', in J.K. Satia and S.J. Jejeebhoy (eds), *The Demographic Challenges: A Study of Four Large Indian States*. Bombay: Oxford University Press, 114–148.

Satia, J.K. and S.J. Jejeebhoy. 1991. *The Demographic Challenge: A Study of Four Large Indian States*. Bombay: Oxford University Press.

Singh, P.K., R.K. Rai, M. Alagarajan and L. Singh. 2012. 'Determinants of Maternity Care Services Utilization among Married Adolescents in Rural India', *PLoS ONE*, 7(2): e31666.

Sinha, U.P. and R.K. Sinha. 1994. *Population and Development in Bihar*. Delhi: B.R. Publishing Corporation.

Sample Registration System (SRS). 2012. Statistical Report. New Delhi: Office of the Registrar General and Ministry of Home Affairs.

Subramanian, S.V., L.K. Ackerson, G.D. Smith and N.A. John. 2009. 'Association of Maternal Height with Child Mortality, Anthropometric Failure, and Anemia in India', *The Journal of the American Medical Association*, 301: 1691–1701.

UNICEF. 2009. *The State of Asia-Pacific's Children 2008: Child Survival*. New York: United Nations Children's Fund.

Visaria, L., S. Jejeebhoy and T. Merrick. 1999. 'From Family Planning to Reproductive Health: Challenges Facing India', *International Family Planning Perspectives*, 25: S44–49.

Appendix

Table A1

Details of State Level Selected Variables

S.No.	*Abbreviated Name*	*Description of the variable*	*Source*
1	Population	Total Population	Census, 2011
2	Decennial Growth Rate	Decennial Growth Rate for 2001–11	Census, 2011
3	TFR	Total Fertility Rate	SRS Bulletin, 2012
4	CBR	Crude Birth Rate	SRS Bulletin, 2012
5	CDR	Crude Death Rate	SRS Bulletin, 2012
6	Neonatal Mortality	Neonatal Mortality Rate	SRS Bulletin, 2012
7	PNMR	Post-Neonatal Mortality Rate	SRS Bulletin, 2012
8	IMR	Infant Mortality Rate	SRS Bulletin, 2012
9	U5MR	Under-Five Mortality Rate	SRS Bulletin, 2012
10	MMR	Maternal Mortality Ratio	SRS Bulletin, 2012
11	CPR	Couple Protection Rate	Family Welfare Statistics, 2011
12	Current Users	Currently using any contraception	NFHS–3: 2005–06
13	Unmet Need	Total Unmet Need of Family Planning	NFHS–3: 2005–06
14	Unmet Need Limiting	Unmet Need for Limiting Methods	NFHS–3: 2005–06
15	Unmet Need Spacing	Unmet Need for Spacing Methods	NFHS–3: 2005–06
16	Mean Age at Marriage	Mean Age at Marriage for Girls, 2009	Family Welfare, 2011
17	% Married below 18	Women Married Below 18 (20–24 Yrs)	Family Welfare, 2011
18	Exclusive Breastfed	Exclusive Breastfeeding up to 6 Months	NFHS–3, 2005–06
19	Full ANC	Per cent Mothers received Full ANC	NFHS–3, 2005–06
20	Institutional Delivery	Women delivered in Health Institutions	NFHS–3, 2005–06
21	PNC	Women undergone for postnatal care within 48 Hrs of delivery	NFHS–3, 2005–06
22	Full Immunization	Children age 12–23 months received one dose of BCG, three doses of DPT and Polio and one dose of measles	NFHS–3, 2005–06

Table A2

Descriptive Statistics of Variables Included into District Performance Index

Variables	*Mean*	*Std. Deviation*
Total Fertility Rate	3.6	0.44
Birth Order 3 & Above	47.5	3.35
Full ANC	5.7	2.32
Institutional Delivery	53.6	12.91
PNC within 7 days of delivery	64.1	13.70
Full Immunization	66.0	11.39
Use of any FP Method	44.1	6.22
Infant Mortality Rate	51.9	6.29
Under–5 Mortality Rate	73.5	12.52
Maternal Mortality Ratio	295.2	34.18
ORS given to Child	72.7	22.43
Child treated for ARI	97.6	5.48

9

Children Undernutrition Status in Bihar and Uttar Pradesh

Estimates using Svedberg's Composite Index of Anthropometric Failure (CIAF) Method

H. LHUNGDIM

The Millennium Development Goals (MDGs) recognize the importance of food and good nutrition as the basic human need essential to eradicate extreme poverty and hunger. Child malnutrition, especially undernutrition, remains a challenging and pervasive problem that impinges on development of both mental and physical health of the child, and ultimately affecting productivity and national economic growth. According to WHO (1995), children who are underweight or stunted are at greater risk for childhood morbidity and mortality, poor physical and mental development, inferior school performance and reduced adult size and capacity for work. In India, despite government's effort to combat hunger and undernutrition for many decades through Maternal and Child Health (MCH) and Integrated Child Development Services(ICDS) programmes, yet millions of children still suffer from both acute and chronic malnutrition, particularly in the bigger states, commonly referred to as 'Empowered Action Groups' (the EAG states), but more prominently in states like Madhya Pradesh, Jharkhand and Bihar.

According to the Global Hunger Index (GHI),[1] since 2006 India has shown relative improvement and placed among the 'alarming' and 'serious' categories (scoring between 17 and 25 on a 100-point scale). By 2014, India's ranking improved to 55 (among 76 emerging economies) scoring 17.8, still trailing behind countries like

Thailand, China, Ghana, Iraq, Sri Lanka and Nepal. This sharp reduction in the percentage of underweight children has helped India improve its hunger record. It is said that India's improved ranking is due to its progress in dealing with underweight children. However, India remains home to the largest number of chronically malnourished and stunted children under five (GHI, 2014).

In the recent years, in contrast to the economic growth observed, decline in malnutrition levels among children has been sluggish. For instance, in the early 1990s, over half of children (53%) age under-4 years were found underweight (weight for age) and 52 per cent were stunted (NFHS–1, 1992–93). The underweight scenario continued to remain discouraging among children under age 3 (47% in NFHS–2, 1998–99), and also among children under-5 (46% in NFHS–3, 2005–06) (IIPS and Macro International, 2007; IIPS and ORC Macro, 1992, 2000).

Studies illustrate that deprivation in child undernutrition is caused by many factors such as income inadequacies, socio-economic marginalization and other forms of human insecurities, particularly in India. It has been argued that poverty, measured in terms of wealth index, has considerable impact on malnutrition, indicating a disproportional burden on the poor that explains for more than half of the inequality in malnutrition. Thus, signifying the importance of poverty-nutrition inequality linkage in worsening malnutrition and leading to unequal nutritional outcomes among children (Poel et al., 2007; Mazumdar, 2010; Kanjilal et al., 2010).

This paper examines and re-estimates undernutrition level among under-5 years in Bihar and Uttar Pradesh (UP), the two most populous states in India, using both WHO growth standards (WHO Multicenter Growth Reference Study Group, 2006), which uses underweight (weight-for-age) as composite index for chronic and acute malnutrition, and that of Svedberg's (2000) Composite Index of Anthropometric Failure (CIAF) method. For this purpose, data of the National Family and Health Survey–3 (NFHS–3) has been used and analysed.

Demographic and Health Context of Maternal and Child in Bihar and Uttar Pradesh

According to 2011 Census, India's population is 1.21 billion, of which both Bihar (103.8 million) and UP (199.5 million) constitute about 25 per cent of the total population. Both these states are also characterized by low sex ratio, high fertility and mortality, and part of the EAG states. These two states also have very large size of children (0–9 years) and adolescents (10–19 years) (47–50%) and with low working population age 15–59 (52% in Bihar and 56% in UP).

As per 2011 estimates by Officer of the Registrar General and Census Commissioner, India (ORGI), the total fertility rate (TFR) of Bihar and UP was 3.6 and 3.4 children respectively. In case of mortality indicators also, both these states show a much higher risk levels. For instance, in 2011 the share of under-5 mortality was about 25 per cent in UP and 24.1 per cent in Bihar. Besides, the two states also have a high maternal mortality ratio (MMR) of 292 per 1,00,000 in UP/Uttarakhand and 219 in Bihar/Jharkhand (ORGI, 2013).

Both the states, due to their enormous population size, show a huge share and riskier state of maternal and child health status in the country. However, although the levels indicated are still high, the two states have experienced gradual improvement over the years since the introduction of the National Rural Health Mission (NRHM) in 2005.

Methodology

Data

To examine the undernutrition level among children age under–5, the study uses data of National Family Health Survey–3 (2005–06). NFHS is a large-scale, multi-round survey conducted based on representative sample of households throughout India. The survey provides state and national information on issues such as fertility, infant and child mortality, the practice of family planning, maternal and child health, reproductive health, nutrition, dietary habits, anaemia, utilization and quality of health and family planning services. NFHS–3 coverage in Bihar was 3,016 households and 3,818 women interviewed, and in UP it was 10,026 households and 12,183 women, in which children under-5 numbered about 6–7,000 in each state.

Method Applied

Nutritional status of children under age five years (U–5) has been measured according to three anthropometric indices, viz. height-for-age (chronic or stunting), weight-for-height (acute or wasting), and weight-for-age (underweight, the composite index) based on WHO growth standard (IIPS and Macro International, 2007), which consider for each index a Z-score below minus two standard deviations (–2 SD) from the median of the reference population. Each index provides different information about growth and body composition of children who are classified as chronically malnourished (stunted), acutely malnourished (wasted), and underweight (both acute and chronic malnutrition). A further lower Z-score below minus three standard deviations (–3 SD) classified as 'severely' malnourished (Dibley et al., 1987).

Svedberg (2000) proposed methods that provide a comprehensive estimate (or a better aggregated indicator), as the three conventional measures have been found to overlap or lack robustness, by developing a single and more comprehensive index known as 'composite index of anthropometric failure' (CIAF). Scholars who had applied this modified measure pointed out huge variation in the estimates of malnourished children and/or those missed by conventional indices. Therefore, as they argued, conventional measures are inadequate to give a true estimate or burden of undernutrition among children in a population, and failure to capture those at risk would be simply devastating (Nandy et al., 2005; Seetharaman et al., 2007; Bose and Mandal, 2010; Ao and Lhungdim, 2014). Svedberg also argued that, '... the *W/A* indicator does not identify the *sum* of those who are stunted and/or wasted. The *W/A* indicator will in fact miss some of the children who are undernourished in the two latter dimensions. The total prevalence of anthropometric failure in a population will thus be underestimated by the weight-for-age indicator (as well as by any of the other two)' (Svedberg, 2000).

For the purpose of this study, the modified method of anthropometric failures (Nandy et al., 2005) has been used. The original method developed by Svedberg (2000) has six subgroups of anthropometric failures, which has been extended/modified by Nandy et al. (2005) to include an additional subgroup Y (children who are only underweight, but not stunted or wasted). All the subgroups of anthropometric failures in the CIAF method are listed below (Svedberg, 2000; Nandy et al., 2005):

- Group a (No failure),
- Group b (Wasting only),
- Group c (Wasting and underweight),
- Group d (Wasting, stunting and underweight),

- Group e (Stunting and underweight),
- Group f (Stunting only), and
- Group y (Underweight only).

The modified Composite Index of Anthropometric Failure (CIAF) can be expressed symbolically as:

$$CIAF = (1 - a)/(a + b + c + d + e + f + y) = (1 - a)/1$$

The present study uses the modified method of CIAF to derive new estimates of undernourished children (anthropometric failures) in Bihar and UP, and comparing the estimates with that of the conventional measures (e.g. underweight) across selected socio-economic and demographic variables such as:

- *Child characteristics:* Sex, and Size of the child at birth.
- *Mother characteristics:* Education, Working status, Ante Natal Care (ANC) status, and Body Mass Index (BMI).
- *Household characteristics:* Place of residence, Economic status (wealth quintile/index), and Ethnicity (social groups).

Besides the bivariate analysis applied to examine the relationship between two variables which is the outcome and the exposure variables, a multivariate logistic analysis has been applied to assess adjusted effects of socio-economic and demographic characteristics on the outcome variables.

Results and Findings

Overall Nutritional Status of Under-5 Children in India

According to the WHO growth standards, NFHS–3 results indicated that nearly 43 per cent of under-5 children in India can be categorized as underweight, but when using the composite index of anthropometric failure (CIAF) method as developed by Svedberg (2000) Nandy et al. (2005), at least 61 per cent of children have nutritional problem (failure). As shown in Table 1, the scale of undernutrition or anthropometric failure among under-5 children is found highest in Central India (71%), followed by East India (65%) and North India (62%).

Similarly, under-5 children who are underweight (as per WHO) is much smaller despite the fact that Central India shows the largest share of undernutrition with 57 per cent. In case of UP and Bihar, the proportion of underweight children age under-5 is 42.3 and 56.1 per cent respectively.

Table 1

Proportion of Children Under-5 with any Anthropometric Failure (CIAF) in India by Region, 2005–06

Undernutrition/Region	*East*	*North*	*Central*	*Northeast*	*West*	*South*	*India*
CIAF (any failure)	64.8	61.5	70.7	55.9	60.7	51.4	61.4
Underweight (WHO)	48.9	39.7	56.9	35.4	39.8	31.9	42.5

Prevalence of Undernutrition (Anthropometric Failure) among Under-5 Children in Bihar and UP as Indicated by CIAF Method

Results using both methods show that proportion of children under-5 who are underweight (WHO standards) or with any anthropometric failure (CIAF) is much higher in Bihar than Uttar Pradesh (Table 2). According to the WHO growth standards, Bihar has over half (56%) of children age under-5 who are underweight compared to about 42 per cent in Uttar Pradesh (NFHS–4, 2005–06). However, the CIAF method shows a much higher anthropometric failure among children (71% in Bihar and 66% in UP). However, the state average or prevalence of nutritional status conceals the reality presence within the subpopulations in both the states.

A very high level of anthropometric failure among children observed when associating it with different characteristics of the child, mother and household, particularly in Bihar is alarming (70–80% in some cases).

As indicated in Table 2, in both the states the female child is found more undernourished or more likely to have anthropometric failure than the male child, particularly in Bihar. Also it is seen that the size of a child at birth (as reported by the mothers) seems to have impact on the nutritional status. For instance, children considered to be 'small' at the time of birth are more likely to suffer or at higher risk of anthropometric failure than those born with average or large size. Similarly, among mother's characteristics, her education, nutritional status, and ANC visit indicate huge influence on children's nutritional status than her age. Therefore, mothers who are illiterate, underweight, and did not avail of any ANC are nearly twice more at risk of having undernourished children. Among these characteristics, education shows the most difference. The anthropometric failure among children of illiterate mothers is nearly twice (1.9 times) in Bihar (76%) and 2.2 times in case of UP (72%) than among the most educated mothers.

Mother's health care during pregnancy has also indicated association with the current nutritional status of the children. For example, the proportion of children (age under-5) with anthropometric failure is highest among children (above 70%) whose mothers had not availed of any ANC, as compared with mothers who had full ANC (40–50%). A similar pattern is also found with mother's nutritional status as represented by BMI.

Table 2

Proportion of Under-5 Children who are Malnourished (Anthropometric Failure) by CIAF Method According to Selected Characteristics in Bihar and Uttar Pradesh, 2005–06

Selected Characteristics	*UP*	*Bihar*
Sex of Child		
Male	65.0	69.2
Female	67.8	72.3
Size of Child		
Large	63.4	68.3
Average	64.4	70.5
Small	74.8	74.8
Mother's Age		
15–19	67.0	69.6
20–24	65.5	69.5
25–29	66.3	68.5
30–49	67.2	75.1
Mother's Education		
No Education	71.9	75.5
Primary	63.9	63.6
Secondary	56.8	59.7
Higher	32.5	40.1
Body Mass Index (BMI)		
Underweight	72.6	76.2
Normal	64.4	67.3
Overweight	48.9	41.6
Ante Natal Care (ANC) Visit		
No	73.1	75.2
Partial	64.8	62.4
Full	41.8	51.5

Cont'd...

...*Cont'd*

Residence		
Urban	59.4	64.3
Rural	68.0	71.5
Wealth Index		
Poorest	75.9	79.7
Poorer	69.2	73.3
Middle	67.8	68.7
Richer	59.2	58.0
Richest	40.5	39.6
Caste		
Schedule Tribe	71.0	80.3
Schedule Caste	77.6	56.3
Other Backward Classes	68.0	70.7
Others	56.4	62.2
Total	66.3	70.7

Results of Regression Analysis

There is also evidence of wide disparity or inequality in the level of malnutrition or anthropometric failures within the two states by socio-economic and demographic indicators, as indicated by results of the logistic regression. Overall, in both Bihar and UP, children who are female, small sized at birth, having mothers with no education, having mothers who have not availed ANC, belonging to schedule groups, and from poor economic status are found highly prone to malnutrition or risk of anthropometric failure ($p<0.00$). From among the selected variables, most of them indicated significant association with anthropometric failure. Clearly, the bivariate and multivariate analyses illustrate inequality in undernutrition across and within the two states.

The degree of risk of malnutrition varies within the subpopulations in both Bihar and UP. In case of UP, it is seen that children born with small size are nearly twice (1.7 times; $p<0.001$) more likely to have anthropometric failure. Other variables that indicated significant association with malnutrition or anthropometric failure are mothers with no education, those underweight, mothers with no ANC, from poorer wealth/households, and urban residents. Interestingly, sex of child and age of mother are not statistically significant, despite the fact that more female children and children of older women suffer from anthropometric failure.

In the case of Bihar, children are 1.5 times more likely of suffer from anthropometric failure if born with small size as compared with large size children, and mothers over 30 years compared with younger mothers (p<0.10). The association or odds of risk of anthropometric failure is also found statistically significant for those underweight, mothers who had not availed any ANC during pregnancy, poorest households (nearly 70% higher than the richest quintile) and belonging to scheduled tribe.

Table 3

Odds Ratios from Logistic Regression Analysis Assessing the Association between Explanatory Variables and Anthropometric Failure (CIAF) among Under-5 Children in Bihar and UP, 2005–06

Variables	*Bihar*	*UP*
Sex of Child Male (R)		
Female	1.18	1.04
Size of Child at Birth Large (R)		
Average	1.12	1.03
Small	1.40*	1.70***
Mother's Age: 15–19 (R)		
20–24	1.2	1.01
25–29	1.19	1.19
30–49	1.53*	1.16
Mother's Education No education (R)		
Primary	0.83	0.78*
Secondary	1.22	0.79**
Higher	0.74	0.44***
Body Mass Index (BMI): Underweight (R)		
Normal	0.65***	0.72***
Overweight	0.40**	0.61***
Antenatal Care (ANC): None (R)		
Partial	0.66**	0.82**
Full	0.62**	0.50***
Wealth index: Poorest (R)		
Poorer	0.75	0.81*
Middle	0.87	0.81*
Richer	0.48***	0.66***
Richest	0.33***	0.47***
Social Group: Schedule Tribe (R)		

Cont'd...

...Cont'd

Scheduled Caste	0.57	0.79
Other Backward Classes	0.81	0.88
Others	0.55**	0.74**
Residence: Urban (R)		
Rural	0.94	0.74**

Note: (R) = Reference category; Statistically significant level: * $p<0.05$, ** $p<0.01$, and *** $p<0.001$.

Conclusion

The level of malnutrition or undernutrition among under-5 children is very high both in Bihar and UP, as indicated by both methods (underweight and anthropometric failure). The CIAF method simply illustrates the fact that more children are actually at the risk of undernutrition (66% in UP and 71% in Bihar), which is concealed when considering underweight (42% in UP and 56% in Bihar). Besides, it is also clearly revealed that within the subpopulations anthropometric failure is rife and at alarming level. In both the states, children most affected by anthropometric failure or undernutrition (over 75%) are those whose mothers are uneducated, belonging to poorest households, and of scheduled caste/tribe. Therefore, maternal education, ANC, nutritional status of mothers (BMI), and household economic status emerged as very important intermediate factors on nutritional status of children in both Bihar and Uttar Pradesh.

The present state of undernutrition in both Bihar and UP is very alarming, particularly as indicated by the CIAF estimates. Such very high level of undernutrition among children entails concerted efforts by the state machineries to seriously put in place remedial actions at the earliest to contain and bring to an acceptable level, including vigorously implementing the various maternal and child-related welfare schemes.

Note

1. As mentioned in the GHI 2014 Report, the calculation of the global hunger index is as below:

   The Global Hunger Index (GHI) is designed to comprehensively measure and track hunger globally and by country and region. It is calculated each year by the International Food Policy Research Institute (IFPRI).

The GHI highlights successes and failures in hunger reduction and provides insights into the drivers of hunger. To reflect the multidimensional nature of hunger, the GHI combines three equally weighted indicators in one index number:

(i) Undernourishment: The proportion of undernourished as a percentage of the population (reflecting the share of the population with insufficient calorie intake).

(ii) Child underweight: The proportion of children younger than the age of five who are underweight (low weight for age reflecting wasting, stunted growth, or both), which is one indicator of child undernutrition.

(iii) Child mortality: The mortality rate of children younger than the age of five (partially reflecting the fatal synergy of inadequate dietary intake and unhealthy environments).

The GHI ranks countries on a 100-point scale. Zero is the best score (no hunger) and 100 is the worst, although neither of these extremes is reached in practice. A lower GHI score implies better nutritional standard and a higher rank for a country (GHI, 2014).

References

Ao, M. and Hemkhothang Lhungdim. 2014. 'Re-estimating Malnourishment and Inequality among Children in North-east India', *Economic and Political Weekly*, XLIX(6), February 8: 53–64.

Behrman, J.R. and B.L. Wolfe. 1984. 'More Evidence on Nutrition Demand: Income Seems Overrated and Women's Schooling Underemphasized', *Journal of Development Economics*, 14: 105–128.

Bentley, M.E. and P.L. Griffiths. 2003. 'The Burden of Anemia among Women in India', *European Journal of Clinical Nutrition*, 57: 52–60.

Bose, K. and Gopal Chandra Mandal. 2010. 'Proposed New Anthropometric Indices of Childhood Undernutrition', *Malaysian Journal of Nutrition*, 16(1): 131–136.

Das, S. and Kaushik Bose. 2009. 'Report on Anthropometric Failure among Rural 2-6 Years Old Indian Bauri Caste Children of West Bengal', *Anthropological Review*, 72: 81–88.

Dibley, M.J., J.B. Goldsby, N.W. Strehling and F.L. Trowbridge. 1987. 'Interpretation of Z-score Anthropometic Indicators Derived from the International Growth References', *American Journal of Clinical Nutrition*, 45(5) 749–762.

Global Hunger Index. 2014. Issue Brief No. 83, Bonn, Washington, D.C. and Dubai: IFPRI, Concern Worldwide and Welthungerhilfe.

Gopalan, C. and Bani Tamber Aeri. 2001. 'Strategies to Combat Undernutrition', *Economic and Political Weekly*, 36(33): 3159–3169.

Gragnolati, Michele, Meera Shekar, Monica Das Gupta, Caryn Bredenkamp and Yi-Kyoung Lee. 2005. India's Undernourished Children: A Call for Reform and Action. Health Nutrition and Population Discussion Paper, The World Bank.

International Institute for Population Sciences (IIPS) and ORC Macro. 1992. *National Family Health Survey (NFHS-1), 1992-1993, India*. Mumbai: IIPS.

——. 2000. *National Family Health Survey (NFHS-2), 1998-1999, India*. Mumbai: IIPS.

International Institute for Population Sciences (IIPS) and Macro International. 2007. *National Family Health Survey (NFHS-3), 2005-2006, India*. Vol. 1, Mumbai: IIPS and Macro International.

Kanjilal, B., Papiya Guha Mazumdar, Moumita Mukherjee and M. Hafizur Rahman. 2010. 'Nutritional Status of Children in India: Household Socio-economic Condition as the Contextual Determinant', *International Journal for Equity in Health*, 9(19): 2–13.

Levinson, F.J. and L. Bassett. 2007. *Malnutrition is Leading Killer of Children but Cost-Effective Interventions Can Reduce Global Effects*. Washington, D.C.: Population Reference Bureau.

Malavika, Subramanyam A., Ichiro Kawachi, Lisa F. Berkman and S.V. Subramanian. 2011. 'Is Economic Growth Associated with Reduction in Child Undernutrition in India?', *PLoS Medicine*, 8(3): e1000424.

Mazumdar, S. 2010. 'Determinants of Inequality in Child Malnutrition in India', *Asian Population Studies*, 6(3): 307–333.

Menon, P., Anil Deolalikar and Anjor Bhaskar. 2009. *India State Hunger Index: Comparisons of Hunger across States*. Washington, D.C., Bonn and Riverside: International Food Policy Research Institute, Welthugerhilfe and University of California.

Mukhopadhyay, D.K. and A.B. Biswas. 2011. 'Food Security and Anthropometric Failure among Tribal Children in Bankura, West Bengal', *Indian Pediatrics*, 48: 311–314.

Nair, K.R.G. 2007. 'Malnourishment among Children in India: A Regional Analysis', *Economic and Political Weekly*, 42(37): 3797–3803.

Nandy, S., Michelle Irving, David Gordon, S.V. Subramanian and George Davey Smith. 2005. 'Poverty, Child Undernutrition and Morbidity: New Evidence from India', *Bulletin of the World Health Organization*, 83(3): 210–216.

Office of Registrar General, India (ORGI). 2013. Special Bulletin on Maternal Mortality in India 2010–12, Sample Registration System, New Delhi: ORGI.

Poel, Ellen Van de, Ahmad Reza Hosseinpoor, Caroline Jehu-Appiah, Jeanette Vega and Niko Speybroeck. 2007. 'Malnutrition and the Disproportional Burden on the Poor: The Case of Ghana', *International Journal for Equity in Health*, 6(21): 1–12.

Prema, Ramachandran. 2007. 'Poverty Nutrition Linkages', *Indian Journal of Medical Research*, 126: 249–261.

Radhakrishna, R. 2005. 'Food and Nutrition Security of the Poor: Emerging Perspectives and Policy Issues', *Economic and Political Weekly*, 40(18): 1817–1821.

Radhakrishna, R. and C. Ravi. 2004. 'Malnutrition in India: Trends and Determinants', *Economic and Political Weekly*, 39(7): 671–676.

Seetharaman, N., T.V. Chacko, S.L.R. Shankar and A.C. Mathew. 2007. 'Measuring Malnutrition: The Role of Z Scores and the Composite Index of Anthropometric Failure (CIAF)', *Indian Journal of Community Medicine*, 32(1): 35–39.

Som, Suparna, Manoranjan Pal, Bishwanath Bhattacharya, Susmita Bharati and Premananda Bharati. 2006. 'Socio-economic Differentials in Nutritional Status of Children in the States of West Bengal and Assam, India', *Journal of Biosocial Sciences*, 38: 625–642.

Subramanyam, Malavika A., Ichiro Kawachi, Lisa F. Berkman and S.V. Subramanian. 2010. 'Socio-economic Inequalities in Childhood Undernutrition in India', *PLoS ONE*, 5(6): 1–9.

Svedberg, P. 2000. *Poverty and Undernutrition: Theory, Measurement and Policy*. New Delhi: Oxford India Paperbacks.

United Nations Children's Fund (UNICEF). 2000. *The State of the World's Children 2003 Report*. New York: UNICEF.

Valerie, Kozel and Barbara Parker. 2003. 'A Profile and Diagnostic of Poverty in Uttar Pradesh', *Economic and Political Weekly*, 38(4), January: 385–403.

Viswanathan, B. and J.V. Meenakshi. 2006. 'The Changing Pattern of Undernutrition in India: A Comparative Analysis across Regions', UNU-WIDER, Research Paper No. 2006/118.

WHO. 1995. *Physical Status: The Use and Interpretation of Anthropometry*. Report of a WHO Expert Committee, WHO Technical Report Series 854, Geneva: World Health Organization.

WHO Multicentre Growth Reference Study Group. 2006. WHO Child Growth Standards: Length/Height for-Age, Weight-for-Age, Weight-for-Height and Body Mass Index-for-Age Methods and Development, Geneva: World Health Organization.

10

Issues of Out-migration from Uttar Pradesh and Bihar

N. JAYENTA MEITEI

Mobility is a unique human nature and has been crucial to conspicuous population dynamics that have been seen throughout the history of man around the world. Migration of people affects the socio-economic and demographic structures of both the terminal places. If it does not bring favourable conditions in general, problems naturally arise at either places. On the other hand, it is also due to certain unfavourable conditions, along with other factors, that drive people to migrate. Hence, there are always issues on why people move out of a place and into another place. There are theories which view migration as a boon to development. For example, the Lewis-Fei-Ranis model (Lewis, 1954; Ranis and Fei, 1961) regarded rural-urban migration as essential to economic development, where shift of surplus labour from rural areas to labour deficit urban areas by dint of wage difference facilitate industrialization as well as capital flow to the backward areas. The criticism to this theory is that in certain cases, the migrants may not be pulled by the wage difference or other opportunities in the urban areas but pushed by unfavourable conditions in the source region. In developing countries like India, the push factors are often more prominently persistent leading to rather overcrowding of labour and expansion of informal sector in urban areas. Unskilled labour out-migrants are being pushed out from rural India due to poverty, exploitation of landless or marginal farmers by big landlords, exploitation of backward castes by higher castes, lack of credit and other facilities in agriculture, and lack of employment diversification

(Mahadevia, 2002). At the receiving end too, these unskilled labours find it difficult to get some reliable jobs in the growingly capital-intensive industrial sector.[1] Such labour migrants naturally end up in informal sector where the nature of employment is unreliable, hazardous and exploitative. Government should intervene to tackle with the issues associated with migrants so that the fruit of migration may be harvested. India does not have a specific migration policy so far. Mention may be made of two key legislations which pertain to migration issues, namely, *Inter-state Migrant Workmen (Regulation of Employment and Conditions of Service) Act of 1979* and *Contract Labour (Regulation and Abolition) Act of 1970.* Practically, these protective measures are largely violated and made ineffective by manipulation of the employment procedures (ibid.).

As far as demographic issues are concerned in India, the two states viz. Uttar Pradesh (UP) and Bihar draw scholarly attention since these two states not only account for a huge share of the total population of the country but also exhibit similar demographic problems and challenges, of which the issue of mass out-migration to other states is one. Uttar Pradesh and Bihar are the two major states which are sending out migrants, most of which are in search of employment. In fact, the Census (2001) figures show that these two states account for the largest number of out-migrants i.e. 22.5 (UP) and 12.8 (Bihar) per cent of the total out-migrants from all the states. The Census data also indicate that the two states record the highest net out-migration rates, viz. –3.9 and –4.4 per cent respectively. These figures mean that for every 100 people in UP and Bihar, the number of out-migrants exceeds that of in-migrants by about four times. The traditional cause of rural out-migration from Bihar is rooted agricultural crisis induced by various reasons like ineffective land-reforms, sporadic floods and droughts. Besides this, worsened law and order situations, corrupt administration and closure of industries added to the outflow of migrants (Deshingkar et al., 2006). As per the bulk of out-migrants, the two states draw attention on the issue and its associated causes and consequences within the states as well as in other states where the migrants move.

Inter-state migrants are usually considered as the long-distance movers among internal migrants. Such type of migrants moves in response to labour market dynamics. UP and Bihar have suffered prolonged poverty, agrarian distress, unemployment and ineffective law & order conditions since the time of Independence.

Introduction of Green Revolution in Punjab and Haryana during 1970s created demand for unskilled labours thereby. It initiated a flow of out-migrants from the rural areas of Bihar and eastern UP to Punjab and Haryana. This stream of out-migration gained momentum during the decades that followed. Using census data (1961–2001), Kundu and Saraswati (2012) pointed out that UP and Bihar have been predominantly out-migrating since the time of Independence, and got their respective rural male net out-migration rejuvenated during 1991–2001. This trend suggests that labour out-migration from the two states has gained momentum in the recent past. According to the findings of a qualitative survey, it is found that out-migration from rural Bihar has increased further during the early 2000s (Deshingkar et al., 2006).

This analysis seeks to understand the recent patterns of out-migration from UP and Bihar, and to check whether the traditional factors of out-migration are still relevant in these states. The present study relies on the migration data given by the National Sample Survey (NSS) 64th Round (2007–8) dataset.[2] The NSSO (2010) defines *an out-migrant as any former member of a household who left the household, any time in the past, for stay outside the village/town provided he/she was alive on the date of survey.* The present study is only concerned with *inter-state out-migrants* whose present place of enumeration is a state in India other than the state of last usual place of residence. In other words, those migrants whose last usual places of residence are UP and Bihar, and present place of enumeration are any of the remaining states of India are taken into account for analysis.

UP and Bihar: Background

The geographical location of the UP and Bihar with reference to other states may be understood from Map 1 given below a later section. Uttar Pradesh is the most populous state accounting for 16 per cent (nearly 200 million) of the total population of India, whereas Bihar is the third most populous state in India accounting for 9 per cent (nearly 104 million) of the total population of the country (Census of India, 2011). These two states together accommodate one-fourth of the total population of India. Both the states are densely populated too. UP has a population density of 828 persons/sq. km and Bihar has 1,102 persons/sq. km in 2011. They invariably show poor performance in most of the development indicators. Effective literacy rate (ELR) is 69.7 per cent in UP and 63.8 per cent in Bihar in 2011.[3] In fact, Bihar records the lowest literacy rate among the states. Sex ratio is 908 in UP and 916 in Bihar against the national average of 940 females/1000 males in 2011.

UP and Bihar constitute the poorest states of India with intolerably low income. In UP, the real per capita monthly income was ₹ 1,509 and in Bihar, ₹ 1,272 (at 2004–5 prices) during 2011–12. These figures are even less than half of the national average which is ₹ 3,167.[4] Huge proportion of the people in these states is living below the poverty line. These states perform badly in Human Development Index (HDI), Gender Equality Index, implementation of health and social welfare programmes, agricultural and industrial development. While the economies of UP and Bihar are predominantly agrarian, crop productivity is invariably low for most of the cereals due to lack of capital investment, poor irrigation (except in western UP), ineffective implementation of land-reforms and severe fragmentation of holdings, lack of transport and marketing facilities (Deshingkar et al., 2006). Cultivation and farm labour provide the major share of employment especially in rural areas.

Data and Methods

As mentioned above, all the quantitative inferences given below are sourced from the NSS 64th Round (2007–8) dataset given by the National Sample Survey Organisation (NSSO). This dataset includes a schedule (Schedule 10.2) on 'Employment-unemployment and Migration', which provides micro-level information on migration as well as other demographic and socio-economic particulars of 572,254 sample household members from all the states. Out of this all-India sample, an inter-state migrant population of 23,209 individuals are extracted. As per the NSSO (2010) definition, *a household member whose last usual place of residence (LUPR), anytime in the past, was different from the present place of enumeration (PoE) is considered as a migrant, provided he/she had stayed in the LUPR continuously for six months or more.* Out of the inter-state migrant population, a sample of 7,683 individuals are further extracted as the out-migrants from UP (4,765) and Bihar (2,918), and hence taken into account for the analysis. The process of extraction of out-migrants from the originally inter-state migrant population is based on the relationship between Protector of emigrants (PoE) and LUPR of a migrant, i.e. *a migrant moving from place 'A' (LUPR) to place 'B' (PoE) can be considered as an out-migrant from place 'A' but as an in-migrant in place 'B'*. With these two variables (PoE & LUPR) as rows and columns representing the states/UTs, a *matrix* is constructed where the inter-state migrants are all fitted according to their respective PoE and LUPR status. From the matrix, out-migrants from any states/UTs as well as in-migrants to any states/UTs can be computed. Similarly, those migrants whose LUPR is either UP or Bihar and whose PoE is any other states/UTs of India are considered as out-migrants from UP and Bihar.

In-migration rate is computed as the number of (inter-state) in-migrants in a state divided by the total population of the state expressed in percentage. *Out-migration rate* is the number of (inter-state) out-migrants from a state divided by the total population of the state expressed in percentage. In-migration rate minus out-migration rate gives *net-migration rate*, which literally indicates whether a state is predominantly in-migrating or out-migrating. If the net-migration rate is positive, then it is called *net in-migration rate.* If the net-migration rate is negative, then it is called *net out-migration rate.* Univariate (simple frequency table), bivariate (cross tabulation) and multivariate (logistic regression model) tools are employed to understand the various aspects of out-migration.

Results and Discussions

The National Sample Survey (NSS) data indicate that UP and Bihar show very high out-migration rates (see Figure 1). About 6 persons out of every 100 population have migrated out of these two states. As of 2007–08, UP and Bihar respectively account for 20.5

Figure 1

Migration Rates in UP and Bihar

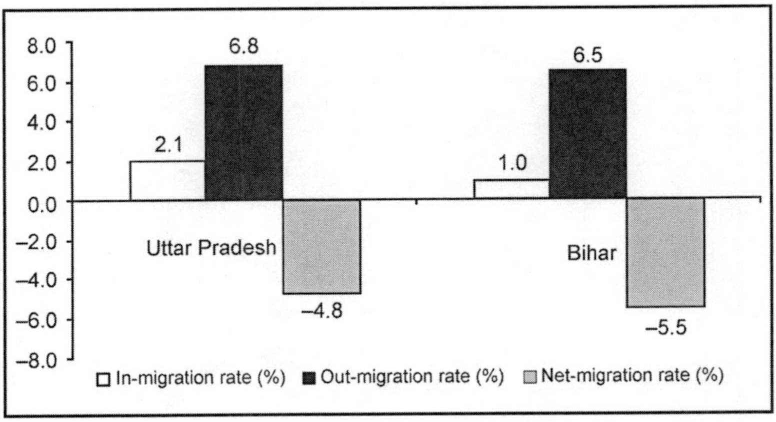

Source: NSS 64th (2007–8).

and 12.5 per cent of the total out-migrants from all the states. In other words, every third out-migrant belongs to either UP or Bihar. They have scored net out-migration rates of –4.8 and –5.5 per cent respectively showing their predominantly out-migrating scenario. The major destinations of UP and Bihar out-migrants comprise Delhi (18.4%), Maharashtra (11.7%), West Bengal (10.5%), Uttarakhand (8.7%), Haryana (6%), Punjab (5.1%), M.P. (5.1%), Gujarat (5%) and so on. It may be mentioned that UP is also a major destination of Bihar migrants (Map 1).

Map 1

Destinations of Out-migrants from UP and Bihar

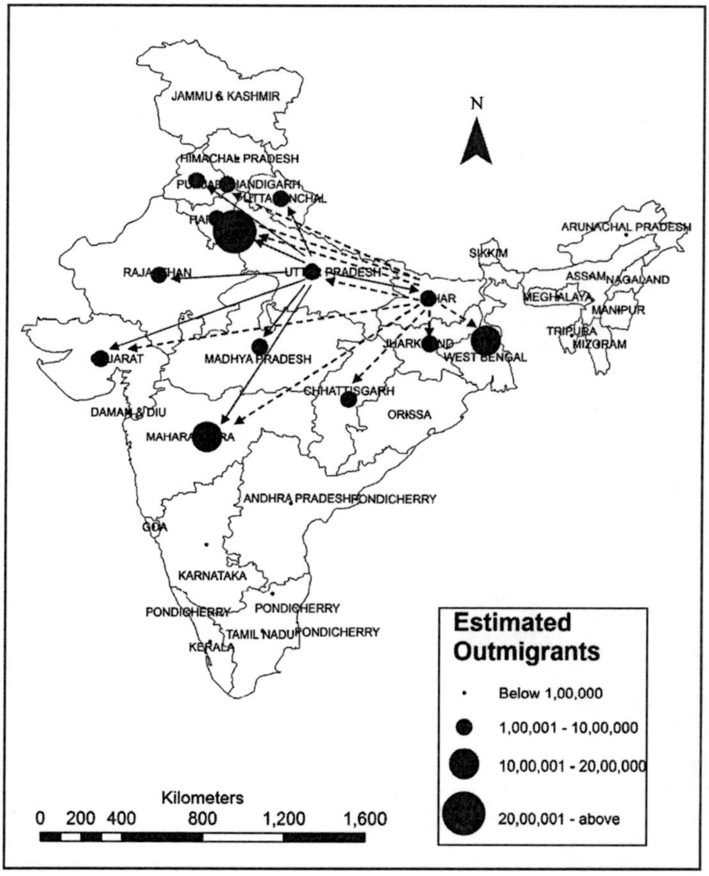

Source: NSS 64th (2007–8).

The NSS data include 17 various *reasons of migration* which are hereby grouped into 6 reasons viz. (1) employment related, (2) studies, (3) forced, (4) marriage, (5) move with parent/earning member and (6) others. Both UP and Bihar show very similar pictures as far as reasons of out-migration are concerned. Employment related reasons account for nearly 40 per cent of all the UP and Bihar out-migrants, of which the latter has greater employment seeking behaviour. Other major reasons of out-migration from UP and Bihar include move with parent/earning member (30%) and marriage (26%).

Table 1

Out-migrants (in %) from UP and Bihar by Reasons

Reasons of out-migration	*UP*	*Bihar*	*Total*
Employment related	37.5	43.0	39.6
Move with parent/earning member	30.3	28.4	29.6
Marriage	27.7	23.6	26.1
Others	0.9	0.8	0.8
Studies	1.4	1.3	1.4
Forced migration	0.7	0.6	0.7

Source: NSS 64th (2007–8), schedule 10.2.

As far as *streams of out-migration* are concerned, long distance migrants usually follow rural-urban and urban-urban streams. In the same manner, 55.5 per cent of the UP and Bihar out-migrants combined move from rural to urban and another 20 per cent from urban to urban. Regarding *duration of migration*, last year out-migrants at the time of survey account for only 5.6 per cent. There are relatively more out-migrants with longer duration of migration. Marriage is the main reason for longer duration of out-migration since it bears a motive of permanent stay. Even employment related migrants and their companions (move with parent/earning member) tend to stay longer in course of time. For example, among out-migrants with more than 15 years of stay, marriage migrants account for 43.4 per cent and employment related migrants account for 31.2 per cent, whereas among less than 1 year out-migrants, employment related account for 51 per cent.

Table 2

Reasons of Out-migration and Duration of Out-migration (in percentages)

Reasons of Out-migration	*Duration of Migration (years)*					
	Below 1	*1–5*	*6–10*	*11–15*	*Above 15*	*Total*
Employment related	50.8	45.3	41.0	36.5	31.2	39.3
Move with parent/ earning member	36.9	32.8	33.4	31.2	21.6	29.4
Marriage	5.8	15.1	20.5	28.5	43.4	26.1
Studies	2.8	2.7	0.4	0.7	0.5	1.3
Forced migration	0.0	0.0	0.2	0.1	0.3	0.2
Others	3.7	4.0	4.6	3.0	3.0	3.7

Source: NSS 64th (2007–8), schedule 10.2.

It is interesting to see how the reasons of out-migration vary across other attributes of the out-migrants like age, sex etc. Employment related migrants are dominantly male, whereas female migrants mostly move with parents/earning member or for marriage reasons in UP and Bihar.

Regarding the *age-structure* of the out-migrants, it is known that majority of the employment related migrants are in 15–59 age-group, whereas those moving with parent/earning member are children (0–14 age-group). As far as *educational attainment* of the out-migrants is concerned, 30.8 per cent of the UP and Bihar out-migrants are illiterate, most of whom move for marriage reasons or move with parent/earning member. Among the literate migrants, majority of them are either primary or secondary completes. Of the employment related migrants, primary completes are 46.7 per cent and secondary completes are 21.8 per cent. Higher educational attainment among the out-migrants including employment related migrants is marginal.

The NSS data provide information on *occupational status* (usual activity status) of out-migrants (see Table 3). Various usual activities have been classified into 6 occupational groups, viz. (1) self-employed, (2) employed – regular salary/wage earner, (3) employed – casual wage labour, (4) unemployed, (5) students and (6) others (including domestic works, renters, pensioners, beggars, disabled etc.). Nearly half of the UP and Bihar out-migrants are engaged in economic activities. This includes self-employed migrants

(15.7%), employed as regular salary/wage earner (25%) and employed as casual wage labour (6.9%). But still, a sizable chunk of migrants (37%) is engaged in unproductive domestic works.

Table 3

Out-migrants (%) from UP and Bihar by Occupational Status

Occupational Status	*Before Migration*	*After Migration*
Self-employed	11.0	15.7
Employed: regular salary/wage	6.4	25.0
Employed: casual wage	8.6	6.9
Unemployed	13.2	0.7
Students	12.3	9.5
Others	48.6	42.3

Source: NSS 64th (2007–08), Schedule 10.2.

The data also provide occupational status of migrants before migration (at the time of leaving LUPR). Hence, it is convenient to look into the temporal changes in activities of the migrants. Also it makes possible to find out how much the purposes (reasons) of migration have been fulfilled. At the time of leaving their LUPR, 26 per cent of the out-migrants were engaged in economic activities but after migration, 47.5 per cent of them have been engaged in economic activities. It is because most of the formerly unemployed people and some others, who were not in the labour force, have now entered into employment sector. However, there are still shortfalls which can be pointed out as per the reasons of migration reckoning. The reasons of migration are, in another sense, the intentions of the migrants at the time of move. All those employment related out-migrants intended to take up certain productive activities and hence are supposed to be in labour force, but in ground reality, not all of them are in labour force.

Remittances sent by the out-migrants can be used as a reference to the usefulness and significance of migration to the home economy. Of the total employment-related out-migrants from UP and Bihar, 72.4 per cent have sent remittance (during the last year of the survey) and they are all engaged in economic activities. However, 22.4 per cent of those engaged in economic activities have not sent remittances. The exact reasons for not sending remittances are not known due to limitation of the data. The average amount of remittances sent during last 365 days of the survey (2007–8) was nearly ₹ 13,000. The most important use of remittance is buying food items, followed by education of household members, health care and household consumer durables.

As mentioned already, two binary logistic regression models are used to find out the *factors of out-migration* in this context. Appendix I & II respectively show the net effects of demographic and socio-economic variables on the mass out-migration and employment-related out-migration from UP and Bihar. Sex, age-groups, marital status, household size, social status, religion, monthly household consumer expenditure and educational attainment are found to be significant factors of out-migration. According to the first model, persons in the age-groups (15–59) and (60 plus) especially married females, household members from middle and higher income groups, and those having higher social status are more likely to out-migrate from UP and Bihar. On the other hand, male members, unmarried persons, those belonging to bigger household size and lower social strata are less prone to out-migration.

In the second model, sex, age-groups, marital status, social status, monthly household consumer expenditure and educational attainment are found to be significant factors of employment-related out-migration from UP and Bihar. Unlike in the first model, male members are more likely to migrate than female ones in search of employment. The probabilities of out-migration among the age-groups 15–59 and 60 plus are many times more in this case. Employment-related migrants tend to have higher educational attainment as compared to that of overall migrants.

Conclusion

The bulk of out-migrants moving out of UP and Bihar accounts for one-third of all out-migrants from the states. This volume of migrants suggests that there are certainly issues and challenges faced by the migrants at their place of origin. As per the data, the major reason of out-migration is for employment purposes. When employment reason comes up, there is a question on availability of employment in the places of origin. Occupational status in UP and Bihar shows that, at the time of leaving LUPR, only 26 per cent of the out-migrants were in employment sector but after migration, this proportion has risen upto 47.5 per cent. It has clearly illustrated that unemployment or underemployment is a prominent push factor which exerts people to migrate out of UP and Bihar. This does not mean that there are no pull factors of this out-migration. Majority of the migrants move to urban centres in economically more developed states/UTs like Delhi, Maharashtra, West Bengal, Punjab, Gujarat etc. wherein the sprawling townships and cities provide employment opportunities either in formal or informal sector and attract in-migrants. However, marriage is a major reason for those who move to nearby states although it is inter-state movement.

Both male and female household members are equally mobile in UP and Bihar. However, employment seeking behaviour is much more prominent among the male migrants than female ones. Not only women are less educated and skilled than men but also female migrants move due to marriage or in association with parent/earning member. Male out-migrant who are in search of employment/better employment, are in lack of higher educational attainment and technical skills. Most of them are hardly educated beyond secondary level. Less than 2 per cent of all the out-migrants from UP and Bihar gets technical education. Hence, lack of education and technical skills limit the migrants' window of employment opportunities at their destinations and induce them to work in informal sector because there is already overcrowding and strong competitions for jobs in the cities. Without having good knowledge of the employment scenario in the destinations, people just move out of their homes having been pushed by unemployment and lack of capital. Subsequently, some out-migrants remain unemployed or engaged in unproductive activities. According to the NSS data, this proportion of employment related out-migrants who remain out of labour force constitutes about 6 per cent.

Factors of out-migration and employment related out-migration exhibit certain deviations. For all migrants, female members are more likely to out-migrate than male members on account of marriage and associated move with parent or earning member, but in case of employment migration, male members are many times more likely to out-migrate than females. Literally, women in UP and Bihar are economically very inactive. Social status of individuals is another issue reflected in migration too. People in lower social strata (castes) are so suppressed that they are very much less likely to migrate out as compared to those of upper castes. Social and economic freedoms are prerequisite for a venture to move.

Despite of different datasets, the records of Census 2001 and NSS 64th (2007–8) tend to show a trend of increasing net out-migration from UP and Bihar. Lack of employment generation against rapid increase in population force the migrants to move out in search of employment or better employment. Other than marriage reason, a number of out-migrants also move in association with income earner of the household. Due to lack of good education and technical skills, these employment seeking out-migrants often find themselves in difficulties. Unprecedented mass labour migrants to cities like Delhi, Mumbai, Bangalore (Bengaluru), Kolkata etc. give pressure on limited civic amenities and subsequently lead to emergence of slums thereby. Hence, out-migration is not the final solution although people opt for available alternatives. State governments need to intervene and create ample employment opportunities like the Mahatma Gandhi National Rural Employment Guarantee Act (MGNREGA) scheme at home states.

Notes

1. Various studies have observed evidences of capital-intensive industrial development in the last few decades hitting a blow to rural-urban migration, thereby making urbanization process more exclusionary to rural unskilled out-migrants (Kundu, 1986; Kundu and Gupta, 1996; Kundu and Saraswati, 2012).
2. Census 2011 has not released migration data so far.
3. National ELR average is 74 per cent (2011).
4. <http://planningcommission.nic.in/data/datatable/index.php?data=datatab> as accessed on 8 August 2015.

References

Census of India. 2001. Migration Tables (D-series). New Delhi: Registrar General of India, Ministry of Home Affairs, GoI.

——. 2011. Provisional Population Tables. New Delhi: Registrar General of India, Ministry of Home Affairs, GoI.

Deshingkar, P., S. Kumar, H.K. Chobey and D. Kumar. 2006. *The Role of Migration and Remittances in Promoting Livelihoods in Bihar*. London: Overseas Development Institute.

Kundu, A. 1986. 'Migration, Urbanisation and Inter-regional Inequality: The Emerging Socio-political Challenge', *Economic and Political Weekly*, 21(46): 2005–2008.

Kundu, A. and L.R. Saraswati. 2012. 'Migration and Exclusionary Urbanisation in India', *Economic and Political Weekly*, 47(26 & 27): 219–227.

Kundu, A. and S. Gupta. 1996. 'Migration, Urbanisation and Regional Inequality', *Economic and Political Weekly*, 31(52): 3391–3398.

Lewis, A.W. 1954. 'Economic Development with Unlimited Supply of Labour', *Journal of the Manchester School of Economic and Social Studies*, 22(2): 139–191.

Mahadevia, D. 2002. *The Poverty and Vulnerability of Migrant Workers in India: A Post-earthquake Study in the State of Gujarat*. Ahmedabad: Centre for Environmental Planning and Technology.

National Sample Survey Organisation (NSSO). 2010. Migration in India 2007–08. NSS 64th Round Report No. 533, New Delhi: Ministry of Statistics and Programme Implementation, GoI.

Ranis, G. and J.C. Fei. 1961. 'A Theory of Economic Development', *American Economic Review*, 57: 538–565.

Appendix I

Effects of Demographic and Socio-economic Variables on Out-migration from UP and Bihar: Results from Logistic Regression Model I

Covariates	*Beta coefficients*	*Odds Ratios*
Sex		
Female®		
Male	1.085	.338**
Age-groups		
0–14 years®		
15–59	1.336	3.804**
60 above	.580	1.786**
Marital status		
Married®		
Unmarried	–1.396	.247**
Household size		
1–3 members®		
4–6 members	–1.503	.223**
7 above	–2.975	.051**
Social status		
High (GEN) ®		
Middle (OBC)	–1.410	.244**
Low (SC&ST)	–.823	.439**
Religion		
Hindu®		
Others	–.176	.839**
Monthly HH consumer expenditure		
Below ₹ 2,501®		
₹ 2,501–5,000	1.020	2.773**
₹ 5,001–10,000	2.328	10.262**
₹ 10,001 above	3.032	20.743**
Educational attainment		
Illiterate®		
Literate (informal)	.230	1.259*
Primary	.153	1.165**
Secondary	–.263	.769**
Higher secondary	–.701	.496**
Diploma	–.557	.573**
Graduate	–.880	.415**
Post graduate	–1.380	.252**

Note: ®: Reference category; **p < 0.01, *p < 0.05 level of significance

Source: NSS 64th (2007–8), schedule 10.2

Appendix II

Effects of Demographic and Socio-economic Variables on Employment-related Out-migration from UP and Bihar: Results from Logistic Regression Model I

Covariates	*Beta Coefficients*	*Odds Ratios*
Sex		
Female®		
Male	2.167	8.732**
Age-groups		
0–14 years®		
15–59	4.726	112.839**
60 above	3.722	41.336**
Marital status		
Married®		
Unmarried	–.748	.473**
Social status		
High (GEN) ®		
Middle (OBC)	–1.677	.187**
Low (SC&ST)	–1.083	.339**
Monthly HH consumer expenditure		
Below ₹ 2,501®		
₹ 2,501–5,000	–.646	.524**
₹ 5,001–10,000	–.137	.872**
₹ 10,001 above	.313	1.368**
Educational attainment		
Illiterate®		
Literate (informal)	.599	1.821**
Primary	.641	1.898**
Secondary	.398	1.488**
Higher secondary	–.065	.937
Diploma	.533	1.704**
Graduate	.169	1.184*
Post graduate	–.144	.866

Note: ®Reference category; **$p < 0.01$, *$p < 0.05$ level of significance

Source: NSS 64th (2007–8), schedule 10.2

11

Socio-Economic Analysis of Migrant Workers in Mumbai

A Case Study of Auto-rickshaw and Taxi Drivers from Uttar Pradesh

RUCHI SINGH

Migration is often an adopted strategy by rural poor to diversify income and risks. Literature highlights that migration is not always a result of urgency and shocks. In recent era, migration has become foremost way to diversify resources. There are various strands of literature on migration as risk and income diversification strategy across various disciplines. This paper tries to explore various existing literature on migration as one of the most prominent source of risk, insurance and income diversification by the rural poor in Uttar Pradesh. Out-migration from Uttar Pradesh has increased manyfold in past two decades as per NSSO and Census data. With a widespread poverty and scarce income opportunities in Uttar Pradesh migration is a key poverty reduction and income diversification instrument for rural households. Households send members abroad to migrate as part of diversified (ex-ante) income portfolio strategy (Ghobadi et al., 2005). Socio-economic characteristics of migrants have also been discussed in detail. Literature shows that there are very few studies on socio-economic status of auto and taxi drivers (Ali, 2013; Alam and Alam, 2013). Various other studies also mentioned that remittances from migrant members increase household liquidity and may contribute to alleviate binding credit constraints in productive activities (Katz and Stark, 1986; Paulson, 2003). There is strong interrelationship between the determinants of migration as a family strategy and people left behind (Mendola, 2004). Mincer (1978) also mentions that migration is a family decision as whole to diversify risk. Various studies found that social capital have positive impact on migration (Haug, 2008; Faist et al., 1997; Pries, 2004; Fawcett, 1989).

Objective

To carry out empirical analysis to understand socio-economic characteristics of migrants from Uttar Pradesh to Mumbai (case study of auto rickshaws and taxi drivers)

Data and Methodology

Auto rickshaw and taxi are familiar means of transportation in Indian cities which is a livelihood for rural immigrants. The paper will analyse the socio-economic conditions of auto rickshaw and taxi drivers with objectives to assess the arrival and previous occupation, to examine their age group, marital status, religion, caste, and analyse educational level, residential conditions at destinations, basic and civil amenities and facilities in Mumbai.

The paper has undertaken exhaustive literature review to disentangle existing literature on migration as risk insurance and income diversification strategy. To support the objective and theoretical findings and to understand the socio-economic conditions of migrants, the study undertakes a primary survey of 50 auto rickshaw and taxi drivers at Andheri, Khar East, Chembur, Deonar and Jogeshwari in Mumbai. Snowball methodology has been employed for selection of sites. The study is based on primary data. The direct questionnaire method was used to gather information from respondents. The collected data were tabulated and analysed with the simple statistical techniques. The limitation of the study is that it is limited to migrants from UP only, that too even migrant engaged only in auto/taxi driving. This paper is qualitative in nature and is a kind of preliminary study to understand socio-economic conditions of male out-migrants from Uttar Pradesh in Mumbai.

The paper is divided in four parts. Part one will be dealing with Introduction, Objectives and Methodology adopted. Part Two draw attention to exhaustive Literature on migration as risk and income diversification strategy. Part Three will confer Results and Discussions with the help of case study of migrant auto and taxi drivers in Mumbai from Uttar Pradesh. In results and discussions section we will highlight two major findings. We will discuss socio-economic conditions of auto and taxi drivers and analyse migration as part of risk and income diversification strategy by the rural poor in UP. Paper in very brief will talk about the role social capital plays in facilitating migration from rural UP. Part four will be concluding remarks.

Review of Literature on Migration as Poverty Reduction and Income Diversification Strategy

This section deals with existing literatures which observe migration as risk insurance and income diversification strategy. Lindstrom et al. (2012), mentions that household economies in developing societies emphasize the role of income pooling and risk diversification as a common strategy that households use to self-insure against risk. Long-term and temporary migration is often the principal means by which households diversify their sources of income and protect themselves against environmental shocks in case study in Ethiopia. De Weerdt and Hirvonen (2013) found in their study conducted in Tanzania that those who migrated out of the region grew three times richer than those who remained at home. Study also found that migration works as risk sharing and income diversification strategy. Study by Brauw et al. (2011) highlights that migration and remittances can be used by rural households as a means of insurance, investment and income augmentation. Demurger et al. (2010) in their paper analyses the factors that drive rural households and individuals in their income-source diversification choices in North China Township. De Haan (2000) in his study found that high income differential doesn't always lead to high migration. Author concludes the paper by mentioning that migration should not only be seen as a reaction to socio-economic circumstances but it is a strategy of households for income diversification. Sakho-Jimbira and Bignebat (2008) in their study found that migration and local diversification are substitutes, implying that migration is a form of insurance. Facilitating role played by networks in migration has also been mentioned. Migration and remittances are widely seen as major components of diversification strategies aimed at coping with risky environments in developing countries is major finding of the study in Kakamega district in Kenya (Giesbert, 2007). Konseiga (2005) in one of the study in Burkina Faso also highlighted the importance of migration as survival strategy in the study confronted with severe scarcity of natural resources. Migration is income diversification strategy in rural poor (Rosenzweig and Stark, 1989; Waddington, 2003).

Mendola (2004), uses cross-sectional data from two rural regions of Bangladesh to test whether migration is a form of income diversification strategy or not and found from empirical analysis that it acts as a very important source of income diversification strategy. The insurance motives for migration has been emphasized by the New Economics of Labour Migration (NELM), according to which greater income uncertainty may encourage out-migration as a risk and income diversification strategy (Stark and Bloom, 1985).

Migration is one of many strategies households utilize to manage risk and uncertainty. Study probes into role of migration as poverty reduction strategy for rural households in rural Afghanistan (Ghobadi et al., 2005; Deshingkar and Start, 2003; Ellis, 2003). Waddington (2003) in the paper theoretically review the literature to examine the links between poverty and migration. Paper also highlights the facilitating role of network in migration. Migration can be seen as poverty reducing and income diversification strategy, which involves refashioning sources dispersed in space into family livelihoods (Nyberg-Sorenson et al., 2002).

One of the studies in China found that migration represents a key form of arbitrage: especially for the poor, human capital may represent the largest share of wealth, and migration allows this human capital to receive higher returns (Kinnan et al., 2012). Guilmoto and Sandron (2001) mention that for residents of developing countries, decision to migrate or not to migrate is to minimize risks. De Haan (2000) also highlights the fact that migration is part of active livelihood strategies, but is also determined by social context, and is determined by social norms and structures. Household composition, gendered ideologies and social contacts and networks determines who migrates and who can profit from opportunities arising elsewhere. Paulson (2003) in his study highlights that migrants often maintain important connections with their origin communities. In particular, many migrants provide support to non-migrants, usually closed ones in forms of remittances. The results of the study show that insurance motives play an important role in explaining migration patterns. Bigsten (1998) also considers migration a household decision in which a family allocates labour to the urban or rural sector depending on the marginal products of combined wages.

Results and Discussions

Socio-Economic Characteristics of Auto and Taxi Drivers from Uttar Pradesh in Mumbai

Table 1 shows that most of the migrants are from eastern Uttar Pradesh. This signifies that as western part of UP is both developed and have industrial areas, eastern part is underdeveloped and lack any other kind of income earning opportunities apart from agriculture. Majority of the migrants belong to families whose primary occupation was farming. At origin most of the migrants (78%) were studying before migrating to Mumbai. Data suggests that no one came for study purpose in Mumbai. There are just 8 per cent migrants who were doing farming at origin and 78 per cent were studying before leaving origin and only ten per cent was the share of migrants who were doing both farming and studying simultaneously at origin before migration. Moreover, most of the migrants, as per reports by autorickshaw and taxi drivers, left studies either because they failed at some level in education or came to Mumbai with help of social networks (relatives or friends) for employment in Mumbai.

Table 1

Auto and Taxi Drivers by Place of Origin and by Previous Occupation both at Origin and Destination.

Place of Origin of Autorickshaw and Taxi Drivers in Mumbai (in %)					
Pratapgarh	*Jaunpur*	*Sultanpur*	*Gazipur*	*Bhadohi*	*Sant Kabir Nagar*
36	22	14	12	10	6

Previous Job at Origin and Destination (in %)		
	Origin	*Destination*
Auto/Taxi Driving	0	20
Farming	8	–
Casual worker (Worker at Petrol Pump, Watchman, Milkman, Vendors, Mechanic, Electrician, etc.	4	80
Studying	78	–
Farming and Studying	10	–

Majority of migrants started working as casual workers before the present occupation of auto rickshaw or taxi driving. The reason behind getting engaged in other jobs instead of auto rickshaw and taxi driving is that most of them were learning driving while staying in Mumbai and were engaged in some jobs and others were waiting for driving license to be made.

Auto and Taxi Drivers by Religion, Caste, Age and Level of Education

Data highlights that all of the migrants were Hindu by religion. It might be coincidence but as respondents mentioned hundred per cent of migrants were Hindus.

Most of the migrants belong to Rajput/Kshatriya and Brahmin (88%), whereas SC (12%) and OBC (8%) account for very less number of migrants from rural UP. One of the justifications of higher number of migrants as reported by many migrants from upper caste is that they can't do such low status kinds of jobs at their origin and that will be against their social prestige and status. One can't do such kind of menial jobs at origin and so left hometown in search of jobs and seeing others doing well in Mumbai.

Table 2

Auto Rickshaw and Taxi Drivers by Religion and Caste, Age and Level of Education

Religion (in %)	*100 (Hindu)*
Caste (in %)	
Rajput/Kshatriya	36
Brahmin	52
OBC (Baniya)	8
SC (Kori)	12
Level of Education (in %)	
Educational Qualification	*Percentage of Migrants*
Primary Education	22
Secondary Education	48
Higher Secondary	16
Graduate	14
Age in Years	
Age	*Per cent*
25–30	12
30–35	16
35–40	18
40–45	18
45–50	6
50–55	30

Table 2 highlights that most of the migrants are in age group 50–55 but, if we look in detail, we can see that taken all age groups together, the highest number of migrants are in between age group 30–45.

Level of education plays a very important role in social development of humans. Table 2 explains that literacy was hundred per cent in case of auto and taxi drivers from Uttar Pradesh. Everyone has primary education. It shows that more than half of the respondents had education up to secondary level. Around 16 per cent are having education till higher secondary level and 14 per cent of migrants are graduates.

Majority of migrants mentioned that, they were studying before coming to Mumbai. They didn't leave studies because of lack of income or in search of employment, but had been called by relatives who were doing well in Mumbai (54%) or had failed in one or other standards (14%). Almost 18 per cent of migrants reported that less source of income also accounts for leaving school or college.

Monthly Incomes, Previous Destination and Reason for Leaving Home Town of Auto and Taxi Drivers from Uttar Pradesh

Table 3 shows that half of auto rickshaw and taxi drivers were earning between INR 11,000 and 15,000 followed by 38 per cent respondents with an income between INR 5,000–10,000. There are very few (8%) who earn around Rupees 16,000–20,000. As reported by migrants it was found that those who earn more than Rupees 15,000 have other sources of income as well in Mumbai. They have other part time jobs as well, along with primary occupation of auto or taxi driving. Some are having their own some kind of shop as well. Data also suggested that those who belong to earning category of Rupees 20,000 to Rupees 25,000 have other occupation as well, such as agent for some private limited company, mechanic or electrician.

Data analysis shows that for most of the migrants, Mumbai was their first destination. Around 78 per cent of respondents reported that Mumbai was their first place of migration. The reason for this can be that most of the respondents' relatives or friend were already there in Mumbai and were also doing well. Network played a role in migration of auto and taxi drivers to Mumbai from eastern Uttar Pradesh. Most of the migrants reported that they are staying in the region of the people from the same origin. Remaining migrants reported Kanpur, Lucknow and Haryana as their first place of movement. Major reasons for migration are less income and facilitating role of networks.

Table 3

Monthly Incomes, Previous Destination and Reason for Leaving Home town of Auto and Taxi Drivers from Uttar Pradesh

Monthly Incomes (in %)	
Monthly Income (in ₹)	*Percentage of Migrants*
5000–10,000	38
11,000–15,000	48
16,000–20,000	8
20,000–25,000	6
Previous Destination (in %)	
Mumbai	78
Kanpur	10
Haryana	4
Lucknow	8
Reason for leaving Rural Home Town (in %)	
No future in hometown, Unviable land holding	16
Less source of Income	33
Liabilities (Sisters or daughters marriage)	7
Lots of people were doing well in Mumbai (Network or social capital)	40
Other reasons	4

Residential Conditions of Auto and Taxi Drivers in Mumbai

Most of the respondents mentioned that they live in very bad and pathetic conditions at destination. Although findings are indicative of improvements in the well-being of migrant workers over time, several of the long duration migrants and natives in the cities still lead a low quality life. The paper, therefore, argues in favour of urban employment programmes.

Around 98 per cent of migrants are living in slums (Jhuggis) of very small area. Per square feet of dwellings is very small and even in that there resides 4–5 members in one room. Kitchen too is within room itself. All of them are sharing toilets and bathrooms on rent basis. They use Bombay Municipal Corporation (BMC) water and have to pay monthly rent as well for their small room. There are just two per cent migrants who either own a personal room or home in Mumbai or don't spend on monthly rent. All the rooms were without toilet and sanitation facilities. Even for cooking, majority of the migrants are using kerosene instead of LPG in Mumbai.

Migration as Risk Insurance and Income Diversification Strategy

The major outcome of the study from literature review and from data analysis shows that migration acts as one of the most often adopted risk and income diversification strategy (33%) and network effect (40%) by rural poor in Uttar Pradesh (Table 3). This implies network plays a very crucial role in facilitating migration as it reduces the transfer cost of migration both in physical and monetary terms. Data highlights that most of the out-migrants from UP to Mumbai were studying before migration and migrated just to diversify income at households by remittances. The family as a whole decide and send members to Mumbai to have and additional earning to diversify income and minimize risks if it arises in near future.

Table 4

Amount Remitted per Month, Use of Remittances of Auto and Taxi Drivers at Origin and Changes felt by Migrants after Migration

Amount of Remitted Money per Month (in %)		
INR1,000–5,000	*INR 5,000–10,000*	*No Remittance*
78	20	2

Use of Remittances by Households at Origin (in %)				
Daily expenses & Children's education	*Medicine*	*Marriage Purpose*	*Loan Repayment*	*Others (Buying Home Land, Livestock etc)*
70	14	8	5	3

Major changes after Migrating to Mumbai (in %)				
Increase in Household Income	*Increase in Social status at Origin*	*Increase in Expenditure*	*Increase in Assets (Both at Destination and Origin)*	*Others (No Change, etc)*
31	42	10	6	11

Family size and Composition (in %)		
Parents	*Brothers (2–4)*	*Cousin Brothers*
12	82	6

Table 4 shows that majority (78%) of the auto and taxi driver migrants remit between ₹ 1,000–5,000. This remitted amount acts as diversified income in the income portfolio of rural household and also acts as a stabilizer against certain risks and failures associated with agriculture and thus reduces the vulnerability of poverty. Studies also show that a remittance reduces the uncertainty of a family income, provides investment funds and livelihoods for those with small lands and are poor (De Haan, 2000). Remittances diversify household income, co-insure household and migrants and can also enhance the social status of the migrant and his/her household in sending area (Waddington, 2003). The 20 per cent of migrants who remit between Rupees 5,000–10,000 have other part time occupation as well, along with auto and taxi driving as main primary occupation.

Most of the amount remitted is used in meeting daily expenses and children's education (70%) by household in origin. This denotes that with rural income alone the households are unable to meet the basic needs. Migration also contributes in human capital formation, as most of the remitted money is used in children's education. Medicine accounts for 14 per cent share of total remittances. Loan repayment accounts for 5 per cent which indicates most of the households have nothing left after daily expenses to pay loan. Marriages of siblings and children also account less, i.e. only 8 per cent as the amount remitted is only 1,000–5,000 and moreover that too is spent mostly on education and daily expenses. Almost all migrants responded that in case of urgent situations such as marriages in family, accidents, severe illness, crop failure, etc. they dispatch huge amount by taking loans and removing their savings.

Bigger family size encourages male migration in rural Uttar Pradesh. Around 82 per cent of auto rickshaw and taxi drivers reported that they belong to big family size and composition. Around 82 per cent of them have 2–4 brothers and someone is always there to look at homesteads and agriculture when they are in Mumbai. Bigger family size households diversify their resources by sending one or more members abroad and allowing someone to stay back to look at agriculture and livestock. Remittances act as shock stabilizers in case of emergencies and in regular days helps in smoothening household consumption. Some studies also support this fact that migration decisions strongly depend on household size and composition (Demurger et al., 2010). Household composition may play a role, as households with fewer earning members may be less likely to take up opportunities for migrant work (De Haan, 2000).

Around 42 per cent of migrants reported increase in social status and 32 per cent showed increase in household income. From the data set we found that around 90 per cent of migrants have farming as main occupation at origin. Migrants reported that earnings from farming are insufficient to meet the daily needs at origin, thus remittances increases the household income. Increase in social status implies that most of the migrants belong to big family size households and farming is the primary occupation for majority of them at origin. Though farming does not yield much revenue these days, the remittances helps in meeting even the daily expenses, so migrants are often respected by family households for an alternative as insurance mechanism in case of emergencies. Another major reason for increase in social status and respect can be accounted to the fact that, as farming is the only occupation at home and all members are engaged in agriculture only, there arises disguised unemployment. So migration is the most opted option to get rid of disguised unemployment and also diversify household income.

Migration as Ex-ante Strategy Adopted by Rural Poor as Against Poverty and Risk in Uttar Pradesh

Data analysis highlights the fact that majority of the migrants have farming as main household income earning occupation at origin. Most of them have land resources, home and livestocks at origin (88%). This indicates that migration is not ex-post strategy adopted by poor as against poverty and risk in Uttar Pradesh rather is ex-ante strategy by entire family as in portfolio and income diversification management. Migration is perceived as preplanned strategy by households to avoid certain kinds of adversity, and poverty is a major one.

Role of Network in Migration from Rural Uttar Pradesh

Literature shows that migration network, often known as social capital, plays a crucial role in facilitating migration (Haug, 2008; Demurger et al., 2010; Munshi, 2003). Though some studies also found that migration network sometimes acts as an entry barrier, such as facilitating caste based, region based network only and working as entry barrier for other potential migrants.

Most of the migrants came to Mumbai with the help of relatives, friends and father. Data analysis highlights that only 3 per cent of the migrants reported that they came on their own in search of job, whereas rest 97 per cent of auto and taxi drivers mentioned that they came to Mumbai with the help of relatives (72%), friends (16%) and father (09%) respectively. This denotes that most of the migrants already had someone from origin in Mumbai promoting migration. Moreover, they also cut the transfer cost of migration in both physical and monetary terms. In reasons for migration also we found that most of the migrants migrated to Mumbai because there are already many people in Mumbai and also they are doing well. We can say that network plays a very important role in migration from rural eastern Uttar Pradesh in the present case study.

Table 5

Role of Social Capital in Facilitating Migration

Minimum No. of Weeks of getting Job in Mumbai after Migration (in %)		
Number of Weeks	*Percentage of Migrants employed*	*Cumulative Percentage of Migrants employed*
1	21	21
2	36	57
3	24	81
4	17	98
5	2	100

Migration referred by (in %)	
Relatives	72
Friends	16
Father	09
Self	3

Majority of the migrants got jobs within three weeks of migration. Respondents mentioned that social capital (friends and relatives) reduces the monetary cost and physical cost of searching jobs at destination of migration as well as chances of being unemployed for longer time to least. The study also found that most of the migrants were employed very soon in some other occupation before joining as auto and taxi drivers. Cumulative percentage of migrants employed shows that almost hundred per cent of migrants were engaged in some work within five weeks of migration. Migrants reported that their relatives and friends already have looked for some part time job in Mumbai while they learn auto/taxi driving and their driving licence is made to get employed as auto/taxi drivers. So they already were offered with some job such as watchman, vendor, electrician, etc. meanwhile they were learning driving. Again it is visible that network be it caste based, region based or occupation based helped a lot in migration from eastern rural Uttar Pradesh. Various studies also found that migration networks allow better understanding of processes of work in their birth and their dynamics (Guilmoto and Sandron, 2001). Same study also found that migration by itself is a powerful force that serves to reduce uncertainty in developing countries.

Conclusion

Using thorough literature review and field survey on auto and taxi drivers from UP in Mumbai, the central finding of the paper is that migration works as strategy to enhance livelihoods of rural poor. Data analysis found that migration reduces the uncertainty of family income, provides investment funds, and livelihoods for those with limited earning in eastern rural Uttar Pradesh. The paper also found that social capital also plays a very crucial role in migration by reducing transfer cost of migration at destination. Another major finding of the study is that most of the migrants are from eastern UP. NSSO 64th Round also highlights that majority of male out-migration is from eastern Uttar Pradesh. Remittances act like auxiliary income for rural households engaged only in farming as primary occupation. Remittances are used in daily expenses, children's education and medicines at origin, thus providing additional pecuniary resources to meet basic needs and diversifying income.

The study also found that bigger family size encourages migration. The family with more adults or children are more likely to migrate. Based on the findings from literature and data analysis, migration may be well understood as a family decision to diversify income, risk insurance and poverty reduction strategies by rural poor in eastern Uttar Pradesh.

We can conclude by mentioning that migration by means of remittances diversify household income, co-insure household and migrant, and can also enhance the status of migrant and his/her household in sending area. We can wind up by stating that migration enhances their status at origin though they experience disrespect and powerlessness at destination. Migration helps in smoothening household consumption and acts as income diversification strategy.

References

Alam, Rukhsana and Asraful Alam. 2013. 'Socio-Economic Analysis of Van-Rickshaw Puller (Manual) in Rural Areas: A Case Study', *Indian Streams Research Journal*, 3(11): 1–5.

Ali, M. 2013. 'Socio-Economic Analysis of Rickshaw Pullers in Urban Centres: A Case Study of Uttar Pradesh, India', *International Journal of Advanced Research in Management and Social Sciences*, 2(1): 98–109.

Bigsten, A.A. 1998. 'Note on the Modelling of Circular Smallholder Migration', *Economics Letters*, 28: 87–91.

Brauw, Alen de, Valeries Mueller and Tassew Woldehanna. 2011. Insurance Motives to Remit: Evidence from Matched Sample of Ethiopian Internal Migrants. Discussion Paper 01090, International Food Policy Research Institute, Development Strategy and Governance Division Markets, Trade and Institutions Division.

Christiaensen, L., J. Weerdt and Y. Todo. 2013. 'Urbanization and Poverty Reduction: The Role of Rural Diversification and Secondary Towns', *Agricultural Economics*, 44(4 & 5): 435–447.

De Haan, A. 2000. Migrants, Livelihoods, and Rights: The Relevance of Migration in Development Policies. Social Development Working Paper No. 4, London: Department for International Development.

De Haas, Hein. 2010. 'Migration and Development: A Theoretical Perspective', *International Migration Review*, 44(1): 227–264.

De Weerdt, Joachim and Kalle Hirvonen. 2013. Risk Sharing and Internal Migration. Policy Research Working Paper Series 6429, The World Bank.

Demurger, Sylvie, Martin Fournier and Weiyong Yang. 2010. 'Rural Households' Decisions Towards Income Diversification: Evidence from North China', *China Economic Review*, 21(1): 32–44.

Deshingkar, Priya and Daniel Start. 2003. Seasonal Migration for Livelihood in India: Coping, Accumulation and Exclusion. Working Paper No. 220, London: Overseas Development Institute.

Ellis, F. 2003. A Livelihood Approach to Migration and Poverty Reduction, Norwich, Paper Commissioned Department for International Development (DFID), UK: ODG/DEV.

Faist, T. 1997. 'The Cucial Meso Level', in T. Hammer, G. Brochman, K. Tamas and T. Faist (eds), *International Migration, Immobility and Development*. Oxford: Berg, 187–217.

Fawcett, J.T. 1989. 'Networks, Links and Migration Systems', *International Migration Review*, 23(3): 671–680.

Ghobadi, Negar, Johannes Koetti and Renos Vakis. 2005. Moving Out of Poverty: Migration Insights from Rural Afghanistan. Afghanistan Research and Evaluation Unit, The World Bank.

Giesbert, Lena. 2007. Seeking Opportunities: Migration as an Income Diversification Strategy of Households in Kakamega District of Kenya. Working Paper No. 58, German Institute of Global and Area Studies.

Guilmoto, Z. Christophe and Fredric Sandron. 2001. 'The Internal Dynamics of Migration Networks in Developing Countries', *Population: An English Selection*, 3(2): 135–164.

Haug, Sonja. 2008. 'Migration Networks and Migration Decision-Making', *Journal of Ethnic and Migration Studies*, 34(4): 585–605.

Katz, Eliakim and Oded Stark. 1986. 'Labor Migration and Risk Aversion in Less Developed Countries', *Journal of Labor Economics*, 4(1): 134–149.

Kinnan, Cynthia, Shing-Yi Wang and Yongxiang Wang. 2012. 'Credit Constraints, Job Mobility and Entrepreneurship: Evidence from a Property Reform in China', *Review of Economics and Statistics*, 94(2): 523–551.

Konseiga, Adama. 2005. Household Migration Decisions as Survival Strategy: The Case of Burkina Faso. Bonn Discussion Paper No. 1819, The Institute of Study of Labour (IZA).

Lindstrom, David P., Craig Hardley and Tefera Belachew. 2012. The Role of Migration and Income Diversification in Protecting Households from Food Insecurity in Southwest Ethiopia. Session 59: Economic Change and Migration: International Perspectives. Population Association of America, Annual Meeting Programme, San Francisco, CA, May 3–5.

Mendola, Mariapia. 2004. Migration and Technological Change in Rural Households: Complements or Substitutes? University of Milan-Bicocca and Centro Studi Luca d'Angliano, Development Studies Working Papers.

Mincer, Jacob. 1978. 'Family Migration Decisions', *Journal of Political Economy*, 86(5): 749–773.

Munshi, K. 2003. 'Networks in the Modern Economy: Mexican Migrants in US Labour Market', *Quarterly Journal of Economics*, 118(2): 549–599.

Nyberg-Sorenson, N., Nicholas Van Hear and P. Engberg-Pedersen. 2002. The Migration-Development Nexus: Evidence and Policy Options. Centre for Development Research Study, Migration Development Links: Evidence and Policy Options, Copenhagen, CDR 2000, February.

Paulson, A. 2003. Insurance Motives for Migration: Evidence from Thailand. Working Paper, Kellogg School of Management, Northwestern University, Evanston, IL.

Pries, L. 2004. 'Determining the Causes and Durability of Transnational Labour Migration between Mexico and the United States: Some Empirical Findings', *International Migration*, 42(2): 3–39.

Rosenzweig, Mark R. and Oded Stark. 1989. 'Consumption Smoothing, Migration, and Marriage: Evidence from Rural India', *Journal of Political Economy*, 97(4): 905–926.

Sakho-Jimbira, Maam Suwadu and Celine Bignebat. 2008. Local Diversification of Income Sources versus Migration: Complements or Substitutes? A Case Study from Rural Senegal. Paper presented in 37th Australian Conference of Economists, Gold Coast, Queensland, Australia, September 30–October 3.

Stark, Oded and Davi E. Bloom. 1985. 'The New Economics of Labor Migration', *American Economic Review*, 75(2): 173–178.

Waddington, Clare. 2003. Livelihood Outcomes of Migration for Poor People. DRC Working Paper No. T1, Development Research Centre on Migration, Globalisation and Poverty, University of Sussex, Brighton.

12

Migration in Empowered Action Group States

Some New Facts

D.P. SINGH

Government of India has constituted Empowered Action Group (EAG) in the Ministry of Health and Family Welfare in 2001 consisting of eight Indian states, namely, Bihar, Chhattisgarh, Jharkhand, Madhya Pradesh, Orissa (now Odisha), Rajasthan, Uttaranchal (Now Uttarakhand) and Uttar Pradesh. The objective of EAG is to bring down various social and health related parameters which are much higher in these states as compared to non-EAG states. The population growth, fertility, mortality, social and health indicators in these states constituting of 261 administrative districts affects directly and indirectly the overall progress of the country. These EAG states also are economically backward states in terms of high poverty level, high population pressure and unemployment problem.

The present paper makes an attempt to understand migration level and trend in EAG states vis-à-vis non-EAG states. Data from national sample survey 2007–08, India Human Development Survey (IHDS) 2005 and special tables at district level migration from census of India 2001 are used.

Migration Level

Nearly 45 per cent of total population of India lives in these eight EAG states and occupy 43 per cent of land area of country. According to 2001 census, 338 million person (73.5%) reported that they were born at same place while nearly 16 per cent moved within districts, 6.6 per cent between districts and 2.8 per cent between states. Out of 8

EAG states, state of UP, Rajasthan, Odisha and Bihar reported more people moving out of state than people coming into the state. States of Jharkhand, Madhya Pradesh, Chhattisgarh and Uttarakhand show similar number of people moving in and out of the state.

Table 1

Volume and Percentage of Migrants, 2001 Census (Figure in '000)

	Non Migrants	*Intra-district*	*Inter-district*	*Interstate - In-Migrants*	*Interstate - Out-Migrants*
Bihar	63,009 (75.92)	13,663 (16.46)	4,532 (5.46)	1,582 (1.91)	5,543 (6.68)
Jharkhand	19,685 (73.05)	4,286 (15.91)	1,177 (4.37)	1,781 (6.61)	1,502 (5.57)
Madhya Pradesh	42,401 (70.26)	10,793 (17.88)	4,848 (8.03)	2,237 (3.71)	2,068 (3.43)
Chhattisgarh	14,049 (67.43)	4,252 (20.41)	1,513 (7.26)	969 (4.65)	861 (4.13)
Odisha	25,942 (70.48)	7,674 (20.85)	2,472 (6.72)	659 (1.79)	964 (2.62)
Rajasthan	40,610 (71.87)	10,316 (18.26)	3,735 (6.61)	1,731 (3.06)	2,753 (4.87)
Uttar Pradesh	1,26,484 (76.10)	25,134 (15.12)	11,608 (6.98)	2,808 (1.69)	9,627 (5.79)
Uttarakhand	5,479 (64.54)	1,510 (17.79)	532 (6.27)	867 (10.21)	927 (10.92)
India	7,21,460 (70.14)	1,81,800 (17.67)	76,841 (7.47)	42,431 (4.13)	

Source: Census of India 2001, D1 Table: Population classified by Place of birth and Sex.

According to HDI survey the percentage of migrant household were nearly 15.8 per cent as compared to non-EAG states who recorded nearly 31 per cent (Table 2). Among EAG states Highest percentage of migrant household were in Orissa and Chhattisgarh while lowest in Bihar state. In rural areas of almost all EAG states recorded less than 10 per cent of migrant households while urban areas of Chhattisgarh, Odisha and Jharkhand states reported more than 64 percentage migrant households. Urban areas of Bihar and Rajasthan recorded less than 50 per cent as migrant households. High rate household migration in tribal belt of Chhattisgarh, Jharkhand and Odisha may be attributed to availability of many natural resources in terms of coal and minerals.

Table 2

Percentage of Migrant Household, HDI 2005

States	*Rural*	*Urban*	*Total*
Bihar	5.0	47.1	9.7
Jharkhand	4.6	64.2	14.3
Madhya Pradesh	7.3	51.0	18.7
Chhattisgarh	8.1	74.1	20.8
Odisha	13.3	66.3	20.9
Rajasthan	5.0	45.6	15.0
Uttar Pradesh	5.1	55.0	15.3
Uttarakhand	6.6	54.5	16.3
EAG States	6.6	55.1	15.8
Non-EAG States	19.4	53.5	31.3
India	13.5	53.9	25.1

Source: HDI 2005.

Duration of Residence of Migrant Households

Response to 'How many years ago did your family first come to this village/town/city' provides the temporal information about household migration. Table 3 provides the duration residence of household migration. Nearly 12 per cent of households migrated during five-year preceding household survey while nearly one-fifth migrated during 1990 to 2000 and another one-fifth during 1980–90. Migration in urban areas during 1980–90 and 1190–2000 was at higher level as compared to rural areas. Similar trend is observed between rural and urban areas of EAG and Non-EAG states.

Table 3

Duration of Residence of Migrant Households in EAG and Non-EAG States

Duration of Residence	*EAG*			*Non EAG*		
	Rural	*Urban*	*Total*	*Rural*	*Urban*	*Total*
2000–2005	7.1	14.9	12.3	7.5	15.1	12.0
5–14 (1990–2000)	16.2	27.0	23.5	14.3	25.7	21.1
15–24 (1980–1990)	18.1	21.0	20.1	19.4	22.0	20.9
Before 1980	58.5	37.1	44.1	58.9	37.2	45.9
Total	100.0	100.0	100.0	100.0	100.0	100.0

Source: HDI 2005.

Short-term Migration

In last two NSS rounds – 55th and 64th, data on short-term migration was collected based on whether a person stayed 30 days or more and less than 6 months away from his usual place of residence for employment or search of employment. Table 4 presents the short term migration rates in EAG states in rural and urban areas. In these two rounds there was slightly different duration of cut-off as in NSS 55th round any person stayed away from village or town for 6 month or more while 64th round it was between 30 days and 6 month during 365 days. The short-term migration was found as 1.3 per cent in 2007–08 and 1.2 per cent during 1999–2000. Short-term migration was higher in rural areas as compared to urban areas, lower socio-economic group such as SC and ST reported higher migration than OBC and others. Education-wise up to middle educated and higher educated show higher rate than illiterates. Short-term migration was higher in EAG states than non-EAG states. Further analysis according to monthly per capita expenditure shows that lower economic strata groups reported much higher short-term migration than upper economic groups.

Table 4

Percentage Distribution of Persons Temporarily Staying away for Employment by Sex, Social Groups and Educational Category, 2007–08 and 1999–2000

	EAG/Non-EAG States	*NSS 64th (2007–08)*			*NSS 55th (1999–2000)*		
		Rural	*Urban*	*Total*	*Rural*	*Urban*	*Total*
Persons	Total	1.7	0.4	1.3	1.3	1.1	1.2
Male	EAG	3.3	0.7	2.8	1.6	1.5	1.6
	Non-EAG	2.3	0.6	1.7	1.5	1.1	1.4
Female	EAG	0.4	0.1	0.3	0.8	1.1	0.8
	Non-EAG	0.7	0.1	0.5	1.0	0.8	1.0
Total	EAG	1.9	0.4	1.1	1.2	1.3	1.2
	Non-EAG	1.5	0.4	1.6	1.3	1.0	1.2
ST	EAG	2.6	0.4	2.4	3.1	1.9	2.9
	Non-EAG	3.8	0.4	3.4	0.7	1.0	1.8
SC	EAG	2.3	0.6	2.1	1.2	1.5	1.2
	Non-EAG	1.5	0.4	1.2	0.9	0.8	1.3
OBC	EAG	1.8	0.5	1.6	0.9	1.2	1.1
	Non-EAG	1.1	0.4	0.9	2.1	1.2	1.2

Cont'd...

...Cont'd

Others	EAG	1.3	0.2	0.9	0.8	1.2	0.8
	Non-EAG	1.2	0.3	0.8	0.9	0.9	1.1
Illiterate	EAG	1.6	0.4	1.5	1.2	1.5	1.2
	Non-EAG	1.6	0.4	1.4	1.3	0.9	1.3
Up to Middle	EAG	2.1	0.4	1.8	1.1	1.1	1.2
	Non-EAG	1.5	0.4	1.1	1.4	0.9	1.0
Secondary and Above	EAG	2.4	0.3	1.5	1.6	1.5	1.3
	Non-EAG	1.2	0.4	0.8	1.0	1.1	1.3

Source: Computed from NSS 2007–08 and 1999–2000 based on raw data.

Return Migration

In NSS 64th round, an additional question was added to ascertain return migration. The question was whether the place of enumeration was usual place of residence (UPR) any time in the past. The return migration rate in both rural and urban areas was 12 and 11 per cent. However, the return migration rate was found much higher for males in rural areas as compared to female return migration. This indicates that higher percentage of male migrated from rural areas return back to rural areas. Return migration to EAG and non-EAG states indicate that little higher percentage of return migrant in rural areas in EAG state than non-EAG state. In urban areas, return migration in non-EAG state was found comparatively higher than EAG states. The comparison with 49th round data indicates that female return migration increased much more in rural as well as urban areas.

Table 5

Return Migration Rate per 1000 in EAG and Non-EAG States,

Sector	*EAG and Non EAG States*	*NSS 64th 2007–08*			*NSS 49th 1993*		
		Male	*Female*	*Total*	*Male*	*Female*	*Total*
Rural	EAG	261	105	115	245	28	53
	Non-EAG	227	107	124	182	50	71
	All	238	106	120	198	43	66
Urban	EAG	90	81	84	58	35	44
	Non-EAG	126	117	121	62	54	57
	All	117	105	109	61	49	54

Source: Computed from NSS 64th round, 2007–08 and NSS 49th 1993.

Poverty in EAG States

The poverty level in EAG states always has been higher than non-EAG states. Even though estimated poverty level in rural and urban areas is getting narrowed down as nearly one-third of population lives below poverty line in the country. The poverty situation in many EAG states is much higher than the country as whole. Out of eight EAG states, seven states namely Bihar, Jharkhand, Madhya Pradesh Chhattisgarh, Odisha, Uttarakhand and Uttar Pradesh shows nearly half of population in rural areas living in below poverty. In urban areas of all EAG states except Jharkhand recorded higher poverty than all-India urban. The data available from HDI survey suggest that rural poverty in six states is higher than all-India and again urban poverty in six states is higher than all-India. The results of HDI survey shows surprisingly, Bihar as lower poverty state as compared to country level which probably seems grossly underestimated. The per capita income based on HDI survey reported much lower in state of Bihar, Jharkhand, Madhya Pradesh, Chhattisgarh, Odisha, and Uttar Pradesh. Based on these estimates it may be concluded that EAG states remain economically poor and backward. State of Madhya Pradesh and Rajasthan even reported higher poverty level in urban areas as compared to rural areas (Table 6).

Table 6

Poverty Level and per capita Income in EAG States based on NSS and HDI Survey

States	*NSS 2004–05 (Revised Estimate)*		*Percentage Below Poverty – HDI 2005*			*Per capita Income*		
	Rural	*Urban*	*Rural*	*Urban*	*Total*	*Rural*	*Urban*	*Total*
Bihar	47.91	44.94	12.4	18.1	13.0	3339	6857	3530
Jharkhand	51.85	21.75	52.7	20.7	47.4	4175	13654	4833
Madhya Pradesh	45.19	48.94	41.1	41.5	41.2	3530	6328	4125
Chhattisgarh	50.37	42.15	64.0	32.2	57.9	4800	12000	5306
Odisha	53.23	48.40	37.8	25.8	36.1	3096	9000	3450
Rajasthan	26.91	40.34	20.1	27.9	22.0	5732	9000	6260
Uttarakhand	48.00	39.65	35.4	14.7	31.2	6000	12800	6857
Uttar Pradesh	45.78	42.95	29.0	23.0	27.8	3605	8235	4300
All-India	36.38	34.45	22.0	18.5	21.0	4712	11444	5999

Sources: NSS Estimate from Mahendra Dev and Ravi (2008); Calculated from raw HDI household data and per capita income from Desai et al. (2010).

Migration Rate and Economic status

Economic motivation has been found to be the main factor among male migration in India as well as in many Third World countries. Based on last NSS data of 2007–08, male and female migration rate in EAG and non-EAG states according to deciles groups of monthly per capita expenditure is presented in Figure 1 and 2. Migration data suggest that as economic status of person increases propensity to migrate also increases. Lower economic status people are less migratory in both EAG states as well as non-EAG states. It seems that people from lower economic group find much more difficult to move or may not be aware about the benefit they may get after moving. A detail analysis shows people from lower economic group prefer moving short distances as compared to long distance which require further social and economic support to settle at place of movement. It is difficult to draw clear relation between economic status and migration rate because economic status also gets reflected in their characteristics such as education level, skill and occupation choices. Based on presented relation between economic status it can be suggested that people from middle and higher economic status are more mobile as compared to lower economic status and also for reaping the benefit of their movement.

Figure 1

Male Migration Rates by MPCE in EAG and Non-EAG States, 2007–08

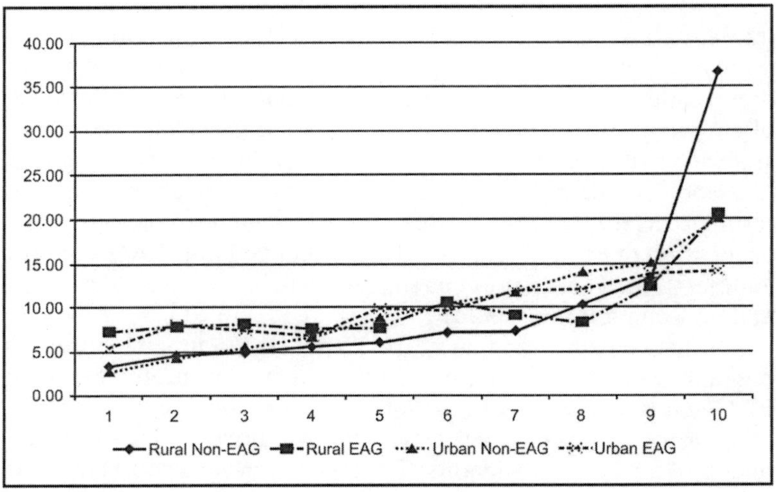

Female migration rate shows increasing trend in non-EAG states in both rural and urban areas while in EAG states female migration rate declines as economic status increases (Figure 2).

Figure 2

Female Migration Rates by MPCE in EAG and Non-EAG States, 2007–08

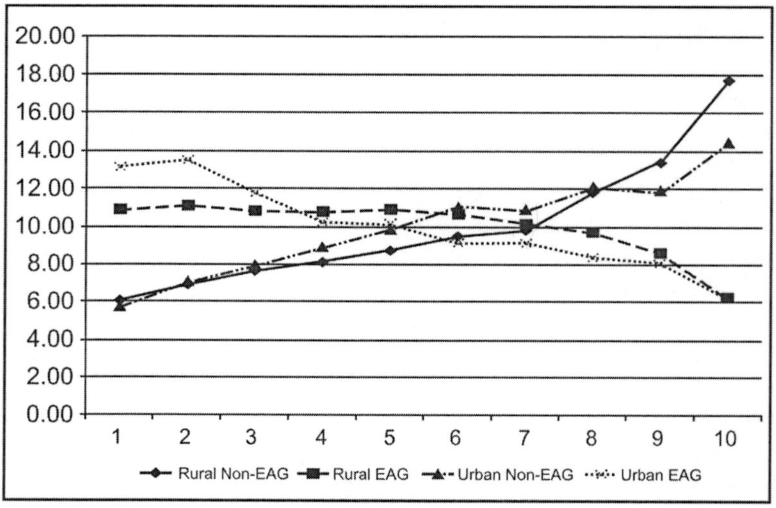

Characteristics of Household Migration

Bi-variate and binary logistic regression is used to find out determinants of migration in India. Dichotomous dependent variable is migrant household if household reported number of years ago his family first came to the place of enumeration – village/town/city or non-migrant household if household reported to live at the place of enumeration as forever. The independent variables used in the analysis are households below poverty line, income group household, religion, social groups, land ownership, place of residence as rural or urban, educational level of head of household, occupation of head of household and EAG and non-EAG states of enumeration. Table 7 presents the bivariate distribution of migrant and non-migrant household.

It may be observed that nearly 53 per cent of urban reported as migrant households as compared to 13.5 per cent in rural areas. In EAG states, about 15.8 households reported to have moved from other place to place of residence while in non-EAG state nearly one-third reported as migrants. The income level of household was negatively related to migration of households. Caste and religion shows that among progressive caste as well, religion increases the migration chances. The occupational status of household and education level suggests positive impact on migration level. Ownership of agriculture land affects negatively migration level. Nearly 12.1 per cent of land owners reported as migrant, while 35.6 per cent of non-owners as migrants.

Table 7

Distribution Migrants and Non-migrants Households by Selected Characteristics

Characteristics of Head of Household	*Migrant*	*Non-Migrant*	*Total*
Total	25.1	74.9	
Rural	13.5	86.5	28.7
Urban	53.9	46.1	71.3
EAG states	15.8	84.2	40.3
Non-EAG	31.3	68.7	59.7
Below Poverty Line			
Yes	18.5	81.5	21
No	26.8	73.2	78.9
Income Quintile			
Poorest	13.1	86.9	19.7
2nd	16.9	83.1	19.3
Middle	23.7	76.3	19.5
4th	31.1	68.9	19.7
Richest	41.9	58.1	19.3
Brahmin	35.2	64.8	5.1
OBC	21.9	78.1	40.8
SC	21.4	78.6	22
ST	18.4	81.6	7.8
Other	33.7	66.3	24.3
Hindu	24	76	82.3
Muslim	27	73	11.4
Christian	50.6	49.4	2.7
Sikh	25.2	74.8	1.4
Buddhist	35	65	0.8
Jain	40.1	59.9	0.3
Tribal	8.5	91.5	1
Education			
Illiterate	87.1	12.9	23.4

Cont'd...

...Cont'd

Till Primary	80.1	19.9	15.7
Till Middle	72.4	27.6	35.7
Higher Secondary	70.4	29.6	10.4
Graduate and Above	59.3	40.7	14.6
Occupation of Head			
Cultivation	10.1	89.9	25.1
Allied Agriculture	15.9	84.1	1
Agriculture Labour	11.1	88.9	15.4
Non-Agriculture Labour	26.1	73.9	18
Artisan	31.7	68.3	6
Petty Trade	34.9	65.1	4.2
Business	38.7	61.3	5.5
Salaried	46.2	53.8	17.8
Profession	35.9	64.1	0.9
Pension-Rent	35.8	64.2	3.4
Others	26.9	73.1	2.8
Own or cultivate any Agriculture Land			
Yes	12.1	87.9	44.7
No	35.6	64.4	55.3

Source: HDI 2005.

Multivariate Analysis of Determinants of Household Migration

As seen above most of selected characteristics show clear social and economic differences between migrant and non-migrant households. To further analyse the individual impact each selected variable controlling the effect other variables, bivariate logistic regression was applied and results are presented in Table 8. The outcome variable is migrant or non-migrant household while rural urban residence, EAG and non-EAG states, household income and whether they fall below poverty line or not, Occupation and education of head of household, ownership of agriculture or cultivable land, Caste and religion of household are considered an as explanatory variable in the in the model. Altogether nine explanatory variables are used in the analysis. The actual and predicted classification of dependent variable shows nearly 76 per cent of cases were correctly classified.

Poverty and income level of household after controlling the effect of other variable indicate that it affects negatively. The chances of migration among above poverty line and increase in income level were much higher than lower income group. Disadvantage and vulnerable group in Indian society are less mobile as compared to progressive caste groups. Muslims were found comparatively less mobile than Hindus while probability among Christians household was much higher than Hindus households. Literacy level of household shows that increase in literacy level is significantly associated with increased chances of migration of household. Occupational distribution of household suggest that agricultural labourers were less mobile than cultivators and allied agriculture related household while other type of households such as business, trade, salaried, professional and artisans are comparatively shown higher chances of migration than cultivators.

Table 8

Result of Multivariate Analysis of Migrant and Non Migrant Households with Selected Characteristics

Background Variables	*B*	*S.E.*	*Sig.*	*Odd Ratio*
EAG state ® non-EAG	–.207	.029	.000	.813
URBAN ® Rural	1.370	.031	.000	3.936
POOR® Non-Poor	–.202	.036	.000	.817
2nd income group ® Poorest	.144	.049	.003	1.155
Middle	.194	.047	.000	1.214
4th income group	.267	.047	.000	1.307
Richest	.296	.050	.000	1.345
OBC ® Brahmin	–.203	.053	.000	.816
SC	–.234	.058	.000	.791
ST	.011	.073	.882	1.011
Others	.015	.054	.781	1.015
Muslim ® Hindu	–.145	.040	.000	.865
Christian	.811	.066	.000	2.250
Sikh–Jain	–.367	.079	.000	.693
Buddhist	.070	.149	.638	1.073
Tribal	–.163	.157	.300	.850
Up to Primary ® Illiterate	.273	.047	.000	1.314
Middle	.258	.041	.000	1.294
Higher Secondary	.216	.052	.000	1.241
Graduate	.302	.051	.000	1.352
Own Land ® No Land	–.539	.039	.000	.583
Agriculture Labour ® Cultivation	–.147	.062	.018	.863
Non-Agriculture Labour	.409	.055	.000	1.505

Cont'd...

...Cont'd

Artisan	.454	.065	.000	1.575
Petty Trade	.522	.069	.000	1.686
Business	.445	.065	.000	1.560
Salaried	.690	.053	.000	1.994
Profession	.645	.119	.000	1.906
Pension-Rent	.305	.073	.000	1.357
Others	.418	.087	.000	1.519
Constant	−1.897	.083	.000	.150

The estimated probability of migration of household is shown in Figure 3. It clearly indicates that education and economic status shows increasing positive probability of migration. The religion and caste group shows upper caste and Christians having much higher probability chances than others. Probability to move to EAG states is lower than non-EAG states after controlling the effect of other factors presented in multivariate analysis.

Figure 3

Probability of Migration of Household by Selected Characteristics

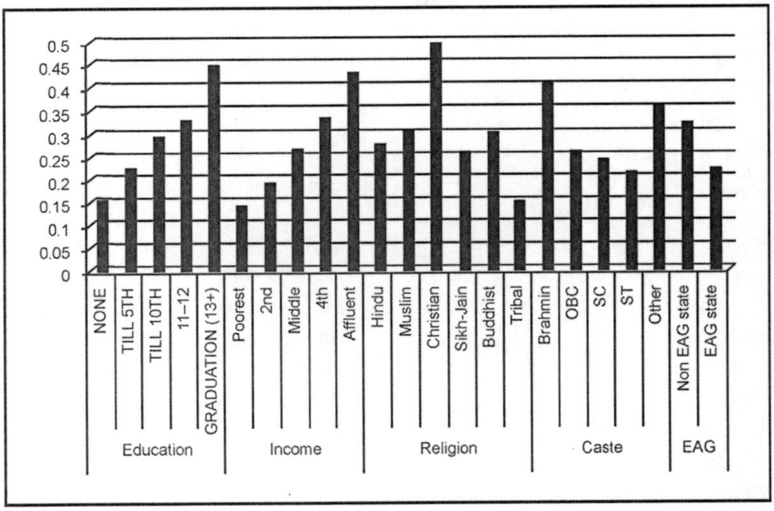

Characteristics of Out-Migrants

Present section discusses some characteristics of out migrants from HDI survey 2005. Detail of out-migrants from household was collected regarding the members who presently are not living in the household and part of family. Table 9 presents some selected characteristics of out-migrants from HDI survey. Nearly 26 per cent households reported that husband has moved out of house and 25 per cent some member of family who send money to households including brother, uncle and other relation. In EAG state absentee husband exceeded much more than in non-EAG out-migrants. Students moving out of household exceed in non-EAG states as compared to EAG states. Nearly 40 per cent out-migrant are reported as single. Out-migrant moving out of country were nearly 10 per cent in EAG states as compared to 1.6 per cent in non-EAG states.

Table 9

Selected Characteristics of Out-migrants in EAG and Non EAG States

Selected characteristics	*EAG state*	*Non EAG state*	*All*
Sample	2,174	2,587	4,761
Who migrated			
Absent husband	33.9	17.5	26.2
Absent wife	3.8	2.6	3.3
Absent parents	5.5	7.3	6.3
Who transfer money to HH	37	42.4	39.6
Student	19.8	30.2	24.7
Marital Status			
Spouse absent	36.2	18.5	27.8
Married	20.6	29.9	25
Single	38.7	45.5	41.9
Widowed	1.8	1.9	1.8
Separated-divorce	1.1	1.8	1.5
No Gauna	1.7	2.4	2
Education			
Up to Primary	21.4	18.3	19.9
Up to Secondary (6–10)	35.9	40	37.8
High Secondary and above	15.7	14.5	15.2
Graduation and Above	9.3	13.9	11.5
Do not Know-Illiterate	17.7	13.3	15.6
Where Migrated			
Same state	46.4	72.9	58.9
Another state	52	17.1	35.5
Abroad	1.6	10.1	5.6
Place migrated			
Same village-Town	6.4	12.6	9.3

Cont'd...

...Cont'd

Another Village	22	26.4	24.1
Another Small city	20	23.6	21.7
Another Large city	51.5	37.5	44.9
Occupation			
Professional-Technical	9	11.7	10.1
Administrative-Executive	2.3	3.1	2.6
Clerical and related	4.8	5.5	5.1
Sales Workers	6.5	11	8.5
Service workers	15.3	15.2	15.3
Farmers	10.6	14.3	12.2
Production-Transport	36.9	28.4	33.2
Labourers NEC	14.7	10.8	13
Caste			
Brahmin	9.5	3.3	6.6
OBC	48.6	34.6	42
SC	18.5	21.3	19.8
ST	6.3	6.9	6.6
Others	17.1	33.9	25
Poor	22.1	9.6	16.2
Non-Poor	77.9	90.4	83.8

Source: Computed from HDI 2005 raw data.

Nearly 22 per cent reported out-migrants from poor households in EAG states as compared to 10 per cent in non-EAG states.

Inter-censual Migration During 1991–2001

As mentioned earlier, EAG states are divided into 261 administrative districts in 2001 census. Migration in India is measured using administrative district as migration defining criteria. If a person moves from one place to other within same district is termed as intra-district migrants while those who cross administrative district to another district within same state are termed as inter-district and those who cross the state are termed as interstate migrants. Based on special table prepared to measure district-wise inflow and outflow of migrants, this paper tries to measure total loss and gain to a particular district through exchange of migrants coming and moving out of district administrative boundary.

Table 10A summarizes the volume of total in-migrants including inter-district and inter-state migrants. Out of 261 administrative districts of EAG states only 5 districts namely Indore, Khordha, Jaipur, Ghaziabad and Lucknow attracted more than 1,00,000 males while 11 districts gained through in-migration between 50,000 to 1,00,000 males during 1991–2001. Nearly half of districts of EAG states received less than 10,000 males. One shall remember in interpreting this in-migration volume that these are all male migrants who might have moved due to economical, social and other factors such as education or moved due to birth. Map 1 shows district-wise in-migration to 261 EAG districts. It seems clear from the map of male in-migration that districts which are either state capital or industrial district and closer to metropolitan district attract more male migrants than districts having not much economic base. In-migration rate indicates that in 93 districts it was less than 1 per cent and in 73 districts it varies between 1 to 2 per cent. District of Shrawasti, Kaushambi and Ballia, all in UP, recorded about 0.25 as in-migration rate. Ghaziabad, Gautam Buddha Nagar, Dehradun, Bhopal and Khordha recorded more than 10 per cent in-migration rate.

Volume of out-migration during 1991–2001 is presented in Table 10B and Map 2. Six districts namely Patna, Ganjam, Jaunpur, Azamgarh, Allahabad and Gorakhpur show more than 1,00,000 males moved out to other districts in the country. Thirty-five districts reported male out-migration between 50,000 to 1,00,000 and 101 districts between 20,000 to 50,000. Districts of Durg, Raipur and Bilaspur in Chattisgarh state reported high level of male out-migration, in spite of having excellent industrial activities and might be interpreted cautiously because these districts were reorganized during the formation of state of Chattisgarh and many new districts were carved out such as Korba, Janjgir-Champa, Mahasamund, and Kawardha.

Out-migration rate was observed highest in Garwal (15.6%) and Almora (13.8%) followed by Chatra (8.6%), Pithoragarh (8.0%), Tehri Garwal (7.4%), Chamoli (6.9%) and Munger (6.9%). The lowest out-migration rate was recorded in Kheri (0.3%), Shrawasti (0.4%) and Kaushambi (0.6%).

Male net-migration volume during 1991–2001 is presented Table 10C and Map 3. Eleven districts of EAG states recorded net gain of 25,000 and more male persons in exchange of people who lived in district and those who migrated to the district from other district in the country. Similarly, new loss was reported by 178 district spread across all the eight EAG states. Maximum new loss of male migrants is recorded in three district of Uttar Pradesh, namely,

Table 10A

District-wise Number of Male In Migrants in EAG States 1991–2001

Volume of Migration	*Bihar*	*Jharkh*	*MP*	*Chattis*	*Orissa*	*Rajasthan*	*UP*	*Uttaran*	*EAG States*
Up to 5,000	13	5	2	0	7	1	10	2	40
5,000–10,000	18	6	8	5	8	9	33	4	91
10,000–20,000	4	1	18	6	10	7	16	3	65
20,001–50,000	1	4	15	3	3	13	7	3	49
50,001–1,00,000	1 Patna	2 Dhanbad Ranchi	1 Bhopal	2 Durg Raipur	1 Cuttuck	1 Ganganagar	2 Gautam Budhha Nagar, Kanpur	1 Dehradun	11
1,00,001 and above	0	0	1 Indore	0	1 Khordha	1 Jaipur	2 Ghaziabad, Lucknow	0	5
Total	37	18	45	16	30	32	70	13	261

Table 10B

District-wise Number of Male out Migrants in EAG States 1991–2001

Volume of Migration	*Bihar*	*Jharkh*	*MP*	*Chattis*	*Orissa*	*Rajasthan*	*UP*	*Uttaranchal*	*EAG States*
Up to 5,000	1	1	1	2	6	0	3	2	16
5,000–10,000	2	5	7	2	4	4	7	3	34
10,000–20,000	6	4	17	7	7	10	15	3	69
20,001–50,000	17	7	20	2	11	14	26	4	101
50,001–1,00,000	10	1 Ranchi	0	3 Durg, Raipur, Bilaspur	1 Cuttack	4 Pali, Nagaur, Jodhpur, Jaipur	15	1 Garwal	35
1,00,001 and above	1 Patna	0	0	0	1 Ganjam	0	4 Jaunpur Azamgarh Allahabad Gorakhpur	0	6
Total	37	18	45	16	30	32	70	13	261

Map 1

Inter-district and Inter-state Male In-Migrant Districts of EAG States

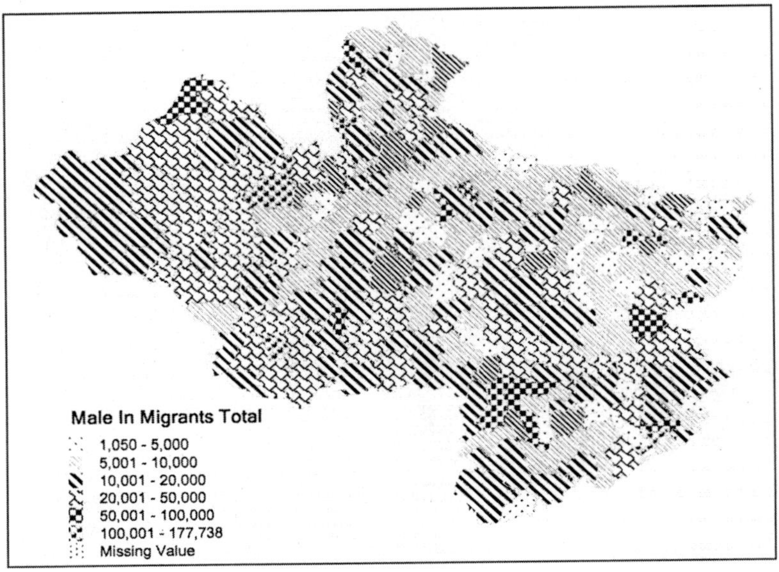

Map 2

Inter-district and Inter-state Male Out-Migrant Districts of EAG States

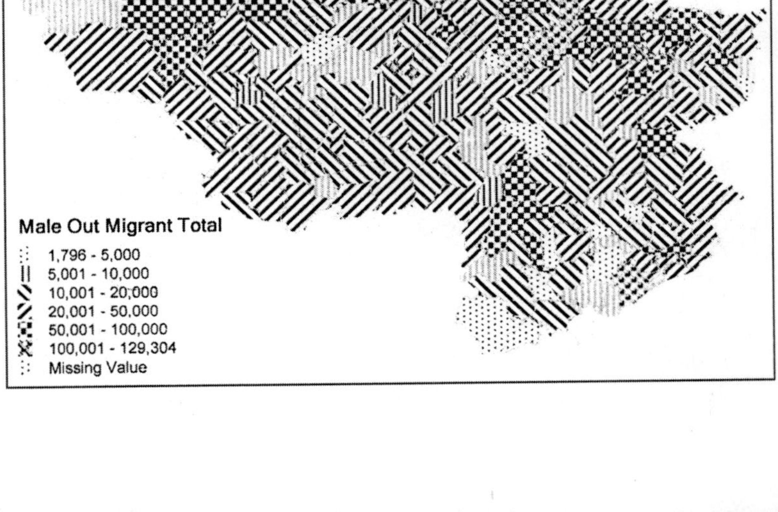

Jaunpur, Azamgarh and Gorakhpur who loss more than 1,00,000 male persons from the district. Ganjam district in Odisha lost nearly 83,000 while Siwan, Madhubani and Dharbhanga districts in Bihar net loss was nearly 80,000 males. Another 10 district in UP namely Allahabad, Pratapgarh, Ballia, Deoria, Bulandsahar, Muzaffarnagar, Basti, Ghazipur and Varanasi recorded net loss was between 50,000 to 76,000. In Bihar, 4 districts reported net male loss between 52,000 to 66,000.

Map 3

Inter-district and Inter-state Male Net-Migrant in Districts of EAG States

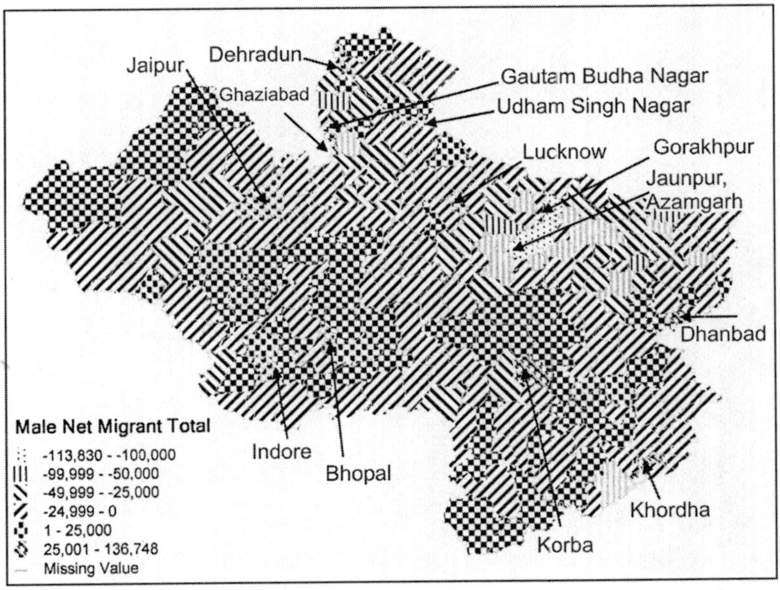

Net migration rate was found highest in Almora (10.3%) followed by Garwal (10.2%). Nearly 10 districts of UP and Bihar net-migration rate varied between –5 to –6 per cent. Chatra district in Jharkhand recorded net loss of –7.8 per cent. In terms of gain of net migration rate was found in Ghaziabad, Gautam Buddha Nagar in UP, Bhopal in MP and Khordha in Odisha between 6 to 10 per cent.

Conclusion

The present paper attempted to analyse migration level and characteristics in EAG and non-EAG states in India. Various sources of information are used such as census, National Sample Survey and

Table 10C

District-wise Number of Male Net-Migrants in EAG States 1991–2001

Volume of Migration	*Bihar*	*Jharkh*	*MP*	*Chattis*	*Odisha*	*Rajasthan*	*UP*	*Uttaran*	*EAG States*
Net Loss more than 1,00,000	0	0	0	0	0	0	3 Jaunpur, Azamgarh, Gorakhpur	0	3
Net Loss of between 50,000 to 99,999	7	0	0	0	1 Ganjam	0	10	0	18
Net Loss of between 25,000 to 49,999	13	1	3	1	0	2	15	2	37
Net Loss up to 24,999	17	10	19	8	17	19	35	5	130
Net Gain of 1 to 25,000	0	6	21	6	11	10	4	4	62
Net Gain of 25,000 and above	0	1 Dhanbad	2 Indore, Bhopal	1 Korba	1 Khordha	1 Jaipur	3 Ghaziabad, Gautam Buddha Nagar, Kanpur	2 Dehradun, Udham Singh Nagar	11
Total	37	18	45	16	30	32	70	13	261

human development survey of 2005. Study suggests that most of EAG states remain as out-migrating states, reflecting lack of employment opportunities in these states. Multivariate analysis of selected characteristics of household suggested that income, education and occupation affects migration level in increasing order. The caste and religion of household shows that lower and vulnerable group of households in addition to poverty level of household migration level was lower than economically and socially better off. Study also highlights the net gain and loss through migration in 261 EAG districts. The intercensual migration data of 1991–2001 shows that out of 261 EAG districts most districts of Uttar Pradesh, Bihar, Odisha and Rajasthan forced more males to out-migrate to other districts within or outside states. Very few districts which are either administrative capitals of state or engaged in industrial activities were able to attract male migrants rather than pushing them out of the district.

References

Bhagat, R.B. 2010. 'Internal Migration in India: Are the Underprivileged Migrate More?', *Asia Pacific Population Journal*, 25(1): 27–45.

Desai, Sonalde B., Amresh Dubey, Brij Lal Joshi, Mitali Sen, Abusaleh Shariff and Reeve Vanneman. 2010. *Human Development in India: Challenge for a Society in Transition*. New Delhi: Oxford University Press, 13.

Deshingkar, P. and S. Akter. 2009. Migration and Human Development in India. Human Development Research Paper No. 13, New York: United Nations Development Programme, Human Development Report Office.

National Sample Survey Office. 2010. Migration in India, NSS 64th round 2007–08. Report No. 533. New Delhi: Ministry of Statistics and Programme Implementation, GoI.

Mahendra Dev, S. and C. Ravi. 2008. 'Revising Estimates of Poverty', *Economic and Political Weekly*, March 8, 8–10.

Singh, D.P. 2005. 'Migration in India: Evidence Based on National Sample Survey Data', *Demography India*, 34(2): 271–298.

——. 2009. Poverty and Migration: Does Moving Help? India Urban Poverty Report 2009. New Delhi: Oxford University Press.

UNDP. 2009. Human Development Report, 2009. New York: Palgrave Macmillan.

13

The Growth Story of Bihar

Some Concerns

VIJAY VIR SINGH

Economic growth is important, not for the sake of it, but for what it allows the state to do with the resources that are generated from it. Equally important is to ensure good use of the resources and pay attention to the character of growth process, including its equity as benefit of growth on equity is not automatic and requires public policies to make growth more inclusive. The growth can be sustainable only when it is more inclusive. Sustainable growth leads to development which is good for the masses.

Bihar, which used to be considered as a laggard/failed state, has emerged as one of the fastest growing state in India in last few years. But the growth story of Bihar is riddled with concerns such as high population growth, high fertility, large number of poor, low employment opportunities, poor health and education indicators etc. The paper makes an attempt to understand the growth reversal story of Bihar and analyse how far higher economic growth has been successful in reducing poverty and improving human development in the state.

The secondary data has been used to assess the pace of change and the focus has been on changes in economic agents and their determinants. The paper concludes that it is too early to visualize Bihar as a growth miracle, but certainly it is moving in the right direction.

Background

Bihar, the third most populous state in India after Uttar Pradesh and Maharashtra, remained one of the poorest for a long time. However, over the past few years, Bihar has been seen as a completely changed and improved state due to one of the fastest growth rates in Indian states. Chanda (2011) finds that Bihar was doing well after India's independence and per capita output in Bihar was around 80 per cent of the country's average. But at the later stage, particularly since 1980s, the state has not performed well and by the early 2000s, the per capita GDP of the state had fallen to about one-third of the national average. Everything had gone wrong with the state; rising law and order problems, low human capital investments, agricultural and industrial stagnation to cite a few. However, since 2005, Bihar experienced a minor miracle by all accounts; recorded one of the fastest growth rates in the country, and law and order has drastically improved. Bihar started experiencing net state domestic product (NSDP) growth from 2002–03 which became evident in the period of 2003–05. Considerable acceleration in growth rate took place 2005 onwards and since then the state economy is growing at over 10 per cent per annum. But even after achieving high economic growth for almost a decade, Bihar continues to be among the economically most backward states with one of the lowest per capita incomes, high incidence of poverty and poor human development indicators.

It is not that efforts have not been made by the state government to reduce the incidence of poverty and improve the health and education status of masses, but the state continues to lag behind the national figures due to its long development backlog. Datta et al. (2012) finds that though the state's Plan expenditure has considerably increased in recent years but per capita development expenditure remains about half of the all-India average. The low per capita income and non-diversification of the economy have led to extremely low labour productivity in the state. The per labour productivity in Bihar is one of the lowest in the country. The per worker productivity of workers in the state was just half of the all-India figure, while in agriculture it was two-thirds of the all-India average.

Another feature of Bihar has been the high population growth. The population of Bihar, according to the 2011 Census, is 104 million (8.6% of India's population) of which nearly 90 per cent lives in the rural areas. Over the last decade (2001–11), the state has witnessed a growth of 25.4 per cent in its population, which is highest amongst the large states of the country. The population is further going to increase as the state has very high fertility rate of 3.7.

One of the implications of this high fertility and rising population is that the population of Bihar is, and will remain, one of the younger populations in future and will give the state a delayed demographic dividend. However, it will depend on how the state goes for skill development of the youth and their employability as most of the current employment in Bihar remains in rural areas.

While analysing Bihar's economic development, it is essential to keep in mind that with the division of the state in 2000 into present Bihar and Jharkhand, Bihar's economy got artificially transformed. But, there was no change in governance and it continued as in the pre-division period. The change in governance in terms of policy and administration took place only after the change in government in 2005, and the period of 2005 onwards makes a clear break from the past. After bifurcation, the vast mineral sector and other big industries went to Jharkhand resulting in the declining share of manufacturing sector in its NSDP and the gap was filled by the services sector. The economy has become more dependent on the services sector, yet remains one of its poorest states. Bihar's income now comes mostly from the services sector, but there is hardy any employment generation in the non-farm sector. Thus, while major share of NSDP of Bihar is coming from the service sector, the economy remained overwhelmingly rural. The 64 per cent of its workforce is still employed in agriculture.

The state is getting high economic growth for almost a decade but it is important to sustain it. The growth can be sustainable only when it is more inclusive and when growth is sustainable, we actually have development which is good for the common man. Economic growth is important, not for itself, but for what it allows the state to do with the resources that are generated. With higher growth, a state can generate more public revenue but it is equally important to ensure good use of that revenue. It is equally important to pay attention to the character of growth process, including its equity and sustainability. As benefit of growth on equity is not automatic, public policies are to be made to make growth more inclusive.

The recent spurt in growth along with improved law and order and the move towards strengthening governance and institutions has generated a great deal of optimism in the state and among other stakeholders. The challenge is to sustain this high growth and making it more diversified and inclusive by overcoming the massive development deficit. The focus of growth needs to ensure that as far as possible all segments of population get advantage of the economic growth of the state.

The objective of this paper is to understand the growth reversal story of Bihar and analyse how far higher economic growth has been inclusive in terms of poverty reduction and human development. The idea is to do it through an examination of outcomes, i.e. changing pattern of economic growth and government expenditure (Section 2), and how far this change has been successful in reducing poverty and improving the human development in the state (Section 3). Section 4 concludes.

Economic Growth and Public Expenditure

As stated earlier, Bihar's economy was growing almost at par with Indian economy in the early 1960s and, in fact, remained so well during the 1970s. It was during the 1980s that Bihar failed to grow fast enough to keep up with the rest of the country. Chanda (2011) finds that during that 1980s the rate of growth of Bihar was 2.3 per cent, while it averaged 3.2 per cent for India as a whole. In fact, it was actually during the second half of the decade, when the pre-liberalization era had begun in India that Bihar fell dramatically behind. The relative GDP per capita of the state, as compared to India, fell from 70 per cent in 1985 to 54 per cent by 1992. When we take the bifurcation of the state into account and the subsequent decline in per capita output, the share falls further to 43 per cent. Moreover, since 1993, which roughly coincides with the beginning of the economic reforms to liberalize the Indian economy, Bihar continued to decline and reduced to 32 per cent in 2005.

With change in regime and governance in 2005, the pace of growth in per capita income reversed and picked up. The state achieved a compounded annual growth of 8.6 per cent during 2005–10 which was higher than the national average of 7.04 per cent over the same period. During this period, Bihar was not the only state which achieved high growth but majority of states were getting comparatively better growth and Indian economy as a whole was growing at a faster pace. The growth story of Bihar becomes important after 2010 when Indian economic growth started faltering. Over the period 2010–12, Bihar's growth further accelerated and compound annual growth rates in per capita income of the state reached almost 13 per cent in 2012–13 (See Table 3). The relative per capita income of the state as compared to India increased to around

61 per cent (₹ 42,036 for Bihar and ₹ 68,757 for all-India at current prices) from 32 per cent in 2005. This change in economic growth is quite significant since 2005, as before that the state has been systematically growing well below the national average.

The research indicates that with economic growth and development the structure of any economy also undergoes changes. This is true of Bihar also. In the beginning of the last decade, the average share of primary, secondary and tertiary sector in total GSDP stood at 32.7 per cent, 13 per cent and 54.3 per cent respectively. With rise in growth, the share of the primary sector has been showing a decline over the years to 29.68 per cent in 2008–09 and then to 24.75 per cent in 2012–13. This shows that the importance of the primary sector has declined steadily over the years while secondary and tertiary sectors are becoming more important for growth. The share of secondary and tertiary has gone up from 13.76 per cent and 54.70 per cent in 2004–05 to 19.65 per cent and 55.60 per cent respectively in 2012–13 (Planning Commission data).

The turnaround in economic activity since 2005 can also be verified by comparing GDP growth figures of Bihar with other few big states similar to Bihar and some advanced states:

- If we take a simple aggregate, the GSDP in Bihar has grown by 34.8 per cent during 2000–05, while comparable states like Odisha had registered 93.6 per cent growth during the same period. Even states which were on a much higher base than Bihar, such as Gujarat, and Maharashtra registered good growth rates of 123.7 per cent and 94.2 per cent respectively (Table 1).
- But between 2005–10, the GSDP of Bihar almost doubled, growing 84 per cent (a simple aggregate) while all the other states were stagnating. Gujarat, which did not even have as high a base as Maharashtra in 2005–06, could only grow 56.2 per cent. This also makes Bihar the biggest GDP gainer in the country (at least among larger states) during 2005–10 (Table 1).
- Bihar was one of the highest achiever of average growth over 2005–12 in India at 11.32 per cent, just behind smaller states like Sikkim and Uttarakhand which achieved a growth rate of 13.4 per cent and 12.2 per cent respectively (Planning Commission, 2012).
- Further, Bihar performed better in BIMARU (Bihar, Madhya Pradesh, Rajasthan and Uttar Pradesh) states also, as rise in economic growth rates over the period of 1994–02 to 2005–11

has been highest (6.4%) in Bihar as compared to other similar states (Table 2).

- If we look at the slowdown in economic growth in India during the period of 2010–13 and analyse how the growth slowdown has been distributed between states, Bihar has remained very stable and continued with more than 10 per cent growth and remained on top of the states ranking in 2012–13 with 14.48 per cent. This is almost thrice the national average. Other backward states – Odisha, Rajasthan, UP, MP, Chhattisgarh and Jharkhand also performed well as compared to the advanced states (Table 4).

Table 1

GSDP Growth at Constant Prices 2004–2005 (in %)

States	*2000–2005*	*2005–2010*
Bihar	34.8	84
Odisha	93.6	56.2
Rajasthan	68.1	49.9
Madhya Pradesh	59.4	53.5
Jharkhand	86.9	35
Chhattisgarh	91.2	60.2

Source: Planning Commission.

Table 2

Average Growth Rates in Bihar vis-s-vis BOMARU States (in %)

States	*1994–02*	*2005–12*	*Change in Growth*
Bihar	4.9	11.3	6.4
Odisha	3.9	8.5	4.6
Madhya Pradesh	4.7	8.3	3.6
Rajasthan	7.3	8.1	0.8

Table 3

Growth Rate of Per Capita NSDP at Current Prices (in %)

States	*2010–11*	*2011–12*	*2012–13*
Bihar	17.49	11.7	12.85
Odisha	17.71	7.76	18.12
Madhya Pradesh	12.23	17.91	15.45
Rajasthan	26.82	20.19	

Source: Planning Commission.

Table 4

GDP Growth Rates (in %) of States during Economic Slowdown

States	*2010–11*	*2011–12*	*2012–13*
Andhra Pradesh	9.66	7.82	5.04
Assam	7.89	6.47	6.88
Bihar	15.03	10.65	14.48
Chhattisgarh	9.75	8.14	8.57
Gujarat	10.00	8.53	N.A.
Haryana	8.37	7.83	7.13
Jharkhand	15.86	7.18	7.83
Karnataka	10.15	4.86	6.19
Kerala	8.05	9.51	N.A.
Madhya Pradesh	7.13	11.81	10.02
Maharashtra	10.24	7.10	7.13
Odisha	7.50	4.92	9.14
Punjab	6.52	5.92	5.19
Rajasthan	15.28	6.11	N.A.
Tamil Nadu	13.12	7.42	4.14
Uttar Pradesh	7.86	6.45	5.52
West Bengal	6.09	6.26	7.50
All India	8.90	6.70	4.50

Source: Economic Times, February 12, 2014.

Table 5

Per Capita NSDP at Current Prices (in ₹)

States	*2010–11*	*2011–12*	*2012–13*
India	54,151	61,564	68,757
Rajasthan	44,709	53,735	N.A.
Odisha	38,878	41,896	49,498
Madhya Pradesh	32,223	37,994	43,864
Bihar	33,348	37,250	42,036

Source: Planning Commission.

As discussed earlier, the population of Bihar has been growing at a high rate and its impact can be seen on per capita income. Due to high population growth rate, the per capita income of the state remains very low. The comparable figures of per capita income at current prices of major Indian states indicates that Bihar still continues to be at the bottom of the ranking of states. However, the impact of the high growth process in recent years can be felt as the gap between the per capita income of Bihar with that of all-India is narrowing down (Table 5 and Figure 1).

Figure 1

Ratio of Per Capita Incomes in Bihar to India (1981–2011)

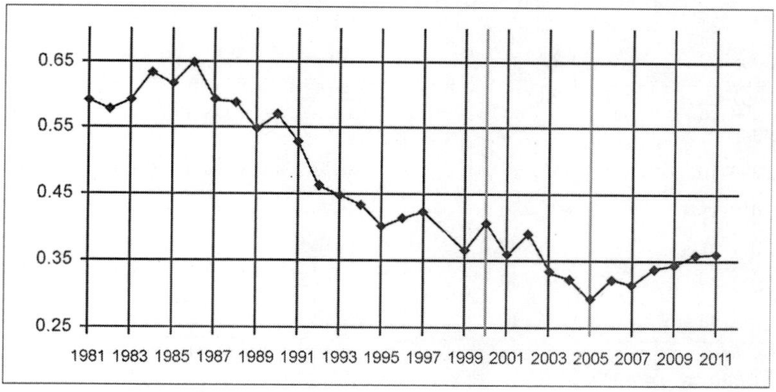

Source: Mukherji & Mukherji (2012).

Further, economic growth is important for development but equally important is how government allocates resources generated out of growth. Rationality in public expenditure is equally important as the economic growth. Many government spendings are specifically aimed at promoting sustained and equitable economic growth. Appropriate government expenditure can play an important role in physical and human capital formation over time, which in turn can boost economic growth when limits to infrastructure or skilled manpower become a constraint in increasing production.

Changing Pattern of Government Expenditure

As discussed above, government expenditure plays an important role in poverty reduction and human development. Keynes justifies the increase in government expenditure, as it may increase the aggregate demand which further stimulates the economic growth and employment. Thus, it is important to allocate revenue generated out of economic growth rationally; higher emphasis on development expenditure and less on non-development expenditure (Table 6 and Figure 2).

Table 6

Development Expenditure in Bihar

Year	*Development Expenditure (₹ Crore)*	*Total Budgetary Expenditure (₹ in Crores)*	*% share of Development Expenditure in Total Expenditure*
2004–05	9,095	20,058.00	45.43
2005–06	12,988	22,568.48	57.55
2006–07	17,304	27,136.47	63.77
2007–08	20,456	31,571.19	64.79
2008–09	17,978	37,181.26	48.35
2009–10	23,622	49,513.1	47.72
2010–11	25,226	57,758.55	43.67
2011–12	38,900	60,181.43	64.64
2012–13	59,640	89,174.51	66.88
2013–14 (BE)	61,910	92,087.93	67.22

BE: Budget Estimate.

Source: Annual Budgets of Government of Bihar for various years.

Figure 2

Restructuring of Public Expenditure in Bihar

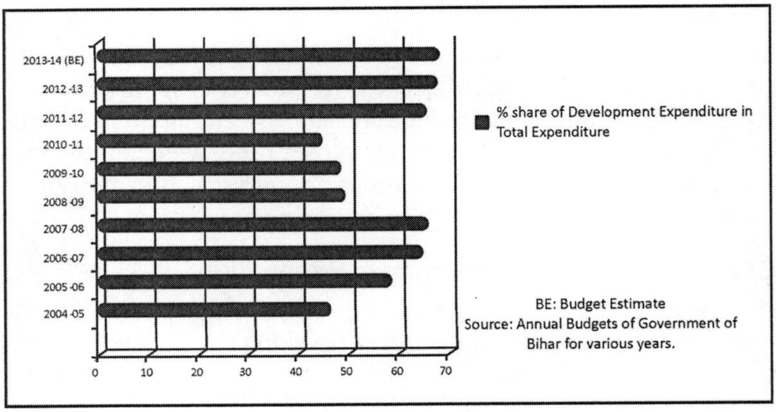

India's GDP has been growing rapidly in most of the years during the period of 2001–10. Mukherji and Mukherji (2012) highlights that rising national incomes have also meant larger tax revenues that can and has been redistributed in this time frame

(Figure 3). Out of rising revenues a numbers of schemes were created, to retire expensive debt for states, etc. that held the potential for improving the fiscal space of a state. While the potential was created at the centre, it was left to individual states to take advantage of these opportunities. They find that Bihar took advantage of this opportunity and undertook many changes that have improved its fiscal space, by expanding it and also reorienting it to promote development expenditures in the state. This was a complete change from the past as the Bihar government sacrificed large potential fiscal transfers from the Government of India designed for anti-poverty programmes because it was unable to complete the relevant bureaucratic procedures. Mathew and Moore (2011) write: 'Bihar has the country's lowest utilization rate for centrally funded programs, and it is estimated that the state forfeited one-fifth of central plan assistance during 1997–2000. The state's Annual Plan expenditure was revised downwards in the course of every year between 1992–93 and 2004–05, sometimes radically… . Between 1997 and 2006, of the 96 billion rupees allocated to Bihar by the Central government in Delhi, over 22 billion rupees could not be drawn and, of the money received, only 64 per cent could be spent'.

If we look at the quality of government expenditure in Bihar it has undergone significant improvement after 2005. The economic survey of Bihar 2012–13 highlights that gap between plan and non-plan expenditure started reducing since 2005–06 when non-plan expenditure was 3.6 times of the plan expenditure. By 2010–11, the non-plan expenditure came down to 1.4 times of the plan expenditure. If we look at the non-salary component of developmental revenue expenditure, it increased from 69 per cent to 74 per cent during this period, while the share of plan expenditure in total expenditure had increased from 35 per cent to 42 per cent. The ratio of plan to non-plan expenditure has also systematically increased from only 53 per cent to a high level of 74 per cent. Further, the expenditure on social and economic services was given a priority and the expenditure on these services accounted for almost half (48%) of the total expenditure in 2011–12 (Government of Bihar, 2013).

Bihar has also done well on per capita development expenditure also. Das Gupta (2012) finds that in spite of quantitative gap in per capita development expenditure between India and Bihar, the compound annual growth rate of per capita development

Figure 3

Ratio of Per Capita Development Expenditure in Bihar to India

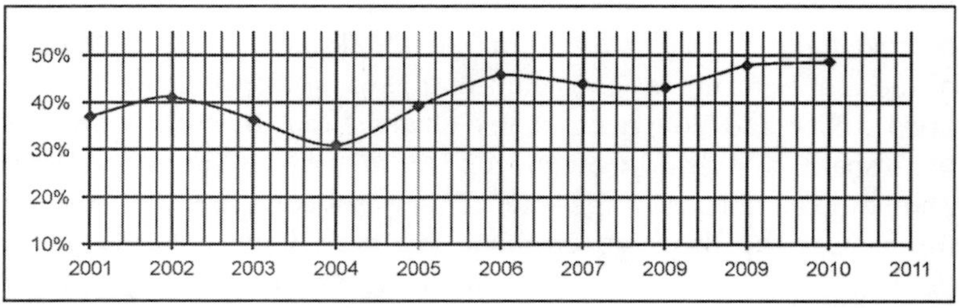

Source: Mukherji & Mukherji (2012).

expenditure in Bihar during 2004–10 has been 16.8 per cent which is higher than national figure of 13.9 per cent. The relative share of development expenditure in the total expenditure of the state government has been continuously increasing since 2005–06 except few years. It reached from 55.55 per cent in 2005–06 to 66.88 per cent in 2012–13 (see Figure 3). Sustaining this effort at government expenditure on development should certainly be playing a key role in reducing poverty and getting higher economic growth.

It indicates that Bihar has not only achieved the higher economic growth but also gone for improving the expenditure pattern of revenue generated by the government. It is also the indication of good governance.

Economic Growth and Welfare

Getting higher economic growth is a necessary condition for economic development but not the sufficient condition as it may or may not lead to development and welfare of masses. For increasing welfare of people's growth needs to be inclusive by ensuring people's participation in it. In other words, attention should be paid not only to growth rates but also to the quality of.growth, the way growth is achieved, who are the players, what mechanisms will take shape, and who will benefit from the growth.

If we want growth to be sustainable, it cannot be achieved without making it inclusive for a very simple reason that if people are not participating in the growth process and are not contributing to the growth process because either they are ill or they are uneducated or both, we are not building their capabilities, obviously, they cannot contribute to growth. Thus, growth cannot be seen just as an end in itself but for the purpose of something higher; making people's life better and developing their capabilities and pulling up workers into gainful employment.

If we look at Bihar, it has been reporting amazing economic growth numbers which gives obvious sense of change and optimism about its future. But more important is to see that what has economic growth delivered for the state and its people? The economic growth certainly has improved the life of masses but there is no visible difference in their poor living conditions. Still a huge number of people live in poverty, and human development indicators are also low. The progress of Bihar on poverty reduction and human development is discussed in the following sections.

Human Development

As discussed earlier, the ultimate goal of economic growth is welfare of all sections of the society. To achieve this goal, the endeavour of the government should be to include all people, particularly underprivileged section of the society, as beneficiary of the buoyant growth process. To ensure this, the focus has to be on social sector development along with proficient system of service delivery.

If we look at Bihar, apart from having large poor population, the state also performs poorly as compared to India in terms of most of the other human development indicators. Human development in Bihar followed national trends since independence. While there was modest improvement in all indicators, there always remained a gap between national and Bihar-specific achievements on human development. Indicators like literacy rate, life expectancy has been below national average while Bihar has been better than the national figure in case of infant mortality rate (IMR). On account of huge disparity in economic outcomes, large disparity in education outcomes, and small differences in the health outcome, Bihar has been the poorest performer among the major states of India in terms of human development indicators. However, human development indicators in the state have been improving over time but not sufficiently to close the gap with the national average (UNDP).

The state government is trying to strengthen the social sector by allocating higher budgetary resources for the sector and better implementation of programmes. The expenditure on social services is growing annually at around 21 per cent and the share of social services in total expenditure is little over one-third (RBI) (Table 7 and 8). But, on account of high growth of population, huge development backlog, and budgetary constraints, the per capita expenditure on social services in Bihar remains barely half of the all-India level.

Table 7

Trends in per cent Share of Social Services in Total Expenditure in Bihar and India

Year	*Bihar*	*All India*
2007–08	35.97	33.29
2008–09	36.09	35.27
2009–10	33.32	35.07
2010–11	37.48	38.01
2011–12	36.02	38.07
CAGR	21.08	21.36

Source: State Finances, A study of Budgets, RBI (Different Issues).

Table 8

Trend of Social Services Expenditure in Bihar

Year	*Total Expenditure on Social Services (₹ crore)*		*Total Expenditure (₹ crore)*		*% share of social Services in Total Expenditure*		*Per Capital Expenditure on Social Services (₹)*	
	All States	*Bihar*	*All States*	*Bihar*	*All States*	*Bihar*	*All States*	*Bihar*
2007–08	2,32,935	10,670	6,99,667	29,669	33.29	35.97	2,039	1,123
2008–09	2,90,831	12,895	8,24,613	34,948	35.27	36.90	2,502	1,329
2009–10	3,38,561	13,301	9,48,368	39,916	35.70	33.32	2,862	1,344
2010–11	4,43,326	20,333	11,63,652	54,257	38.10	37.48	3,683	1,993
2011–12	4,96,729	22,110	13,04,897	61,381	38.07	36.02	4,105	2,126
CAGR	21.36	21.08	17.24	20.85	21.36	21.08	19.5	18.31

Source: State Finances, A Study of Budgets, RBI (different issues).

Poverty

As discussed earlier, the economy of Bihar has traditionally been growing substantially slower than the Indian economy and incidence of poverty has always been significantly higher than the national average. However, the state made progress in reducing poverty along with the general decline in poverty in the country during 1970s and 1980s. But, the difference in levels of poverty continues and even increased with time as the slower growth of per capita income led to slower poverty reduction in the state. By 1990s the state was in poor shape and message going was that the situation in Bihar looks impossible to change.

However, with higher economic growth, higher budgetary allocations for poverty reduction, and improved governance the situation changed since 2005 and poverty ratios continued to follow the standard declining trend. The incidence of poverty declined from 60.6 per cent in 1993–94 to 54.4 per cent in 2004–05. However, the extent of poverty remains quite abject in Bihar as compared to other Indian states as the consumption expenditure continued to be very low (Planning Commission, 2012). The NSSO Consumption Expenditure Survey (2004–05) indicated that Bihar has the lowest level of per capita expenditure in the country.

With rising growth, initially the state had not been able to reduce poverty in a significant way but in later years it has been quite successful in reducing it. If we look at the overall progress in poverty reduction during the period of 2004–11, Bihar shows the biggest decline in poverty; percentage of the population living below poverty line coming down from 54.4 per cent in 2004–05 to some 33.7 per cent in 2011–12 (Planning Commission, 2012).

Table 9

Comparative Track Record of Bihar in Poverty Reduction. (in %)

States	*Reduction in Poverty during 2004–09*	*Reduction in Poverty from 2009–11*
Uttar Pradesh	3.2	8.3
Rajasthan	9.6	10.1
Odisha	20.2	4.4
Madhya Pradesh	11.9	5.1
Jharkhand	6.2	2.2
Chhattisgarh	0.7	8.8
Bihar	0.9	19.8

Source: Planning Commission.

If we look at the performance of Bihar in poverty reduction vis-a-vis states with the highest poverty rates in 2004–05, Bihar performed poorly as compared to other states during the period of 2004 –09 and could reduce poverty by only 0.9 per cent. In 2004–05, 54.4 per cent of Bihar's population or approximately 500 lakh people lived below the poverty line (BPL). The figure reduced marginally to 53.5 per cent in 2009–10. The absolute number of poor people had, however, increased to 540 lakh. While states like Odisha and Madhya Pradesh reduced the percentage of BPL people by 20.2 per cent and 11.9 per cent respectively (UNDP). The reason for the rise in number of BPL people in Bihar may be the major drought in the state in 2009 (Table 9 and 10).

Table 10

Population below Poverty Line in Bihar and India (Figures in %)

Year	*Lakdawala Methodology*		*Tendulkar Methodology*	
	India	*Bihar*	*India*	*Bihar*
1983	44.5	62.2	–	–
1993–94	36.0	55.0	45.3	60.5
2004–05	27.5	41.4	37.2	54.4
2009–10	–	–	29.8	53.5
2011–12	–	–	21.9	33.7

Source: Planning Commission.

The turnaround took place in the period of 2009–11 and Bihar topped the list in poverty reduction. During the period of 2009–11, Bihar performed well and the proportion of BPL people reduced by 19.8 per cent which is the highest in all the states. The number of BPL people, which increased to 540 lakh in 2009–10 declined to 385 lakh in 2011–12. Large reduction in the number of BPL families looks good but the gravity of this number gets further magnified when we come to know that the out of the 269.8 million poor in the country, around 38.5 million still reside in Bihar. Datta et al. (2012) finds in their survey that the living conditions in rural areas in Bihar remains poor as almost half of the houses are Kachcha and almost two-thirds of households do not have electricity connection. Sanitation remains a serious problem.

Now we are discussing empowerment line in place of poverty line. The focus of official poverty line has been on extreme poverty, while empowerment line poses an entirely different question i.e. how much individual consumption is required to meet the basic necessities. This requires the cost of fulfilling eight basic household needs at a level sufficient to achieve a decent, if modest, standard of living rather than just bare subsistence.

Gupta et al. 2014 finds that empowerment line is a measure of individual consumption, yet the ability or willingness to spend money is not wholly sufficient to guarantee a decent quality of life. In addition to having sufficient income, households need physical access to affordable basic services of acceptable quality. Their own purchasing power can meet some needs, such as food and energy, but they also require access to community-level social infrastructure such as health clinics and schools.

As discussed above, the living conditions in rural Bihar are in a dismal condition and majority of rural population does not have access to these eight basic needs. If we analyse Bihar in the light of empowerment, certainly it is in much worst condition than the official poverty line status.

Health

Improved health status is an important indicator of human development and it is important to organize an efficient health service system to attain it. Like other states, most of the people of Bihar also depend on public health facilities. Despite rapid development in the recent time, the improvements in the health sector confront challenges in terms of wide social, regional and gender disparities. In recent years with rising growth, the progress on these challenges is being made. The emphasis has been on access and expansion of public health infrastructure.

Selected Health Indicators

Becker (2007) argues that health plays a key role in shaping human capital through investments made by individuals, hospitals and the government to shape individual and population health, through people's valuation of life itself, and through cross-complementarities with education. In the context of a developing economy, health is first measured through child and maternal health statistics. As in India, the infant mortality rates (IMR) in Bihar is also declining. It has declined from 117.8 in 1981 to 69 in 1991, 62 in 2001 and 52 in 2008 and 48 in 2010 which is very close to the national figure of 47

(Table 18). Bihar has made substantial progress towards universal immunization in recent years.

After analysing NFHS–3 data Mukherji and Mukherji (2012) reveal that majority of women (66%) in Bihar who gave birth in the five years preceding the survey received no antenatal care. Further, only 17 per cent received three or more antenatal care visits and only 19 per cent received care within the first trimester of pregnancy, as recommended. Half of urban women received antenatal care from a health professional for their last childbirth, compared with 32 per cent of rural women. The percentage of women receiving antenatal care in Bihar is less than half the national average (74%) and is also the lowest of any state in India. Mukherji and Mukherji (2012) also highlight that these numbers remained virtually unchanged over the NFHS–2 and NFHS–3 survey periods. A similar lack of care for women emerges in terms of access to a range of other health inputs to maternal care. Thus, maternal health care has not seen any significant strides as child health care. However, the institutional delivery has improved considerably in recent years and maternal mortality rate (MMR) declined from 312 in 2005 to 261 in 2010 but remains much higher than national figure of 212. The number of children born in health institutions is rising continuously.

Table 11

Live Expectancy at Birth by Sex, Bihar and India

	Bihar		*India*	
Year	*Male*	*Female*	*Male*	*Female*
1998–02	61.4	59.5	61.6	63.3
1999–03	61.6	59.7	61.8	63.5
2000–04	61.8	59.9	62.2	63.7
2001–05	62.0	60.1	62.3	63.9
2002–06	62.2	60.4	62.6	64.2
2006–10	67.1	66.7	65.8	68.1
2011–16	69.9	69.1	70.0	71.1

Other indicators used to the judge health status of population are life expectancy at birth, crude birth rate (CBR), crude death rate (CDR). The gap between Bihar and all-India life expectancy at birth figure has been small, particularly in comparison to the systematic gap seen in the economic domain. The gap between all-India figure and the state has further reduced in recent years. During 2002–06, the gap has been considerably reduced to 0.3 years while during 2006–10, the life expectancy for male in Bihar was 67.1 years (projected) which is higher than the national figure of 65.8 years. Life expectancy however, does have a significant gender bias in Bihar. Nationally, women have a higher life expectancy than men; however, in Bihar the trend is just opposite and women have lower life expectancy as compared to men (Table 11).

Table 12

Selected Health Indicators for Bihar and India (2006 to 2010)

Category		*2006*	*2007*	*2008*	*2009*	*2010*
			Crude Birth Rate			
Bihar	Rural	30.7	30.2	29.7	29.3	28.8
	Urban	23	22.9	22.5	22.2	22
	Combined	29.9	29.4	28.9	28.5	28.1
India	Rural	25.2	24.7	24.4	24.1	23.7
	Urban	18.8	18.6	18.5	18.3	18
	Combined	23.5	23.1	22.8	22.5	22.1
			Crude Death Rate			
Bihar	Male	7.4	7.6	7.6	7.2	7.1
	Female	7.9	7.4	6.9	6.8	6.6
	Total	7.7	7.5	7.3	7	6.8
India	Male	8	8	8	7.8	7.7
	Female	7	6.9	6.8	6.7	6.7
	Total	7.5	7.4	7.4	7.3	7.2
			Total Fertility Rate			
Bihar	Rural	4.3	4.1	4	4	3.8
	Urban	3	2.9	2.8	2.8	2.7
	Combined	4.2	3.9	3.9	3.9	3.7
India	Rural	3.1	3	2.9	2.9	2.8
	Urban	2	2	2	2	1.9
	Combined	2.8	2.7	2.6	2.6	2.5
			Infant Mortality Rate			
Bihar	Male	58	57	53	52	46
	Female	63	58	58	52	50
	Total	60	58	56	52	48
India	Male	56	55	52	49	46
	Female	59	56	55	52	49
	Total	57	55	53	50	47

Source: Sample Registration System (SRS), Office of the Registrar General, India, Ministry of Home Affairs, GOI.

The CBR figures in Bihar remain consistently higher than the national figure. However, the difference between CBR of Bihar and all-India has been slightly reduced during 2006–10. Along with improvement in CBR, the CDR also improved to 6.8 in 2010 which was lower than all-India (7.2). In 2006, the CDR in Bihar (7.7) was marginally higher than that for India (7.5). A low CDR implies a better health status (Table 12). But, the combined effect of higher birth rate and lower death rate leads to higher growth rate of population, which is undesirable.

If we look at overall public health infrastructure in the state it is incomplete and poorly staffed at both the preventive and curative levels. People still have to look at private providers for health facilities. However, the state government is trying hard to fulfil the health needs of the population.

Education

Education is the base of human capital. It not only develops basic skills and abilities, but also fosters a value system conducive to national development goals. Dreze and Sen (1995) have provided a useful classification of the benefits of education. Since it is valuable in itself, it is desired not only for itself, for its own sake, but also for its great importance for augmenting the quality of life. Other than economic growth and development, education is known for its critical role in demographic transition too. Female education, in particular, has proved to play an important role in the process of lowering fertility and mortality. So has elementary education been associated with better health outcomes. Strong correlation has been established between literacy and life expectancy by several researchers. It has also been found that the skill of literacy and numeracy improve workers productivity and can affect the allocation of inputs in that schooling has a positive impact on agricultural output and in political and social terms too, schooling is supposed to create and educated population and a more constructive citizenry. Moreover, education empowers and through empowerment affects the larger social process.

Bihar has a long history of quality education but, in the post-independence era Bihar has been one of the laggard states in education. One of the key measures of human capital in the economy is the literacy rate. The census data indicates that literacy rate in Bihar increased from 48 per cent in 2001 to 63.8 per cent by

2011 but it is still 10.2 per cent lower than the national average of 74 per cent. In literacy rate, Bihar has lagged behind national figure since independence; however, the literacy deficit was small, around 5 per cent in 1951. Over the 1960s and 1970s, this gap expanded steadily, so that by the 1981 census, the gap increased to 11 per cent and 14.7 per cent by 1991. The gap between the national and state literacy rate has reduced significantly as compared to the last decade. Like the national trend, the gender gap in literacy rate has reduced significantly in Bihar also. However, Bihar performed better in reducing gender disparity as compared to India as a whole. The gender gap in literacy has come down to 16.6 and 20.1 percentage points for India and Bihar respectively, in 2011 from 21.6 and 26.7 percentage points respectively, in 2001 (Table 13). But, Bihar ranks last in all states in 2001 as well as 2011.

Table 13

Literacy Rates in Bihar and India

Year	*Bihar*			*India*		
	Persons	*Males*	*Females*	*Persons*	*Males*	*Females*
1951	13.5	22.7	4.2	18.3	27.2	8.9
1961	22.0	35.9	8.1	28.3	40.4	15.4
1971	23.2	35.9	9.9	34.5	46.0	22.0
1981	32.3	47.1	16.6	43.6	56.4	29.8
1991	37.5	51.4	22.0	52.2	64.1	32.2
2001	47.5	60.3	33.6	64.8	75.3	53.7
2011	63.8	73.4	53.3	74.0	82.1	65.5

Source: Census of India Reports.

Apart from literacy rates, the other variable keenly tracked with regard to education is the enrolment ratio. According to the Economic Survey 2012–13 of Bihar, the annual growth rate in primary enrolment was 3 per cent during 2006–11, whereas enrolment at the upper primary level grew at 1.2 per cent annually. The ratio of school-age going children out of school also reduced from 14.5 per cent of all school-age going children out of school in 2006 to an out-of-school rate of 4.4 per cent by 2011. This decline has been far more dramatic than the decline seen in rural India, which saw a decline from 8.75 per cent in 2006 to 5.15 per cent by 2011. This is a very substantial achievement in such a short period of time. The dropout rates at the primary level decreased to 39.3 per cent in 2010–11, from 46.1 per cent in 2006–07. At the upper primary stage, it decreased to 55.14 per cent in 2010–11, from 61.8 per cent in 2006–07 (Table 14).

Table 14

Dropout Rate at Primary, Upper Primary, Secondary and Higher Secondary Levels

Year	*Primary*			*Upper Primary*		
	Girls	*Boys*	*Total*	*Girls*	*Boys*	*Total*
2006–07	45.7	46.4	46.1	60.1	62.8	61.8
2007–08	45.2	45.6	45.4	61.1	61.5	61.4
2008–09	44.6	45.1	45	NA	NA	60.3
2009–10	41	43.5	42.5	56.7	60.2	58.8
2010–11	35.3	42.13	39.27	51.31	57.87	55.14
Year	*Secondary*			*Higher Secondary*		
	Girls	*Boys*	*Total*	*Girls*	*Boys*	*Total*
2006–07	79.2	75.4	76.8	82.3	82.7	81.9
2007–08	75.6	72.6	73.7	83.7	82	82.6
008–09	NA	NA	72.1	80.7	79.9	80.2
2009–10	67	69.9	68.8	73.4	76.3	75.2
2010–11	58.85	64.38	62.24	69.42	72.93	71.61

Source: Department of Education, Government of Bihar.

Bihar has been able to reduce the number of out-of-school children by having a larger and larger fraction of the school-going children attending government schools. The proportion of students going to private schools has declined from 13.4 per cent to 5.4 per cent, during 2006–11 period. This indicates a large movement of students from private schools to the public schools which is contrary to the national trend showing the expansion of its enrolment through the private sector during this period (Mukherji and Mukherji, 2012).

The sharp increase in enrolment ratio and reduction in out-of-school children are the result of effective policy implementation and high budgetary allocation by the state government to the education sector. The plan expenditure on education in Bihar has increased by more the 100 per cent during 2007–11. Along with plan expenditure the non-plan expenditure has also increased at an annual growth rate of 5.85 per cent during this period. As a whole, expenditure on education has doubled during this period with an annual growth rate of 13.84 per cent (Government of Bihar, 2012–13).

However, Bihar still remains the state with the lowest literacy rates across all states in India. More children attending school is one aspect of education and another equally important requirement is getting quality education. If we look at quality, the situation in Bihar is poor as in India. The learning outcomes of the children remain quite dismal and show little progress. The Annual Status of Education Reports (ASER) has been regularly illustrating the alarmingly skewed state of affairs in schools. The ASER 2012 has exposed the dismal status of schooling and basic learning in rural India. The Report indicates that on one hand the school enrolment numbers have gone up and school infrastructure has improved, while on the other the attendance and overall ability of children to read have dipped drastically in Bihar. Apart from some skills in mathematics, Bihar's learning levels remains systematically lower than the national average. However, the story of poor quality education is not limited to Bihar only but also to other states.

ASER 2006–11 shows that there is no systematic increase in school attendance in Bihar, even though enrolment ratios are high; Banerji (2011) reports that Bihar has perhaps one of the lowest attendance to enrolment ratios across states in India. Studies (Banerji et al., 2008) suggest that only 65 per cent of those enrolled actually attend school in Bihar. Clearly, delivery of education will be incomplete with low attendance rates.

As discussed above, investment in human capital is an important channel through which the demographic dividends can be reaped. Given that Bihar has the highest ratio of young children (four out of every 10 people in Bihar is under the age of 14) and its high dependence on the services economy, it is important for the state to ensure quality education and skill development in children.

In sum, the question remains, has Bihar changed, and improved from the past? The answer depends on how we look. On economic indicators the state looks quite impressive but at the same time existing human development indicators are still quite unsatisfactory.

The above discussed poverty figures and human development indicators certainly show an improvement but not sufficiently large improvements to close the gap with the national average. Given the huge disparity in economic outcomes, large disparity in education outcomes, and small differences in the health outcome, it is reasonable to expect that Bihar still does poorly on human development indicators. The state still has the lowest literacy rates in the country, highest total fertility rate and decadal rate of population growth, lowest per capita income, home to the large number of BPL people, and one of the lowest human development indicators.

Along with economic growth more attention needs to be given to the human development. This will be possible when all sections of the society participate in the growth process.

Conclusion

The economy of Bihar which has been on declining trend for a long period has now certainly shifted to an expanding economy due to government's active engagement in good governance. The government initiatives undertaken since the last decade have made Bihar the fastest growing state in India. However, the growth story of Bihar has been one of high economic growth most of which is coming from the services sector. The job opportunity remains limited to agriculture sector but growth in agriculture continues to be relatively low. Further, human development indicators are improving but remains below national figure.

The state remains a poor economy with key structural imbalances and is still well below the national average in terms of various human development indicators. A key concern with the growth experienced so far in Bihar has been its lack of inclusiveness; poverty is still very high. To reduce poverty, the focus has to be on raising rural incomes by developing agriculture and allied activities and shifting the people from agriculture to non-agriculture sectors. There is a desperate need to expand the non-farm jobs to absorb the expected high growth of working age population. Unfortunately, manufacturing sector could not pick up in the state but needs to be given priority. Lack of manufacturing sector led to the services sector driven growth. High income is coming from the services sector but majority of population remains employed in agriculture. Possibly, this has been the reason that growth has not made the income distribution more equitable and reduces the poverty ratios significantly. Shifting people from agriculture to services will require quality education and more urbanization. Skill generation through expansion of quality vocational training network is essential. We cannot sustain growth without people's participation in the growth process. Once, judicious use of public revenues, and pulling up workers, particularly from rural areas, into gainful employment work hand-in-hand, the state would be able to eradicate poverty, ill-health, and illiteracy the fastest.

Thus, basic challenge for Bihar is to sustain growth in future and make it inclusive. The state has improved the access of the delivery of public services but still much more is required.

References

Aiyar, S.S.A. 2010. 'Bihar's Economic Miracle: Real, but Fragile', *The Economic Times*, February 21.

ASER Centre. 2007. *Annual Survey of Education Report (Rural) 2006*. Mumbai: Pratham Resource Centre.

——. 2012. *Annual Survey of Education Report (Rural) 2011*. Mumbai: Pratham Resource Centre.

——. 2013. *Annual Survey of Education Report (Rural) 2012*. Mumbai: Pratham Resource Centre.

Banerji, R. 2011. 'Challenging Bihar on Primary Education', *Economic and Political Weekly*, 46(11): 33–39.

Banerji, R., P. Chaudhary and G. Kingdon. 2008. *School TELLS (2007–08) Survey of Rural Primary Schools in UP and Bihar*. London: Institute of Education, University of London.

Becker, Gary S. 2007. 'Health as Human Capital: Synthesis and Extensions', *Oxford Economic Papers*, 59(3): 379–410.

Census of India 2001 Reports.

Census of India 2011 Reports.

Chanda, Areendam. 2011. *Accounting for Bihar's Productivity Relative to India's: What Can We Learn from Recent Developments in Growth Theory?* London: International Growth Centre. http://www.isid.ac.in/~pu/conference/dec_11_conf/Papers/Areend amChanda.pdf

Das Gupta, Chirashree. 2012. Growth and Public Finance in Bihar. IDE Discussion Paper No. 331. http//www.ide.go.jp/English/Publish/Download/Dp/pdf/331.pdf.

Datta, Amrita, Sunil Kumar Mishra, Gerry Rodgers, Janine Rodgers and Alakh N. Sharma. 2012. *Social and Economic Change in Rural Bihar and the Emerging Policy Framework*. New Delhi: Institute for Human Development.

Drèze, J. and A.K. Sen. 1995. *India: Economic Development and Social Opportunity*. Oxford: Oxford University Press.

Economic Times: Various Issues.

Government of Bihar: Bihar Economic Survey of the Year 2006–07, 2007–08, 2008–09, 2009–10, 2010–11, 2011–12 and 2012–13. Ministry of Finance, Patna.

Gupta, Rajat, Shirish Sankhe, Richard Dobbs, Jonathan Woetzel, Anu Madgavkar and Ashwin Hasyagar. 2014. *From Poverty to Empowerment: India's Imperative for Jobs, Growth, and Effective Basic Services.* McKinsey Global Institute, February.

Kumar, Utsav. 2010. India's Demographic Transition: Boon or Bane? A State-Level Perspective. Economics Program Working Paper Series, New York. www.conference-board.org/economics.

Mathew, Santhosh and Mick Moore. 2011. State Incapacity by Design: Inderstanding the Bihar Story. IDS Working Paper No. 366, Institute of Development Studies, UK.

Mukherji, Arnab and Anjan Mukherji. 2012. Bihar: What Went Wrong? And What Changed? Working Paper No. 2012–107, National Institute of Public Finance and Policy, New Delhi.

NSSO. 2011. Employment and Unemployment Situation in India 2009–10. NSS Report No. 537(66/10/1), National Statistical Organisation, Ministry of Statistics and Program Implementation, Government of India, New Delhi.

Planning Commission. 2012. State-Specific Poverty Lines, Number and Percentage of Population Below the Poverty Line by States–2004–5–2011–12.

UNDP in Bihar. http://www.undp.org/content/india/en/home/operations/about_undp/undp-in-bihar/

14

Assessing the Effect of Household Environment on Child Health in Uttar Pradesh

SHALINI I. MESHRAM, ABDUL JALEEL CP
AND B. PASWAN

Survival and health status of children in a population indicate its social and economic development. Ensuring a healthy survival of infants and young children is an important public health concern across the globe. India accounts for about one-fifth of global under-five mortality, which is more than that of any other country (Black et al., 2010). There have been theoretical explanations about the causes of low survivability and adverse health outcomes of children, and concomitant programme interventions to reduce the incidence of infant and child mortality and to improve their health status. Mosley and Chen (1984) suggested that under optimal conditions, child survivability rates for the newborn infant can be expected to reach 97 per cent. But, in the real world, this rate is lowered by social, economic, biological and environmental factors.

Most deaths of children under age five in developing countries have been linked to the household environment (WHO, 2009). A variety of health hazards, including poor air quality, contamination of water and food are present in the household environment (UN, 2002). The source of drinking water has a profound implication for the health outcomes of child. Improved sources of drinking water are less likely to be contaminated, while other sources, such as surface water and open wells, are more likely to carry disease-causing agents (NPC [Nigeria] and ORC Macro, 2004). Mishra and Rutherford (2007) found that the type of cooking fuel used in the household is an important variable, as many children are exposed to toxic pollutants from the use of unprocessed biomass fuel from wood, charcoal, straw and dung. Unprocessed biomass fuels have a high level of toxic indoor air pollutants that have been linked to reduced birth weight, acute respiratory infection (ARI), nutrition deficiency, and child mortality.

Theoretically, degraded household environment is a risk factor and, as a result, members of the households may have poor health outcomes. Children being the most vulnerable to adverse environmental conditions, are more susceptible to diseases. The distinctive physiological nature of children under age five predisposes them to a variety of health hazards within and around the household, including unsafe source of water and poor sanitary conditions. Thus, providing safe drinking water and access to improved sanitation within the household environment can reduce the risk of mortality and morbidity among children under age five (WHO, 2009). This fact has been demonstrated in some developed countries, where childhood mortality has declined through interventions such as the provision of safe drinking water and adequate sanitary facilities (Rutstein, 2000).

Globally, for children under five years of age, acute diarrhoea is the second leading cause of death after pneumonia (WHO and UNICEF, 2009). According to WHO and UNICEF, there are about two billion cases of diarrhoeal disease worldwide every year. Of all child deaths from diarrhoea, 78 per cent occur in the African and South-East Asian regions. Diarrhoea is a leading cause of child death in India. Children in India are extremely vulnerable to diarrhoea because of unsafe water, poor sanitation and hygiene combined with malnutrition. Further, children in India do not routinely receive the vaccine that protects against one of the leading causes of severe diarrhoea. This being the background, this paper tries to examine the linkages between household environmental conditions and the incidence of child loss and diarrhoea in the most populous state of India i.e. Uttar Pradesh. The state being demographically backwards still has high fertility, high infant and child mortality.

Objective, Methods and Materials

The purpose of this analysis is to understand the effect of household environmental factors on child survival and child health in the state of Uttar Pradesh. Analysis is carried out by using data from the third round of District Level Household and Facility Survey (DLHS–3) for Uttar Pradesh conducted in the year 2007–08 by International

Institute for Population Sciences, Mumbai. DLHS–3 surveyed a total of 90,415 households, 87,564 ever-married women aged 15–49 years in Uttar Pradesh. A multistage stratified systematic sampling design was adopted for DLHS–3. In each district, 50 primary sampling units (PSUs) which were census villages in rural areas and census enumeration blocks (CEBs) in urban areas were selected. In rural areas, villages were selected by probability proportional to size (PPS) systematic sampling method and in the second stage households were selected by systematic sampling method. For urban areas in the first stage, urban wards were selected by PPS systematic sampling method, and in the second stage CEBs were selected by PPS sampling method and in the third stage, households were selected by systematic sampling method. The Census of India, 2001 was the sampling frame for DLHS–3.

DLHS–3 provides information on the environmental condition of households and information related to child health and child survival. The response variables (dependent variable) used in this analysis is child loss and incidence of diarrhoea. Data on all live births after first January 2004 were collected, and all eligible women were further asked a question that: 'child still alive?' the response categories were 'yes' or 'no'. If the child was not alive at the time of the survey, then it is considered as a child loss. Further, there is a question on diarrhoea 'Has the child had diarrhoea in the last two weeks?'. This question was asked only for the last two surviving children and the response categories were 'yes' or 'no'. Predictor variables (independent variable) used in this analysis are household environmental conditions such as source of drinking water, type of cooking fuel, availability of a separate room for the kitchen and availability and type of toilet facility. Bivariate and multivariate analysis are carried out to understand the association between household environmental factors and child survival and child health. Binary logistic regression analysis is applied to understand the net effect of the household environmental factors on child survival and child health. In the first model, we included only household environmental factors to examine its effect on child survival. In the second model, we included only household's economic status to examine its sole effect on child survival. In model three we included both household environmental factors and economic status to understand the relative strength of both the sets of predictors on child survival in Uttar Pradesh.

Results

Table 1 presents the weighted percentage distribution of children who were born alive (n = 58548) after first January 2004 by household environmental factors and economic status. It simply portrays what proportion of the children in Uttar Pradesh have the fortune to grow up in a healthy household environment and misfortune to struggle for a healthy life in a degraded household environment. When the source of drinking water is considered, it was found that 88.4 per cent of the children live in those households where the main source of drinking water is tube well/hand pump. Only 6.4 per cent (5.8% through pipe and 0.6% through other improved sources) children are living in those households where drinking water is perfectly safe. Other 5.3 per cent children live in those households where main source of drinking water is other non-improved sources. As far as the type of fuel for cooking is concerned, only seven per cent children live in such households where liquefied petroleum gas (LPG) is in use. About 39 per cent children live in households where they have a separate room for a kitchen. Thus, majority of the children in Uttar Pradesh are likely to come in contact with the toxins that is emitted from solid cooking fuels while burning. When coming to availability of sanitation facility, only 20 per cent children are living in households where they have an improved toilet facility. Whereas, 77 per cent of children in the state have no access to toilet facility at all and thus, they are left with only an option of open defecation. The distribution of children by household's economic status shows that majority (58%) of the children belongs to poorest and poor households (come under lower and lowest wealth quintiles).

Table 1

Percentage Distribution of Children Born alive after First January 2004 by Household Environmental Factors and Economic Status in Uttar Pradesh, DLHS–3

Background characteristics	*Percentage*	*N*
Source of drinking water		
Pipe water	5.8	3,447
Tube Well/Hand pump	88.4	51,716
Other improve	0.6	325

Cont'd...

...Cont'd

Non-improved sources	5.3	3,060
Fuel use for Cooking		
Liquefied Petroleum Gas (LPG)	6.8	4,001
Wood	92.2	53,966
Others	1.0	581
Separate room for kitchen		
Yes	38.7	14,849
No	61.3	23,597
Toilet Facility		
Improved toilet facility	20.1	11,757
No Toilet or Open Space	76.5	44,780
Not improved toilet	3.4	2,011
Wealth Index		
Poorest	31.1	18,180
Second	26.9	15,737
Middle	18.5	10,824
Fourth	15.0	8,800
Richest	8.6	5,007
Total number of children		58,548

Note: All 'N' values are unweighted.

Table 2 gives the bivariate differentials in child loss by each household environmental factor. This shows how the distribution of child loss changes from one group of children to another, where the former have no access and the latter have access to certain household environmental factors. All the household environmental factors (source of drinking water, type of fuel used for cooking, separate room for kitchen and availability of toilet) included in the analysis are found significantly affecting child loss. This means that the availability and non-availability of each of these household environmental factors have the potential to determine the survival and health status of children in Uttar Pradesh. Regarding the source of drinking water, percentage of child loss is lowest for children of those households where source of drinking water is pipe (4.9%). Child loss is significantly higher (6.3, 5.9%) for children in households where wood, others fuel are used respectively as cooking fuel than children of household where LPG is used as cooking fuel. It is further observed that the percentage of child loss is significantly higher in those households where no separate room for a kitchen is available compared to households with a separate room for the kitchen. Child loss is found more among households where no toilet facility is available (7%) and households where only a non-improved toilet is available (6% more) compared to households where improved toilet facility is available (4.7%). Economic status of the households also has a profound impact on child survival. It is found that children of the poorest wealth quintile have higher chances (7.3% more) of mortality than children of the richest wealth quintile (3.3%).

Table 2

Percentage of Child loss by Household Environmental Factors in Uttar Pradesh, DLHS–3

Background characteristics	*Percentage*	*N*
Source of Drinking Water	(9.28)**	
Pipe water	4.9	3,447
Tube Well/Hand pump	6.2	51,716
Other improved	6.5	325
Non improved sources	6.1	3,060
Fuel use for Cooking	(42.90)***	
Liquefied Petroleum Gas	3.8	4,001
Wood	6.3	53,966
Others	5.9	581
Separate Room for Kitchen	(33.03)***	
Yes	4.7	14,849
No	6.1	23,597
Toilet Facility	(58.13)***	
Improve toilet facility	4.7	11,757
No Toilet or Open Space	6.6	44,780
Non-improved toilet	6	2,011
Wealth Index	(123.09)***	
Poorest	7.3	18,180
Second	6.2	15,737
Middle	6.3	10,824
Fourth	5.2	8,800
Richest	3.3	5,007
Total percentage of children	6.1	58,548

Note: All 'N' values are un-weighted; Level of significance: * $p < 0.10$; ** $p < 0.05$; *** $p < 0.01$.

Table 3 presents the weighted percentage of children who have suffered from diarrhoea during the last two weeks prior to the survey date. The distribution is presented by household environmental factors and economic status of the households. Analysis shows that there is no noticeable difference in the percentage of children who suffered from diarrhoea among households with different source of drinking water. Diarrhoea prevalence is 15.6 per cent among children of households where the main source of drinking water is pipe or other improved sources. It is 16.3 per cent among children of households where tube well/hand pump is the primary source of drinking water. However, diarrhoea is 16 per cent and 17 per cent respectively higher among children of households where cooking fuel is wood or others with respect to children of households where cooking fuel is LPG. Further, the prevalence of diarrhoea is significantly higher (16%) among children belonging to households where there is no separate room for the kitchen with respect to children belong to households having a separate room for the kitchen. Availability and non-availability of toilet facility is a significant predictor of diarrhoea among children in Uttar Pradesh. Prevalence of diarrhea is 20 per cent and 16 per cent more among children from households where improved toilet facility is not available, and there is no toilet facility available with respect to children of households where improved toilet is available. Since there is a significant difference in the prevalence of diarrhoea among children of households belongs to the poorest wealth quintile (18.5%) and richest wealth quintile (13%), it can be said that economic status of households is a significant predictor of diarrhoea in Uttar Pradesh.

Table 3

Percentage of Children Suffered from Diarrhoea by Household Environmental Factors and Economic Status in Uttar Pradesh, DLHS–3

Background characteristics	*Percentage*	*N*
Source of Drinking Water	(3.87)	
Pipe water	15.6	2,860
Tube Well/Hand pump	16.3	42,788
Other improve	15.6	277
Non-improved sources	15	2,626
Fuel use for Cooking	(22.84)***	
Liquefied Petroleum Gas	13.2	3,271

Cont'd...

...Cont'd

Wood	16.4	44,797
Others	16.7	483
Separate Room for Kitchen	(23.62)***	
Yes	13.7	12,426
No	15.7	19,631
Toilet Facility	(35.76)***	
Improve toilet facility	14.7	9,695
No Toilet or Open Space	16.3	37,197
Non-improved toilet	20.2	1,659
Wealth Index	(98.83)***	
Poorest	18.5	12,034
Second	16.1	12,502
Middle	16.3	10,135
Fourth	14.7	8,064
Richest	13.1	5,816
Total number of children	16.1	48,551

Level of significance: * p<0.10; ** p<0.05; ***p<0.01.

Determinants of Child loss in Uttar Pradesh

Table 4 demonstrates the results of binary logistic regression where three different models were analysed to examine the factors affecting child loss in Uttar Pradesh. Model 1 examines the influence of household environmental factors such as source of drinking water, type of cooking fuel, separate room for kitchen and availability of toilet facility on child loss. The results of Model 1 show that except source of drinking water, all the household environmental factors included in the model are significantly affecting child loss. For example, child loss is 36 per cent (CI=1.09–1.71) more likely to happen in those households where wood is used as cooking fuel compared to households where LPG is in use. The results show that child loss is 19 per cent more likely (CI=1.08–1.32) in those households where separate room for the kitchen is not available as compared to households with a separate room for the kitchen. Similarly, the odds of child loss are more in households where there is no toilet facility available (OR=1.217, CI=1.07–1.38). In Model 2 effects of household's economic status on child loss is examined. The results of Model 2 confirm the significance of economic status of households on child loss. It tells that child loss decreases with an increase in economic status of household. In Model 3 effects of household environmental factors and economic status on child loss are examined together. When all the variables are taken together (household environmental factors and economic status) in the Model 3, it again confirm the significance of a separate room for the kitchen and economic status of household on child survival. On the other hand, having separate kitchen has significant influence on improved child survival as child loss is more likely to occur in households where there is no separate room available for kitchen (OR=1.141, CI=0.103–1.26). Further, household having good economic status experience less child loss as compared to household having poor economic status.

Table 4

Odds Ratio for Child loss by Household Environmental Factors and Economic Status in Uttar Pradesh, DLHS–3: Results from Logistic Regression Analysis

Characteristics	*Model 1*	*Model 2*	*Model 3*
	Odds ratio	*Odds ratio*	*Odds ratio*
Drinking water source			
Pipe water ®	1.00		1.00
Tube Well/Hand pump	1.14 (0.92–1.43)		1.09 (0.87–1.37)
Other improved sources	1.31 (0.75–2.28)		1.26 (0.72–2.20)
Non-improve sources	1.12 (0.84–1.50)		1.06 (0.79–1.41)
Cooking fuel			
Liquefied Petroleum Gas ®	1.00		1.00
Wood	1.36 (1.09–1.71)***		1.08 (0.83–1.42)
Others	1.41 (0.89–2.41)		1.25 (0.75–2.09)
Separate kitchen			
Yes ®	1.00		1.00
No	1.19 (1.08–1.32)***		1.14 (0.103–1.26)***
Toilet facility			
Improve toilet facility ®	1.00		1.00
No Toilet or Open Space	1.21 (1.07–1.38)***		1.02 (0.88–1.18)
Not improved toilet	1.13 (0.85–1.49)		1.03 (0.77–1.37)

Cont'd...

...Cont'd

Wealth Index		
Poorest ®	1.00	1.00
Second	0.84 (0.77–0.92)***	0.86 (0.76–0.97)**
Middle	0.85 (0.77–0.93)***	0.84 (0.74–0.96)**
Fourth	0.69 (0.62–0.78)***	0.74 (0.64–0.87)***
Richest	0.43 (0.36–0.51)***	0.54 (0.41–0.71)***

Note: ®: Reference Category; Level of significance: * p<0.10; ** p<0.05; ***p<0.01.

Determinants of Diarrhoea Incidence among Children in Uttar Pradesh

Table 5 shows the odds ratio and confidence intervals for incidence of diarrhoea by household environmental factors and economic status. Three different models were analysed to examine the effect of the household environment on the incidence of diarrhoea among children. Model 1 examines the influence of household environmental factors such as source of drinking water, cooking fuel, separate room for the kitchen and toilet facility on diarrhoea among children. The results of Model 1 confirm the significance of toilet facility and separate kitchen in the incidence of diarrhoea. Out of those children who suffered from diarrhoea in the last two weeks prior to the survey, children from the households who do not have improved toilet facility are 55 per cent (CI= 1.30–1.84) more likely to fall ill (suffer from diarrhoea) than children from those households where there is improved toilet facility. Likewise, children from households where there is no separate kitchen are 14 per cent (CI=1.07–1.22) more likely to suffer from diarrhoea than children from households where there is separate kitchen. Model–2 examines the effect of economic status of household alone on the incidence of diarrhoea. The results show that the incidence of diarrhoea among children is lower in rich households as compared to poor households. In Model 3 the net effect of household environmental factors on incidence of diarrhoea has been examined. It has been found that the availability of toilet facility, separate kitchen in the household and household being rich are significant factors affecting incidence of diarrhoea among children. Otherwise, the incidence of diarrhoea is significantly higher in household having non-improved toilet facility. The odds of incidence of diarrhoea is 1.46 in household with non-improved toilet facility. Incidence of diarrhoea is high in household not having separate kitchen (OR=1.106, CI=1.03–1.18) in comparison with households having separate kitchen. According to the wealth status of household, children from household of richest wealth quintile were less likely to suffer from diarrhoea as compared to their counterparts (OR=0.70, CI=0.60–0.81).

Table 5

Odds Ratio for Surviving Children who Suffered from Diarrhoea by Household Environment Factors and Economic Status in Uttar Pradesh, DLHS–3: Results from Logistic Regression Analysis

Characteristics	*Model 1*	*Model 2*	*Model 3*
Drinking water source			
Pipe water ®	1.00		1.00
Tube Well/Hand pump	1.00 (0.87–1.14)		0.97 (0.85–1.12)
Other improved sources	1.11 (0.75–1.64)		1.11 (0.75–1.63)
Non-improve sources	0.85 (0.70–1.03)		0.82 (0.67–0.99)
Cooking fuel			
Liquefied Petroleum Gas ®	1.00		1.00
Wood	1.11 (0.97–1.28)		1.04 (0.89–1.21)
Others	1.30 (0.94–1.80)		1.27 (0.91–1.76)
Separate kitchen			
Yes ®	1.00		1.00
No	1.14 (1.07–1.22)***		1.10 (1.03–1.18)***
Toilet facility			
Improve toilet facility ®	1.00		1.00
No Toilet or Open Space	1.03 (0.95–1.13)		0.91 (0.83–1.01)
Not improved toilet	1.55 (1.30–1.84)***		1.46 (1.22–1.74)***
Wealth Index			
Poorest ®		1.00	1.00
Second		0.84 (0.78–0.90)***	0.83 (0.76–0.92)***
Middle		0.87 (0.81–0.93)***	0.87 (0.79–0.95)***
Fourth		0.75 (0.70–0.81)***	0.73 (0.66–0.82)***
Richest		0.67 (0.61–0.73)***	0.70 (0.60–0.81)***

Note: ®: Reference Category; Level of significance: * p<0.10; ** p<0.05; ***p<0.01.

Discussion and Conclusion

In the first part, this paper analysed the availability of basic household amenities to the children under five years of age in Uttar Pradesh. By doing this, we intended to portray what proportion of the children in the state has the fortune to grow up in a healthy household environment. Disparities exist in the household environment of children in the state. The results show that only six per cent of the children in the state have access to pipe water, only seven per cent children live in households where clean fuel is used for cooking, only 39 per cent children live in households where they have a separate room for the kitchen and only 20 per cent children are living in households where they have an improved toilet facility. Further, it is also found that 58 per cent of the children in the state are belonging to households having low economic status. In conclusion, majority of the children in the state are at a relative disadvantage on basic household amenities and thus, there is an inherent threat of illnesses and disability. In the second part, we analysed how the distribution of child loss varies from one group of households to another based on disparities in the household amenities. We found a significant variation in child loss between households having basic amenities and households not having basic amenities. Child loss is found lowest among those households where: source of drinking water is pipe, cooking fuel is LPG (access to clean fuel), and separate room for kitchen (less chance for indoor pollution) and improved toilet facilities are available. Economic status of the households also has a profound impact on child survival and their health status. Child loss is significantly highest (7.3%) in poorest household than richest household (3.3%). It is a fact that household environmental factors have a profound implication for the incidence of diarrhoea and thus diarrhoea is considered as an outcome variable to understand the health status of children in Uttar Pradesh. We analysed the incidence of diarrhoea among children by household environmental factors and economic status of the households. There is no noticeable difference in the percentage of children who suffered from diarrhoea among households with different sources of drinking water. However, type of cooking fuel used in the household has a significant effect on the incidence of diarrhoea. Incidence of diarrhoea is 16 per cent higher among children of households where cooking fuel is wood with respect to children of households where cooking fuel is LPG. It is also found that having a separate room for the kitchen reduces the chance of children suffering from diarrhoea. Another household environmental factor, that has effect on incidence of diarrhoea, is the availability of toilet facility. Children of households where improved toilet facility is not available are 20 per cent more likely to suffer from diarrhoea than children of households where improved toilet is available. As we saw in the case of child loss, economic status of the households has an inverse reciprocal relationship with the incidence of diarrhoea.

The results of the binary logistic regression to examine the influence of household environmental factors on child loss shows that except source of drinking water, all the other household environmental factors are significantly responsible for the child loss. Child loss is 36 per cent more likely to happen in households where wood is used as cooking fuel, 19 per cent more likely to happen in households where separate room for kitchen is not available and child loss is more in households where there is no toilet facility available with respect to their counterparts. It is also found that child loss decreases with an increase in economic status of household. However, while putting together both environmental factors and economic status of households, having a separate room for the kitchen and being economically better off are the two significant factors on improved child survival in Uttar Pradesh. The results of binary logistic regression analysis carried out to understand the influence of household environmental factors on incidence of diarrhoea prove that the availability of toilet facility and separate kitchen have a significant impact on in the incidence of diarrhoea. Children from the households who do not have improved toilet facility are 55 per cent more likely to suffer from diarrhoea than children from those households where there is improved toilet facility. It is also found that economic status of household has a vital role is determining the incidence of diarrhoea since it is found that diarrhoea prevalence is significantly higher among children in the lower economic strata. However, while putting together both environmental factors and economic status of households the result show that availability of toilet facility, separate kitchen in the household and household being rich are significant factors affecting incidence of diarrhoea among children in Uttar Pradesh.

What we conclude from this analysis is that households where environment is degraded because of indoor air pollution due to burning of wood and other bio-mass fuels for cooking and congestion because of no separate room for cooking are crucial factors that reduce survival probability of children in Uttar Pradesh. Economic status of the household is another important enabling factor for households to improve child survival. In the case of incidence of diarrhoea, availability of improved toilet facility has emerged as the most important factor. As we have seen in the case of child survival, having a separate room for cooking and household being non-poor reduce the chance of children suffering from diarrhoea in Uttar Pradesh. This paper found that economic status of household is a crucial player in determining child survival and child health in Uttar Pradesh. Thus it is very important to ensure the economic development of households to enable them to spend more on health and health care. Economic development at household level also helps people to modify their household environment.

References

Black, R.E., S. Cousens and H. Johnson. 2010. 'Global, Regional, and National Causes of Child Mortality, 2008', *Lancet*, 375: 1969–1987.

Mishra, V. and R.D. Rutherford. 2007. 'Does Biofuel Smoke Contribute to Anemia and Stunting in Early Childhood?', *International Journal of Epidemiology*, 36: 117–129.

Mosley, W.H. and L.C. Chen. 1984. 'An Analytical Framework for the Study of Child Survival in Developing Countries', *Child Survival: Strategies for Research, Supplement to Population and Development Review*, 10: 25–45.

National Population Commission (NPC) [Nigeria] and ORC Macro. 2004. Nigeria Demographic and Health Survey 2003. Calverton, Maryland: NPC and ORC Macro.

Rutstein, S.O. 2000. 'Factors Associated with Trends in Infant and Child Mortality in Developing Countries During the 1990s', *Bulletin of the World Health Organization*, 78: 1256–1270.

UN. 2002. 'The Environmental Performance Review: Uzbekistan', in F. Racioppi and B. Menne (eds), *The Environment and Health Situation in Uzbekistan*. Chapter 12, United Nations, New York.

WHO and UNICEF. 2009. *Diarrhoea: Why Children are Still Dying and What Can be Done*. Geneva: WHO and New York: UNICEF.

WHO. 2009. *World Health Statistics 2009*. Geneva: WHO.

15

Population, Structural Changes and Economic Growth in India

M.R. SINGARIYA

The significance of economic structure gained prominence through the seminal work of Lewis (1954) and other subsequent researchers that include Kuznets (1966), Chenery and Syrquin (1975) and Taylor (1969). Kuznets (1971) and Rostow (1971) claimed that growth is brought by the changes in economy's sectoral composition. These researchers showed that economic structure matters in the development process. In the literature, the term 'structural change' most commonly refers to long-term changes in the composition of an aggregate; this is attributable to changes in the relative significance of sectors in the economy, to changes in the location of economic activity (urbanization), and to other concomitant aspects of industrialization which, taken together, are referred to as structural transformation. In one of his studies on structural transformation, Syrquin (2007: 4), referring to Kuznets, elaborates the concept:

> 'For Kuznets growth and structural change are strongly interrelated. Once we abandon the world of homothetic preferences, neutral productivity growth with no systematic sectoral effect, perfect mobility, and markets that adjust instantaneously, structural change emerges as a central feature of the process of development and an essential element in accounting for the rate of pattern of growth. It can retard growth if its pace is too slow or its direction inefficient, but it can contribute to growth if it improves the allocation of resources…'

Next to Kuznets, there have been other attempts to study structural change and to establish some stylized facts, i.e. the patterns of development followed by most countries. The most well-known studies include Chenery and Syrquin (1975) and Kader (1985), who aimed to demonstrate the shifts in production (from the primary to the secondary to the tertiary sector), which occur as economies grow.

Timmer and Akkus (2008) argue that no country has been able to sustain a rapid transition out of underdevelopment without raising productivity in its agricultural sector. The process involves a successful structural transformation where agriculture, through higher productivity, provides food, labour, and even savings to the process of urbanization and industrialization. A dynamic agriculture raises labour productivity in the rural economy, and pulls up wages. The process also leads to a decline in the relative importance of agriculture to the overall economy, as the industrial and service sectors grow even more rapidly, partly through stimulus from a modernizing agriculture and migration of rural workers to urban jobs.

Most researchers provide evidence that as GDP per capita rises, the share of agriculture in GDP falls. One of the questions that will be addressed in this study is whether this holds true for the Indian economy. In other words, is there a systematic relationship between agriculture, industry and service sector and the level of development? As Chenery and Syrquin (1975) pointed out, 'a development pattern may be defined as a systematic variation in some significant aspect of the economic or social structure associated with a rising level of income or other index of development'. This study analyses the pattern of agricultural growth along the definition of Chenery and Syrquin by utilizing data for Indian economy from 2004–05 to 2011–12, a period that registered higher average growth rates in GDP of over seven per cent. It is interesting to know what happened to the structural pattern of agriculture, industry and service sector during this period of high growth.

Literature Review

Modern analysis of sectoral transformation originated with Fisher (1939) and Clark (1940), who dealt with sectoral shifts in the composition of the labour force. However, they were probably the first to deal with the process of reallocation during the epoch of modern economic growth, and use the form of sectoral division (primary-secondary-tertiary) which, in one way or another, is still with us today (Syrquin, 1988). The most traditional measures of economic structure are sectoral shares of the labour force, consumption patterns, and variables measuring income distribution. Kuznets (1966) examined these three categories in more detail and added the analysis of sectoral shares of GDP and was able to empirically demonstrate that growth is brought about by changes in sectoral composition. Kuznets provided the historical empirics and conceptual framework for modern analysis of the structural transformation, although he used no econometric techniques himself. The first quantitative analysis of patterns in the transformation process was done by Chenery and Taylor (1968) and Chenery and Syrquin (1975).

Historical patterns of economic development of today's developed countries has, no doubt, followed a common pattern and this is well documented by Kuznets (1966) and others. The share of agriculture has seen a steady decline in total output that of industry registered an increase for a considerably long period, and then has shown a decline. And the share of services has steadily increased all through, but the rate of increase seems to have accelerated in the latter half of the twentieth century, the period during which industry has seen a decline in its share and, therefore, is often described as a period of 'deindustrialization' in the developed countries (Rowthorn and Wells, 1987).

The timing of the different phases of structural changes and speed of such changes has, of course, been different between different countries. In the 'pre-modern' era, according to Kuznet's assessment ended at different points of time during the nineteenth century in different countries (e.g. Before 1800 in Great Britain, 1835 in France, 1861 in Italy, 1870 in USA, 1878 in Japan). Agriculture accounted for a half to two-thirds of the total output. It seems to have taken about 75 to 100 years for this share to decline to about one-fourth in the case of most European countries, though similar shift was achieved more swiftly in North America and Japan, the relative latecomers in modern economic development. In spite of differences in time of entering the era of modern development and in the speed of transformation, the share of agriculture had declined to less than 15 per cent in most of these countries by the middle of the twentieth century and has seen a further continuous decline since then, reducing it to less than 5 per cent in all of them, by the end of the twentieth century.

The industry held a share of around 25 per cent at the beginning of the 'modern' development in most of the developed countries of today. It grew steadily and reached the peak of about one-half by 1950s in all these countries, irrespective of the period when they entered the industrialization phase. And all the developed countries have seen a decline in the share of industry in their output since the 1950s. By and large, the changes in the share of industry have been observed to be hump-shaped (Kuznets, 1966; Echevarria, 1997). In most of the countries, industry has the same share in output in the beginning of the twenty-first century as it had in the beginning of their journey to 'modern' economic growth. In 2002, the share of industry in national output in the United Kingdom was 26 per cent, comparable to 23 per cent in 1801; in France, 25 per cent, the same as in 1841; in Germany, 23 per cent compared to 24 per cent in 1841; in Italy, 29 per cent compared to 22 per cent in 1901; and in the USA, 23 per cent compared to 20 per cent in 1841.

The services sector has experienced a secular increase in its share right through the period of modern economic growth in all countries, except for an initial decline in a few countries, namely Great Britain, France and Germany. The share crossed the 50 per cent mark by 1901 in Great Britain, saw a decline till about mid–1950s and crossed 50 per cent again by 1960, by when most other countries, France, Germany, Italy and Japan had crossed this mark for the first time. The United States had hit a 50 per cent mark for services in its GDP earlier. There has been a continuous, and a relatively fast increase in the share of services since the 1960s, and by now, it stands at 68 to 75 per cent in all the countries; the highest being 75 per cent in the case of the United States, followed by the United Kingdom at 73 per cent, France at 72 per cent in 2002. It is somewhat lower at 68 per cent in Japan.

In a comparative study of Papola (2005), agriculture expectedly, registered a decline in its share in GDP in Thailand, Korea, India, China and Malaysia during 1960–2002, the largest decline being in the case of Thailand (from 40 to 9%) and Korea (from 37% to 4%). Thus, while the GDP share of agriculture in China declined from 30 per cent in 1980 to 15 per cent in 2002, its employment share declined from 69 to 47. Corresponding shifts between 1960 and 2002 were: from 50 to 18 per cent in GDP and from 75 to 44 per cent in employment in Indonesia; and from 40 to 9 per cent in GDP and 84 to 46 per cent in employment in Thailand. Only in Malaysia the decline in the labour force in agriculture has been commensurate with that in GDP from 63 to 18 per cent in the labour force. In India, shifts during 1960–2002 have been about 55 per cent, 24 per cent of GDP and from 74 to 60 per cent of the labour force.

Victor Fuchs in his study of 48 US States over the period (1929–1965) also sees the lagging productivity growth of the services sector, as the reason for its rising employment share. On the supply side, agriculture being mainly dependent on a fixed factor of production, namely land, faces a limit on its growth and is subject to early operation of the law of diminishing returns. Industry, especially manufacturing, on the other hand, offers large scope for the use of capital and technology, which could be augmented almost without limit with human effort. Labour supply could constrain expansion of industry, but it is possible to overcome it by introducing labour-saving technological changes. The same applies to services, where application of technologies seems to offer much larger scope, as shown by the experience over the past few decades.

In the case of services, there are also additional reasons why their share in national product increases with industrial development. These arise both out of the technological developments and economic and institutional arrangements compelled by them (Kuznets, 1966). Technological developments facilitate and economically necessitate geographical concentration and large scale based production, leading to larger requirements of transport, storage and communication. In a predominantly rural economy, most of the food is produced close to the consumers; but with an increasingly larger population getting located in urban areas, requirements of transport and trade increase even for reaching food to the consumers. Increasing demand for housing in urban areas leads not only to the expansion of construction activity, but also leads to demand for housing related services, which are generally not common in villages. Further, higher income levels not only give rise to higher demand for personal services such as education, health and recreation, but new, technology based modes of meeting them lead to demand for other services.

Kuznets (1971) saw income elasticity of demand as the primary reason for changes in economic structure, but recognized that other factors, technological and institutional, also play an important role in accelerating these changes. Emphasizing primarily the supply side, Kaldor (1966) considered manufacturing as the engine of growth: agriculture, being subject to diminishing returns is not able to sustain an increasing level of production and income, and, therefore, manufacturing, without such limitations on the expansion of production, is the key to sustained economic growth. The growth of services, according to Kaldor, was induced both by requirements of expanding the industrial sector and rising levels of income.

Victor Fuchs (1968) in his classical study of the emergence of domination of services sector in the United States corroborates the view propounded by Bamoul and concludes that shift to services is largely a result of productivity differentials. He finds that the income elasticity of demand for services is only slightly higher (1.07) than for goods (0.93) and that for non-food goods are similar to that of services. The persistence in development pattern implies that structural differences remain relevant for understanding the development process. However, the interest in structural analysis has decreased considerably since the emergence of the so-called new or endogenous growth theory.

Cornwall and Cornwall (1994) as a structuralist model of Sundrum (1991) show that, whereas new growth theory endorses endogenous growth, it neglects aggregate demand and distributional shifts in output and employment. By analysing the European integration, they show that economic structure matters. Structural changes do not only characterize economic development, they are also necessary for sustaining economic growth. The neoclassical view that sectoral composition is a relatively unimportant by-product of growth has been convincingly questioned by structural economists like Kuznets, who have empirically demonstrated that growth is brought about by changes in sectoral composition. This is so both for the reasons of demand and supply.

However, none of the papers discussed so far explicitly measure structural change or directly examine its empirical link to India's growth rate. This was the innovation of Cortuk and Singh (2011). Using standard definitions of structural change indices, they examine the connection between measures of structural change and growth in India, for the period 1951–2007. They find that there is a structural break in the two time series considered jointly, and this break occurs in 1988. Furthermore, there is a one-way causal relationship between structural change and growth (the former granger causes the latter), but only for the 1988–2007 period. Hence, this analysis provides more objective empirical support for previous informal assertions in the literature.

Ghate and Wright (2012) also examine state-level data, and their analysis and conclusions are worth summarizing here for later comparison with our own results. They do not estimate convergence regressions, but examine the time series of per capita income for 16 states over the period 1960–2003 (hence, a longer period than most convergence studies). Eyeballing the data suggests that a subset of nine states 'diverges' from the others from 1985 onward, in the sense of moving to a higher growth path. These diverging states are Andhra Pradesh, Gujarat, Karnataka, Kerala, Madhya Pradesh, Maharashtra, Rajasthan, Tamil Nadu and West Bengal. The seven remaining states are Assam, Bihar, Haryana, Jammu & Kashmir, Odisha, Punjab and Uttar Pradesh. Note that the two groups had essentially equal per capita incomes up to 1985, controverting suggestions that it was richer states that benefited from India's growth acceleration. Therefore, the Ghate-Wright data do not provide straightforward implications for convergence or divergence among the entire group of states. The grouping of states obtained by Ghate and Wright will be of interest for comparison with our results.

Objectives

The overall objective of this study is to establish simple stylized facts on relationships between population size, per capita income and the shares of agriculture, industry and service sector in Gross State Domestic Product (GSDP). Our specific objective is to see what has happened in high income states in comparisons to low income states and especially in EAG states of India during 2004–05 to 2011–12. We expected a significant negative relationship between the shares of agriculture in GSDP with per capita National State Domestic Product (NSDP) and significant positive relationship between the shares of industry sector & service sector with NSDP per capita.

Methodology & Data Sources

Using panel data collected by the Central Statistical Organization for thirty-two states and UTs of India for the most recent period of 2004–05 to 2011–12 at the constant prices of 2004–05, the present paper highlights the effect of structural change in economic growth in India and discusses state specific impact of structural change on the economic growth of India. As statistical method we have used Ordinary Least Square (OLS) and after panel diagnostics random effect was found unbiased. Further year dummies and state dummies have been used for an in-depth analysis.

The data used in the analysis were drawn from data book for Detachable Carry Handle (DCH); 18 October 2013 published by Central Statistical Organization (CSO). Data on shares of agriculture and agriculture-allied sector, industrial sector, service sector, NSDP per capita, population size were all obtained from the same source. The data used in this study range from 2004–05 to 2011–12, a period when India registered average growth rates of 6.4 per cent per annum. This period is also a period when India experienced relative stability in macroeconomic variables and political situation.

Results

Trend Analysis

It can be observed in Figure 1 that the share of the overall agriculture in GSDP has a downward trend when compared with service sector that had an upward trend. The share of agriculture and allied sector declined from 51.88 per cent in 1950–51 to 14.45 per cent in 2010–11. The steady and significant slow decline in the share of agriculture in total output as a result of its much slower growth has one of the singular features of the process of structural change in India since independence. However, the change within the industry sector shows the different phases of growth and structural changes. The period till the mid-1960s was characterized by a rising industrial output and the period between 1960–1980 was marked as stability in the industrial product. The pattern change in industrial output shifted again in mid-1990s, it saw a reappearance of a trend of declining input productivity in the industrial sector. The size of India's service sector relative to its industrial one started increasing only around 1980. The year 1980 marked a clear upward shift in the pace of growth of the service sector, the share of service sector increased steadily from the end of 1950s, when it stood at around 30 per cent and by 2011 it was close to 57 per cent.

Figure 1

Trends of per cent Share of Agriculture, Industry and Service Sectors in Total GSDP in India during 1950–2011

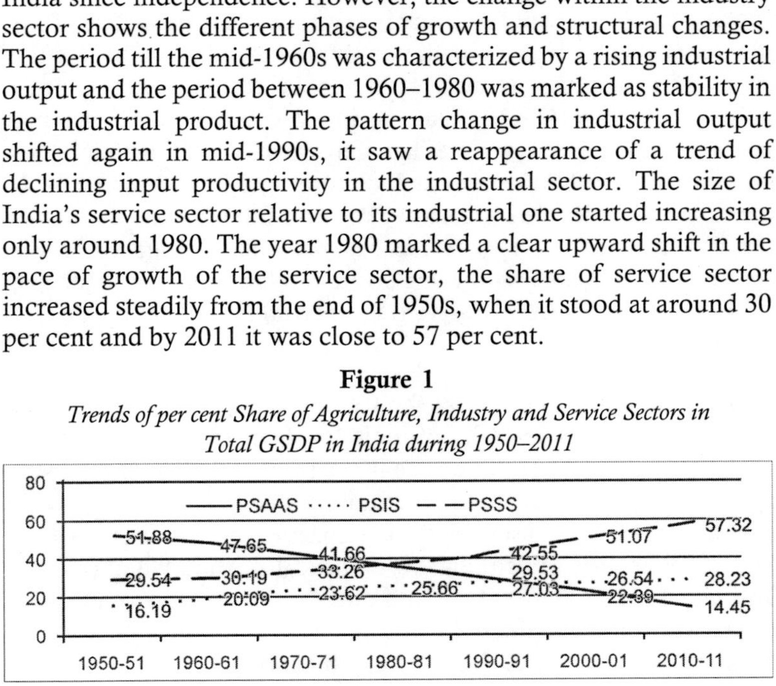

Figure 2

Trends of log Per Capita Net National Income, log Population Size (Millions) and the log of the per cent Share of Agriculture, Industry and Service Sectors in Total GSDP in India during 1950–2011.

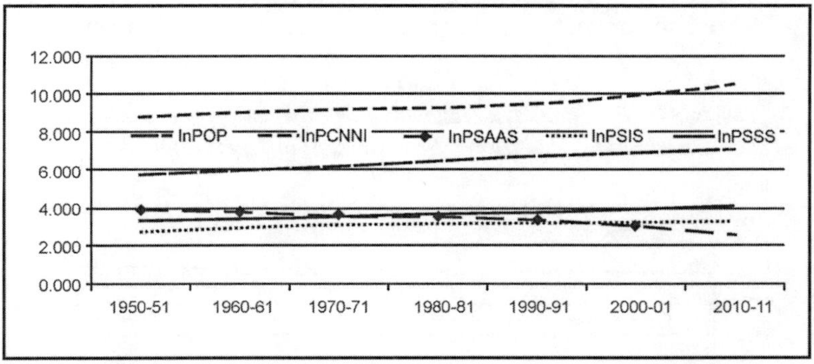

Figure 2 shows that share of agriculture and agriculture allied sector has a downward trend when compared with per capita net national income that had an upward trend during 1950–51 to 2010–11. This observation is consistent with earlier findings which show that as GDP per capita rises, the share of agriculture in GDP falls (Papola, 2005). It can be observed that the share of the industry sector has very slow progress while service sector has noted an upward trend. There are some other observations like, after 1990, population size increasing with diminishing rate and per capita income increasing by an increasing rate, which can be also associated with a speedy decline in agriculture sector

Figure 3

Trends of per cent Share of Agriculture, Industry and Service Sectors in Total GSDP in India during 2004–2013.

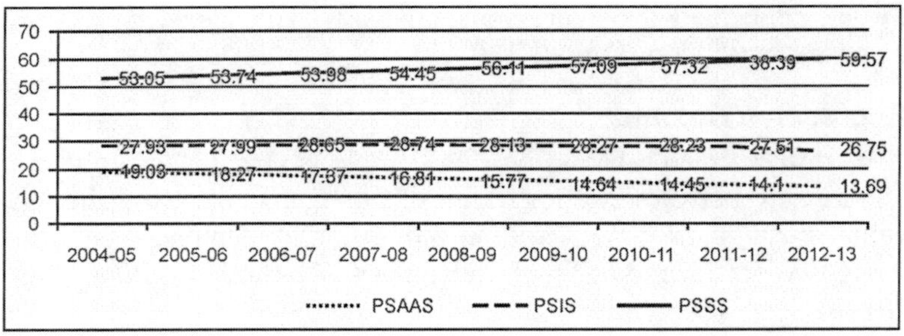

Figure 3 shows year-wise contribution of agriculture, industry and the service sector during the study period only. It can be observed that the service sector has grown up from 53 per cent to 59.5 per cent, while industry sector has slightly declined from 27.93 per cent in 2004–05 to 26.75 per cent in 2012–13. The trend is much steeper for agriculture sector compared to industrial sector during this period.

Figure 4

Trends of log Per Capita Net National Income and log of per cent Share of Agriculture, Industry and Service Sectors in Total GSDP in India during 2004–2013.

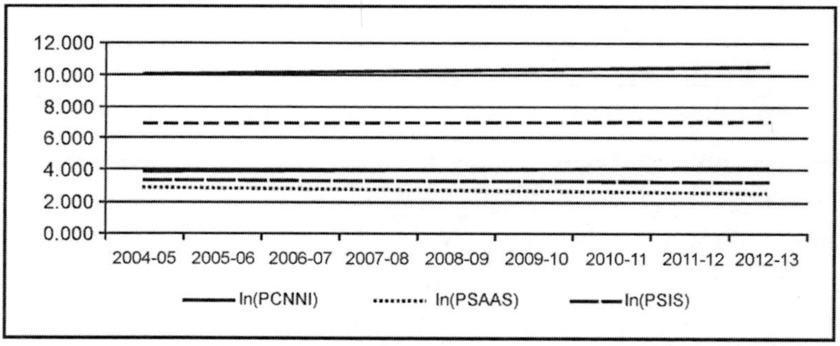

At the next step, we tried to associate shares of agriculture, industry and the service sector to per capita net national income and population size (million). We calculated the logarithm value of all the variables, so as find out trends and their association with per capita net national income and population changes that occurred during the study period. It can be observed from the Figure 4 that share of the service sector is an outlier sector in contributing per capita net national income (NNI). It also shows the downward trend of agriculture and allied sector with per capita NNI as expected, but industrial sector showing the stagnant trend in this period. Although the observations made under trend analysis are revealed, they need to be confirmed by regression analysis. The next subsection discusses regression results.

Regression Results

The study aimed at establishing simple stylized facts on the relationship between the log value of population size and the log value of the share of agriculture and agricultural allied sector for thirty-two states and UTs of India for the period of 2004–05 to 2011–12.

Figure 5

Relationship between log PSAAA and log Population Size (Million) in Indian States during 2004–12

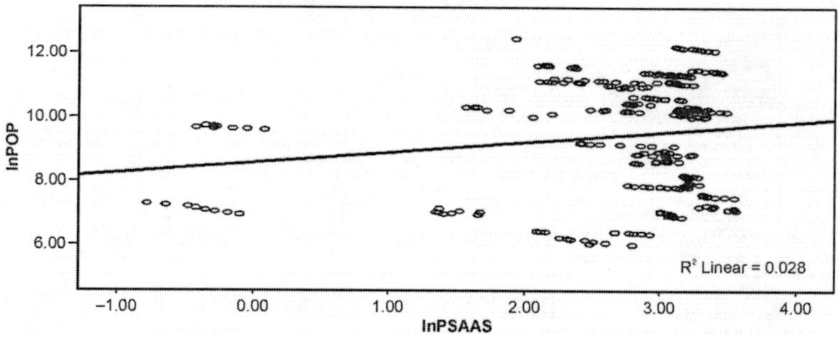

Figure 6

Relationship between log PSIS and log Population Size (Million) in Indian States during 2004–12

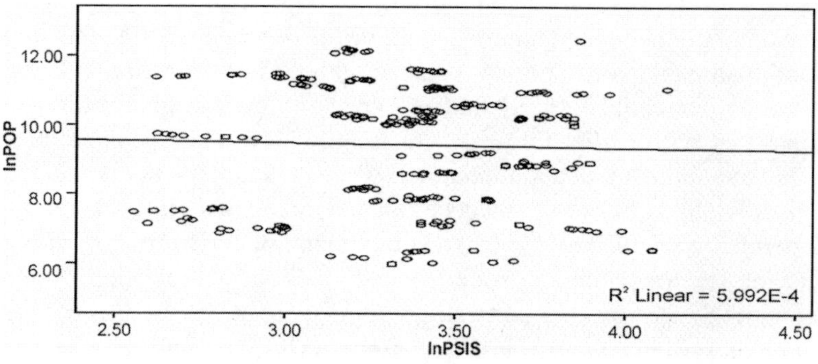

Figure 7

Relationship between log PSSS and log population size (Million) in Indian States during 2004–12

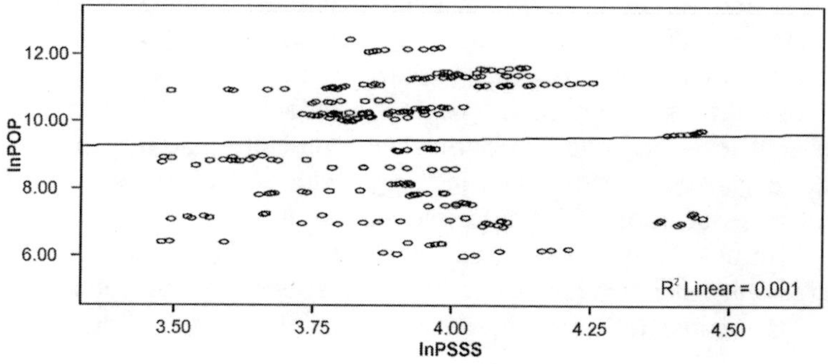

Figure 8

Relationship between log PCNSDP and log Population Size (Million) in Indian States during 2004–12

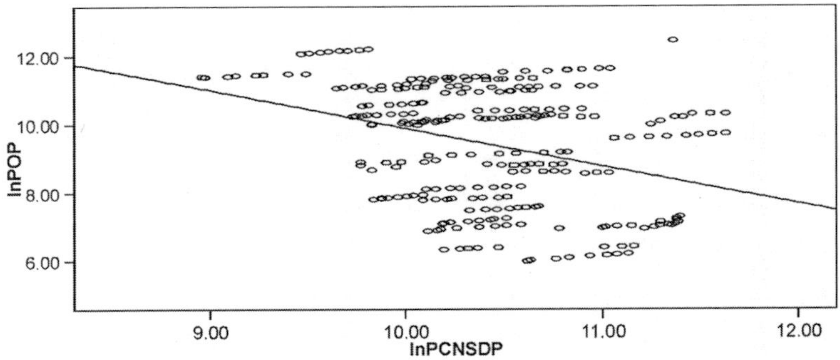

Figure 5 shows a positive association between these two variables. The percentage share of the industry sector has declining trend with population size (Figure 6) while service sector has risen trend population size (Figure 7). Figure 8 demonstrates a negative relationship between the log value of population size and the log value of per capita NSDP that is expected and the observation is consistent with earlier findings which show that as GDP per capita rises, the share of agriculture in GDP falls (Chenery and Syrquin, 1975). Results of random effects models with log per capita NSDP as dependent variable and a log percentage share of agriculture, industry and the service sector as dependant variables show that other things remaining constant one percentage point increase in the percentage share of agriculture and its allied sector in GSDP will decline per capita NSDP by 0.69 points while industry sector and service sector would increase per capita NSDP by 28 and. 52 points respectively (Table 1). Results are consistent with earlier studies, like Victor Fuchs (1968) and Baumol, who concluded that the income elasticity of demand for services is only slightly higher than for goods. When we regressed to the log of percentage share of all sectors of the log value of population size in millions (Table 2), we found significant at the 5 per cent level negative association with agriculture sector, insignificant negative associated with industry sector while insignificant but positive association with the service sector.

Results (Table 3) show log per capita NSDP has statistically significant 1 per cent level negative association while log population size has an insignificant negative associated with a percentage share of agriculture and its allied sector in all specifications. Time trend has negative yet insignificant association in four specifications. Coefficient of dummy for high income states is negative while the coefficients of low income states and EAG states are positive, but all these are insignificantly associated with a percentage share of agriculture and its allied sector for thirty-two states and UTs during 2004–12.

Table 1

Random effect Estimator with Dependent Variable: l_PCNSDP

	Coef.	*(Standard errors)*	*p-values*
Const:	9.28	(0.956)	0.00
l_AAS:	–0.698	(0.047)	0.00
l_IS:	0.288	(0.099)	0.00
l_SS:	0.520	(0.156)	0.00

Note: H = 51.0347 with p-value = prob (chi-square(3) > 51.0347) = 4.80953e–011

Table 2

Fixed effects Estimator as Dependent Variable: l_Population

	Coef.	*(Standard errors)*	*p-values*
Const:	9.45	(1.32)	0.00
l_AAS:	–0.187	(0.07)	0.02
l_IS:	–0.018	(0.139)	0.89
l_SS:	0.138	(0.212)	0.51

Note: $\hat{H}$=4.6767 with p-value = prob (chi-square(3) > 4.6767) = 0.19706

Table 3

Empirical Results from the Structural Changes in Agriculture and Allied Sector

Model	*1 (RE)*	*2 (RE)*	*3 (RE)*	*4 (RE)*	*5 (RE)*
Variable	*Coefficient Std. Error*	*Coefficient Std. Error*	*Coefficient Std. Error*	*Coefficient Std. Error*	*Coefficient Std. Error*
Constant	9.77*	9.50*	9.37*	9.02*	9.45*
	(0.45)	(0.93)	(0.93)	(0.98)	(0.95)
Log Per Capita NSDP	–0.68*	–0.65*	–0.62*	–0.62*	–0.65*
	(0.03)	(0.08)	(0.08)	(0.08)	(0.08)
Log Population Size (Million)	–0.004	–0.002	–0.006	–0.006	–0.0057
	(0.03)	(0.034)	(0.035)	(0.035)	(0.0356)

Cont'd...

...Cont'd

Dummy Time trend		–0.002 (0.006)	–0.004 (0.006)	–0.004 (0.006)	–0.002 (0.006)
Dummy High Income States			–0.364 (0.240)		
Dummy Low Income States				0.363 (0.240)	
Dummy EAG States					0.13 (0.276)
No. of Obs.	256	256	256	256	256
Cow Test	56.5138*	53.444*	55.3679*	55.3679*	60.5068*
Hausman	7.72885**	9.2214**	8.4288**	8.4288*	11.5583*
LM	813.902*	849.969*	835.369*	835.369*	838.407*

Empirical results for structural changes in industry sector shows statistical significant positive association with log per capita NSDP, dummy for low income states and dummy for EAG states while time trend and dummy for high income states have a significant negative association. The size of the population seems to have inconstant and insignificant association with a percentage share of the industry sector in India during 2004–12 (Table 4).

Table 4

Empirical Results from the Structural Changes in Industry Sector

Model	*1 (FE)*	*2 (RE)*	*3 (RE)*	*4 (RE)*	*5 (RE)*
Variable	*Coefficient Std. Error*	*Coefficient Std. Error*	*Coefficient Std. Error*	*Coefficient Std. Error*	*Coefficient Std. Error*
Constant	2.77 (0.55)	–1.37 (0.87)	–2.26** (0.92)	–2.59* (0.98)	–2.06** (0.89)
Log Per Capita NSDP	0.084** (0.04)	0.44* (0.07)	0.55* (0.08)	0.55* (0.08)	0.52* (0.08)
Log Population Size (Million)	–0.03 (0.04)	0.026 (0.02)	0.02 (0.02)	0.022 (0.03)	0.0037 (0.03)
Dummy Time trend		–0.03* (0.005)	–0.037* (0.006)	–0.037* (0.006)	–0.035* (0.005)
Dummy High Income States			–0.34** (0.13)		

Cont'd...

...Cont'd

Dummy Low Income States				0.34* (0.13)	
Dummy EAG States					0.42* (0.15)
No. of Obs.	256	256	256	256	256
Cow Test	26.4119*	21.2968*	22.3038*	22.3038*	20.13*
Hausman	0.405387	13.4738*	6.65917***	6.65917***	6.979***
LM	720.205*	726.532*	727.953*	727.953*	725.67*

Regression results for the share of the service sector have been presented in Table 5, log per cent share of the service sector has positive and significant at 1 per cent level association with log per capita NSDP in India, but its coefficient has changed in negative when we include time trend in the second specification of the model. Table 3, column 1 shows fixed effects while another four specifications are dealt with random effects. There is an insignificant negative association between log values of population and log value of per cent share of the service sector in all specifications excluding first specification that is without any dummy variable.

Table 5

Empirical Results from the Structural Changes in Service Sector

Model	*1 (FE)*	*2 (RE)*	*3 (RE)*	*4 (RE)*	*5 (RE)*
Variable	*Coefficien t Std. Error*	*Coefficient Std. Error*	*Coefficient Std. Error*	*Coefficient Std. Error*	*Coefficient Std. Error*
Constant	2.78* (0.35)	7.34* (0.50)	8.23* (0.49)	8.67* (0.52)	7.92* (0.49)
Log Per Capita NSDP	0.09* (0.02)	–0.32* (0.04)	–0.44* (0.04)	–0.44* (0.04)	–0.39* (0.05)
Log Population Size (Million)	0.02 (0.03)	–0.02 (0.02)	–0.016 (0.016)	–0.015 (0.016)	–0.0010 (0.0165)
Dummy Time trend	.	0.035* (0.003)	0.04* (0.003)	0.042* (0.0033)	0.039* (0.0032)

Cont'd...

...Cont'd

Dummy High Income States			0.44* (0.08)		
Dummy Low Income States				–0.43* (0.08)	
Dummy EAG States					–0.42* (0.09)
No. of Obs.	256	256	256	256	256
Cow Test	52.57*	44.04*	43.88*	43.88*	44.95*
Hausman	0.9077	67.70*	32.24*	32.24*	44.94*
LM	686.29*	690.01*	693.98*	693.98*	695.66*

As far as the dummy of high income states is concerned its coefficient is positive while the coefficient of the log of per capita NSDP is negative and statistical significant at the 1 per cent level. It suggests that high income states have positive associations with the service sector, yet it has influenced negatively to the economic growth in India during the study period. On the other hand, the dummy for low income states and EAG states have negative associations with a service sector and have influenced negatively to the economic growth of India. Hence, EAG states have not performed well in the growth of service sector during the study period. Coefficient of time trend in column 2 is positive and significant, suggesting that there was significant growth in service sector during 2004–11 in thirty-two states and UTs of India. Column 5 includes dummy of EAG which has negative and statistically significant at 1 per cent level association with service sector in India. The coefficient's of dummy for EAG states and log of per capita NSDP are negative and significant at the 1 per cent level while the time trend is positive. Here it is an interesting to highlight, that high income states have a higher positive influence on service sector during 2004–11, while low income states have highest negative influence on the service sector.

At the next step, we tried to analyse state dummies with log per capita net state domestic product at constant prices as dependent variable and population size (million), with some state dummies splitting in high and low per capita NSDP as independent variables. Results of Random Effects Model suggest that states and UTs like Chandigarh, Delhi, Goa, Haryana, Maharashtra, A&N Islands and Pondicherry (Puducherry) have statistically significant at the 5 per cent level positive association between a logarithm value of the population and logarithm value of per capita NSDP (Table 6), while Assam, Bihar, Madhya Pradesh, Uttar Pradesh, Rajasthan, Odisha, Manipur, Chhattisgarh and Jharkhand have significant at the 5 per cent level negative association in this period (Table 7). Some states have sound policies and created productive job opportunities for its population and are able to reap benefits. Some other traditional and slow growing states performed poorly on different accounts in social and physical infrastructure which are still far from the benefits of demographic window. Thus, the impact of population change is not automatic and homogenous throughout the Indian States during the study period. Whether India will be able to capitalize on its favourable age structure depends on how well the EAG states are able to reform their economies.

Table 6

Links between Economic Growth and Population in High Income States of India during 2004–12

	Coefficient	*Std error*	*P Value*
Constant	10.19	–0.38	0.00
Population Size	–0.016	–0.038	0.67
Andhra Pradesh	0.4	–0.3	0.18
Goa	1.39	–0.29	0.00
Gujarat	0.65	–0.29	0.02
Haryana	0.74	–0.29	0.01
Himachal Pradesh	0.56	–0.29	0.05
Karnataka	0.6	–0.29	0.04
Maharashtra	0.79	–0.3	0.01
Nagaland	0.46	–0.3	0.13
Punjab	0.56	–0.29	0.06
Sikkim	0.52	–0.32	0.10
Tamil Nadu	0.64	–0.3	0.03
Uttarakhand	0.46	–0.29	0.12
A & N Island	0.78	–0.32	0.01
Chandigarh	1.26	–0.31	0.00
Delhi	1.32	–0.29	0.00
Puducherry	1.04	–0.31	0.00

LM=213.863 with p-value = prob (chi-square(1) > 213.863) = 1.97316e–048
H=17.5166 with p-value = prob (chi-square(1) > 17.5166) = 2.84813e–005

Table 7

Links between Economic Growth and Population in Low Income States of India during 2004–12

	Coefficient	*Std. error*	*P Value*
Constant	10.38	–0.38	0.00
Population Size	0.047	–0.04	0.25
Arunachal Pradesh	–0.381	–0.35	0.28
Assam	–1.008	–0.35	0.00
Bihar	–1.724	–0.36	0.00
Chattisgarh	–0.868	–0.35	0.01
J & K	–0.73	–0.35	0.03
Jharkhand	–0.438	–0.35	0.22
Kerala	–1.05	–0.35	0.00
Madhya Pradesh	–0.82	–0.35	0.01
Manipur	–0.8	–0.35	0.02
Meghalaya	–0.44	–0.35	0.20
Mizoram	–0.37	–0.35	0.29
Odisha	–0.91	–0.35	0.01
Rajasthan	–0.86	–0.35	0.01
Tripura	–0.43	–0.35	0.22
Uttar Pradesh	–1.31	–0.37	0.00
West Bengal	–0.69	–0.36	0.05

LM=315.272 with p-value = prob(chi-square(1) > 315.272) = 1.55138e–070
H= 10.7685 with p-value = prob(chi-square(1) > 10.7685) = 0.00103241

Conclusions

The growth pattern of different sectors of the economy shows an emergence of the service sector as the major contributor; decline in the share of agriculture sector and industry sector has seen a steep decline during this period. It indicates that some states were able to shift their labour force from low productivity agriculture to higher productivity industry and service sectors, and to increase productivity within those sectors. Results of Random Effects Model suggest that agriculture and its allied sector have statistically significant at 1 per cent level negative association with per capita income, while industry sector and service sectors have a significant positive association with per capita income in India during the study period.

As far as the dummy of high income states is concerned its coefficient is positive, while the coefficient of the log of per capita NSDP is negative and statistically significant at the 1 per cent level. It suggests that high income states have positive associations with the industrial sector, yet it has influenced negatively to the economic growth in India during the study period. On the other hand the dummy for low income states have positive associations with industrial sector and have influenced positively to the economic growth of India. Here it is an interesting to highlight that EAG states have a higher positive influence on industrial sector during 2004–11. High income states' population have influenced positively while EAG states' population have influenced negatively to the industry sector in India during the study period. Low income states time trend is negative while high income states time trend is positive, suggesting that industrial growth has been captured by high income states only.

The findings also show that the service sector has a higher positive influence on per capita income. State dummies show significant positive relationship between service sector and per capita income in Delhi, Chandigarh and Kerala while Arunachal Pradesh, Chattisgarh and Himachal Pradesh have shown significant negative coefficient. The highest negative influence of population size on per capita NSDP has been observed for Bihar followed by Uttar Pradesh. Some bigger states like Maharashtra, Haryana, Gujarat and Tamil Nadu have sound policies and created productive job opportunities for its population and were able to reap benefits of economic growth. Thus, the impact of structural change is not automatic and homogenous throughout the Indian States during the study period. Whether India will be able to capitalize on its favourable growth depends on how well the EAG states are able to reform their economies.

References

Bloom, D.E. and J.G. Williamson. 1998. 'Demographic Transitions and Economic Miracles in Emerging Asia', *World Bank Economic Review*, 12(3): 419–455.

Chenery, Hollis B. 1960. 'Patterns of Industrial Growth', *American Economic Review*, 50(3): 624–654.

Chenery, Hollis B. and Lance Taylor. 1968. 'Development Patterns: Among Countries and Over Time', *Review of Economics and Statistics*, 50(4): 391–416.

Chenery, Hollis B. and Moises Syrquin. 1975. *Patterns of Development: 1950–1970*. Oxford: Oxford University Press.

Clark, C. 1940. *The Conditions of Economic Progress*. London: Macmillan (revised and reprinted in 1951).

Cornwall, John and Wendy Cornwall. 1994. 'Growth Theory and Economic Structure', *Economica*, 61: 237–251.

Cortuk, O. and N. Singh. 2011. 'Structural Change and Growth in India', *Economic Letters*, 110: 178–181.

Denison, Edward. 1985. *Trends in American Economic Growth: 1929–82*. Washington, D.C.: The Brookings Institution.

Echevarria, Cristina. 1997. 'Changes in Sectoral Composition Associated with Economic Growth', *International Economic Review*, 38(2): 431–452.

Fisher, A.G.B. 1939. 'Production: Primary, Secondary and Tertiary', *The Economic Journal*, XV.

Fuchs, Victor R. 1968. *The Service Economy*. New York: National Bureau of Economic Research.

Ghate, C. and S. Wright. 2012. 'The "V-factor" Distribution, Timing and Correlates of Great Indian Growth Turnaround', *Journal of Development Economics*, 99(1): 58–67.

Kader, A. 1985. 'Development Patterns among Countries Reexamined', *The Developing Economies*, 23(3): 199–220.

Kaldor, N. 1966. *Causes of Slow Rate of Growth in the United Kingdom*. Cambridge: Cambridge University Press.

Kuznets, Simon. 1966. *Modern Economic Growth: Rate, Structure, and Spread*. New Haven: Yale University Press.

——. 1971. *Economic Growth of Nations: Total Output and Production Structure*. Cambridge, MA: Belknap Press of Harvard University Press.

Lewis, W. Arthur. 1954. 'Economic Development with Unlimited Supplies of Labour', *Journal of the Manchester School of Economic and Social Studies*, 22(2): 139–191.

Linden, M. and T. Mahmood. 2007. Long Run Relationships between Sector Shares and Economic Growth: A Panel Data Analysis of the Schengen Region. Economics and Business Administration, University of Joensuu, Finland.

Papola, T.S. 2005. 'Structural Changes in the Indian Economy: Some Implications of the Emerging Pattern', *Artha Beekshan*, 13(4).

Rostow, W.W. 1971. *The Stages of Economic Growth*. Cambridge: Cambridge University Press.

Rowthorn, R. and J.R. Wells. 1987. *De-industrialization and Foreign Trade*. Cambridge: Cambridge University Press.

Sundrum, R.M. 1991. *Economic Growth in Theory and Practice*. New York: St. Martin's Press.

Syrquin, Moshe. 1989. 'Patterns of Structural Change', in Hollis Chenery and T.N. Srinivasan (eds.), Handbook of Development Economics, edition 1, volume 1, chapter 7, pp. 203–273, Elsevier.

——. 2007. 'Kuznets and Pasinetti on the Study of Structural Transformation: Never the Twain Shael Meet', ICER working papers 46, ICER: International Centre for Economic Research.

Syrquin, Moshe and Hollis B. Chenery. 1989. Patterns of Development, 1950 to 1983. World Bank Discussion Papers No. 41, The World Bank, Washington, D.C.

Syrquin, Moshe, Lance Taylor and Larry E. Westphal. 1984. *Economic Structure and Performance: Essays in Honor of Hollis B. Chenery*. Orlando: Academic Press.

Taylor, Lance. 1969. 'Development Patterns: A Simulation Study', *Quarterly Journal of Economics*, 83(1): 220–241.

Timmer, P. and S. Akkus. 2008. The Structural Transformation as a Pathway Out of Poverty: Analytics, Empirics and Politics. Working Paper No. 150, Center for Global Development, Washington, D.C.

16

Macro and Micro Perspective on Perception and Gender Gap Towards the Bodily Rights of Women in India

ANKITA SIDDHANTA AND S.K. SINGH

Perception and behaviour are two conjoined aspects where the understanding of one enhances the certainty of the other. Putting this into perspective, an analysis of man's perception about sexual and reproductive rights of a woman on one hand, and woman's views on sexual autonomy and reproductive freedom on the other, will help us to reach to a conclusion about the prevailing demeaning situation of women in India. However, this may or may not be linked to the current unpleasant mishaps occurring in the lives of Indian girls in the form of rape, molestations and sexual assaults. Scholars have argued that men may use force when they lack economic resources to control their partners' behaviour (Felson and Messner, 2000; Goode, 1971) and a man with fewer resources than his partner may bolster his dominance with force (Gartner and Macmillan, 1999).

It is observed that men who are more educated and have better access to information than women are often in a better position than women, in having knowledge about reproductive health. However, they lack interest as they believe that reproductive health has everything to do with contraception, pregnancy, childbirth and STDs and hence, is considered to be of a woman's concern (UNFPA, 2000).

As much as understanding Indian men's perception on bodily rights of women, women's views are also essential to study as researchers have found that women's perceptions define their health seeking behaviours, thereby reflects how women exercise their reproductive rights. Their perceptions of their reproductive rights depend on many cognitive, cultural, emotional, social and political factors (Shabana et al., 2003).

There have been several attempts in the last twenty years to include the concept of sexual and reproductive health, and well-being in the arena of human rights. Though this conceptualization of sexual and reproductive rights has been achieved with a fair success but the privileges are yet to be experienced by women in desirable aspects.

Sexual and Reproductive Rights

According to Hunt (2004), sexual rights include the right of all persons to express their sexual orientation, with due regard to the well-being and rights of others, without fear of persecution, denial of liberty or social interference. International Council on Human Rights Policy (2009) define sexual rights as the right of all individuals, free of coercion, discrimination and violence, to the highest attainable standard of sexual health, including access to sexual and reproductive health care services; seek, receive, and impart information related to sexuality; sex education; respect for bodily integrity; choose their partner; decide whether or not to be sexually active; consensual sexual relations; consensual marriage; decide whether or not, and when, to have children; and pursue a satisfying, safe and pleasurable sexual life.

Programme of Action of the International Conference on Population and Development (ICPD) (1994) has defined reproductive rights as the basic rights of all couples and individuals to decide freely and responsibly the number, spacing and timing of their children and to have the information and means to do so, and the right to attain the highest standard of sexual and reproductive health. This includes the right to make decisions concerning reproduction free of discrimination, coercion and violence, as expressed in human rights documents.

There are several studies worldwide and especially in developing countries in the field of sexual and reproductive rights of women mainly focusing on awareness and perception about these rights of women. A little more than half of the women in urban and four-fifths in rural Bangladesh had the viewpoint that wife beating is justified by husband/man if the wife is unfaithful, refuses sex or does not complete household work. Forty-five per cent urban women and 36 per cent rural women perceived that they had the right to refuse to sex if they are unwilling, sick, and when husbands are drunk or abusive (Wahed and Bhuiya, 2007). Studies done in South Western Nigeria on the awareness of sexual and reproductive rights among adolescents revealed that majority (60%) of the adolescents were aware about the various sexual and reproductive rights. But they were less aware about the contents of the rights as well as the sexual and reproductive health programmes implemented for the adolescents. A major factor identified behind the lack of knowledge about the contents of the rights was lack of education (Ogunlayi, 2005). A large percentage of Nigerian women support wife beating under certain circumstances, including instances when wives refuse to have sex with husbands. Violation of women's bodily rights is accepted as a cultural norm in that region as is evident from the justification of wife beating by both men and women in the region and their disagreement towards the fact that there could be rape within marriage (Oyediran and Isiugo-Abanihe, 2005; Ilika et al., 2002).

Perception of the men regarding the sexual and reproductive rights of women is little different in a developed country like United States. Men are more likely to believe that women play a greater role in a couple's decision of sex but men are more likely to take decisions about contraception. Almost 60–75 per cent men in United States having heterosexual relationship viewed that decisions about sex and contraception are shared responsibility of him and his partner (Grady et al., 1996).

Findings from India is similar to the experiences of several Asian, African and middle eastern developing countries where the marriage patterns are similar (Santhya and Jejeebhoy, 2005). In a study by Pradhan (2008) it had been found that more than 50 per cent of the young women had high equitable view about the gender roles as compared to 35 per cent in case of the young men in Puri district in Odisha, India. Still one-third of the women among the respondents had the view that they were forced to have sex for the first time after their marriage. On the other hand, Singh and Singh (2008) found that 40–50 per cent of women in Bellary, Guntur and Kishenganj districts felt that all the men and their husbands had the right to have sex whenever they wish, irrespective of women's displeasure and unwillingness to have sex. The adolescent males of those areas mostly have a favourable perception towards the sexual rights of the women, but in reality they find coercion and forced sex as a right over their wives. Influence of patriarchy, low status of women and female subjugation in these areas play a major role. In another study by George (1998), it was found that women and men differed in their perception about violation of sexual rights and sexual coercion in Mumbai. They felt sex to be coerced when their husbands forced them for sex against their wishes. On the other hand, men perceived that they had all the rights to have sex in their marriages and that is why the wives had to give consent for sex whenever they wish for it, and force would be justified in the face of unwillingness or refusal. They also believed that they should not have to go elsewhere for sex if they have a wife at home. According to some men, the image of a good woman/wife is one who obeys her husband and is sexually available to him whenever he wants.

Based on the above background, the present study has two objectives:

(1) To study the perception of men and women about the sexual and reproductive rights of women in India.
(2) To study the gender gap between perceptions about the bodily rights of women in India.

Methods and Materials

For the accomplishment of the objectives, NFHS–3 National Family Health Survey (2005–2006) and CHARCA – Coordinated HIV/AIDS Response through Capacity Building and Awareness. (2007–2008 End Line Study Report) data were used.

The study is based on four districts namely, Bellary in Karnataka (known for the prevalence of Devadasi system, where the eldest daughter of a family is offered to the priest), Guntur in Andhra Pradesh (an area where proportion of mobile sex workers has been increasing and extramarital sex has no longer been a taboo), Kanpur in Uttar Pradesh (where dominance of single male migration has been creating a conducive environment for women's vulnerability to HIV/AIDS even in spite of very traditional society having strong patriarchal norms), Kishenganj in Bihar (the bordering district connecting Nepal and Bangladesh and an internationally known route for trafficking of women in sex trade in India from its neighbouring countries). As such, the states of Bihar, Karnataka, Andhra Pradesh and Uttar Pradesh were chosen accordingly for analysis.

NFHS–3 is a nationally representative large scale survey covering more than 1 lakh 24 thousand women, 74,000 men from 1 lakh 9 thousand households selected by Multistage Probability Sampling approach. The number of male respondents in the selected states are 11,161 from Uttar Pradesh, 4,444 from Bihar, 5,698 from Andhra Pradesh and 4,523 from Karnataka. Female respondents comprised of 18,954 from Uttar Pradesh, 9,502 from Bihar, 9,555 from Andhra Pradesh and 7,424 from Karnataka.

Whereas CHARCA study provides a micro-level perspective in the reproductive and sexual rights of young women across 5 districts providing varying cultural contexts. The number of male respondents covered in the CHARCA survey are 328 in Kishenganj, 322 in Kanpur, 317 in Bellary and 213 in Guntur. The numbers of female respondents are 465 in Kishenganj, 632 in Kanpur, 556 in Bellary and 417 in Guntur.

Descriptive statistics and bivariate analysis has been carried out with the two datasets.

The dependent and the independent variables that are used for the analysis are given in tabular form below:

Dependent Variables from NFHS 3 and CHARCA

Data Source	*Objectives*	*Dependent variables*
NFHS–3	The perception of men and women about the sexual and reproductive rights of women. Gender Gap in Perception	Wife beating justified if she refuses to have sex with him; Wife can refuse sex when husband has STD; having sex with other woman and when wife is tired/not in mood. Husband has the right to force wife for sex. Contraception is woman's business, man should not worry; Wife justified to ask husband to use condom if he has STD; Final say on deciding how many children to have.
CHARCA	The perception of men and women about the sexual and reproductive rights of women. Gender Gap in Perception	Woman has the right to refuse sex; Women can say no to sex when not wanted; Women has the right to decide about spacing, number, composition of children, contraceptive method to be used and termination of pregnancy

The independent variables used in the analysis are age, education, place of residence, social status, religion, wealth quintile, marital status, exposure to mass media, alcohol consumption, age at first intercourse, intensity of gender role, age at first marriage, heard about STD, AIDS and number of sexual partners.

Results

Perception of Men about the Sexual and Reproductive Rights of Women

The perception of the men about the sexual rights of women can be understood under the five different circumstances discussed below:

Men's Perception about not Justifying Wife Beating if she Refuses Sex

From the results presented in Table 1, it is evident that Indian men do have a positive perception and positive attitude towards the bodily rights of women. Most of the men in India (92%) perceive that it is not justified to beat wife for sex when she is unwilling. Except in Bihar, this perception in the other states was as high as the national figure.

Table 1

Men's Perception about the Sexual Rights of Women in India and Selected States, 2005–2006

States	*Percentage of men perceiving that wives are justified in refusing sex when husband is having STD*	*Percentage of men perceiving that wives are justified in refusing sex when husband has sex with other woman*	*Percentage of men perceiving that wives are justified in refusing sex when she is tired or not in mood*	*Percentage of men reporting husbands are not justified in forcing wives for sex when she is unwilling*	*Percentage of men not justifying wife beating if she refuses sex*
Bihar (4430)	82.8	86.5	85.5	84.2	91.3
Uttar Pradesh (11161)	88.2	89.6	91.9	93.6	92.6
Karnataka (4530)	83.0	76.4	78.0	90.3	88.7
Andhra Pradesh (5668)	88.3	70.3	83.4	90.8	87.9
India (74331)	81.6	79.4	84.4	91.8	90.1

Figures in Brackets indicate Number (n)

It was found that with increase in age, educational level and wealth status, men have increasingly better perception. Adolescent males in India and states perceived less positively about wife beating but when age increases, more than 90 per cent of men perceive positively. When wealth quintile is considered, close to 95 per cent men from richest quintile perceive that they do not justify beating wife when she refuses to have sex. Lesser percentage of men from the poorest wealth quintile are showing this positive attitude compared to the richest quintile.

Figure 1

Men's Perception about not Justifying Wife Beating if she Refuses to have Sex

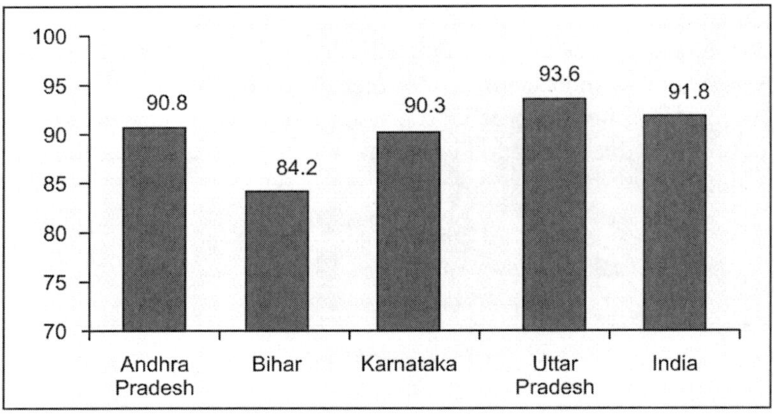

It is evident from the results that rural men of India and the selected states perceive less positively about wife beating than their counterparts in urban areas. With increasing number of sexual partners, and decreasing intensity of gender role, the positive perception is decreasing. Those who are married, have exposure to mass media and have heard about STI and AIDS keep more positive views and do not justify wife beating for sex.

Men's Perception about not Justifying Forcing Wives for Sex when she is Unwilling

Results from Table 1 shows that as high as 90 per cent of men in India do not justify forcing wives for sex when she is unwilling. This percentage is even better in Bihar and Uttar Pradesh. It was found that with increasing age, wealth and education the perception of the men tilted positively towards the bodily rights of women.

More than one-third men in Bihar who have more than two lifetime sexual partners justify forcing wives for sex. In Karnataka, more than three-fourths men who are not exposed to mass media, do not justify forcing wives for sex, when she is not willing as against 91 per cent who are exposed to mass media, throwing light on the fact that exposure to mass media is helping the men to gain positive attitude about the bodily rights of the women. A little less than one-third men who agree to all wife beating circumstances also justify forcing wives for sex even when she is not willing to have sex.

Figure 2

Men's Perception about not Justifying Forcing Wives for Sex when she is Unwilling, by Level of Education

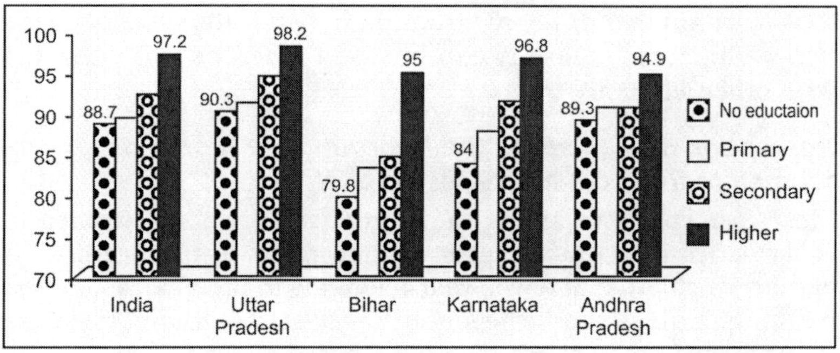

Men's Perception that Wife can Refuse Sex when Husband is having STD and when she is Tired or not in Mood

Four-fifths of men in India have positive attitude opining that wife can always refuse sex when husband is having STD or when wife is tired/not in mood. More men in the age group of 20–35 years compared to other age groups have the positive opinion. About one-third men in rural India do not justify that wife can refuse sex when husband is having STD as compared to one-fourth men in urban India. Except in Karnataka, in all the other states, men from Non-Scheduled Caste, Schedule Tribe and Other Backward Caste categories are having better perception. Currently married men are having better perception regarding the sexual rights of women as more of them perceive that women can refuse sex when husband is having STD or when she is tired.

Men's Perception that Wife can Refuse Sex when Husband has Sex with Other Woman

It has been seen that when unfaithfulness of the husband is linked to wife's refusal to sex, lesser number of men perceive that wife can refuse sex when husband has sex with other women. Table 1 shows that 70 per cent men in Andhra Pradesh perceive that wives can refuse sex when husband has sexual relations with some other women which is much low as compared to other states and national average. Under these circumstances, men of Bihar (86.5%) and Uttar Pradesh (90%) are having a little better acuity than the men from other states and India, thus correlating husband's infidelity and wive's refusal to have sex in a positive path. People with no education and belonging to poorest wealth quintile may be less aware of the contents of the sexual and reproductive rights of women, and thus least number of people from these two categories perceive that woman can refuse sex to husband when he is having sex with other women.

Perception of Men about the Reproductive Rights of Women in the India and Selected States

Men's perception regarding the reproductive rights of women in India varies from the issue of contraception to the decision of number of children to have. Men belonging to urban areas, richest wealth quintile, 'other' category of social status, having exposure to mass media and those who have heard about STI and AIDS agree more positively that wife is justified in asking husband to use contraception when he is having STD and both husband and wife should have right to decide about number of children to have.

Table 2

Men's Perception about the Reproductive Rights of Women in India and Selected States, 2005–2006

States	*Percentage of men who agreed that contraception is only women's business*	*Percentage of men who perceived that wives are justified in asking husband to use condom when he is having STD*	*Percentage of men who perceived that both husband and wife should have the right to decide the number of children to have*
Bihar (4430)	48.8	79.5	80.1
Uttar Pradesh (11161)	13.3	86.2	94.2
Karnataka (4530)	17.3	83.7	90.0
Andhra Pradesh (5668)	26.0	85.9	81.3
India (74331)	21.8	83.2	88.4

Figures in brackets indicate Number (n)

Results from Table 2 depicts that most of the men do not agree to the fact that contraception is only women's business and a man should not have to worry about it. But in case of Bihar about half of the men agree that contraception is only a women's business. Almost 90 per cent men in India, Uttar Pradesh and Karnataka believed that both husband and wife have the right to take decision on the number of children to have.

Perception of Men about the Sexual and Reproductive Rights of Women in the Selected Districts

Coming to micro-level study and analysing district-wise data, it was found from Table 3 that 84 per cent men in Bellary are having the opinion that women can refuse sex as compared to 99 per cent men in Kanpur.

Table 3

Men's Perception about Sexual and Reproductive Rights of Women in some Selected Districts, 2007–08

Districts	*Sexual Rights*		*Reproductive Rights*				
			Women has the right to decide about				
	Women has the right to enjoy sex	*Women can say no to sex when not wanted*	*Spacing of children*	*Number of children*	*Sex composit-ion of children*	*Contrace-ptive method to be used*	*Termi-nation of pregna-ncy*
Kishenganj (322)	93.8	95.0	88.2	84.5	72.2	66.9	72.9
Kanpur (322)	96.6	98.8	97.8	94.1	79.4	64.0	81.9
Bellary (317)	91.2	83.9	86.3	77.9	71.0	91.5	63.4
Guntur (213)	95.3	97.7	91.1	87.9	84.6	96.7	87.9

Figures in brackets indicate Number (n)

When the reproductive rights of the women are taken into account, inter-district variations are observed and it was found that smaller proportion of men in the districts except in Bellary and Guntur are of the opinion that women also have the right to decide about sex composition of their children and she can choose the contraceptive method to be used. The proportion of men perceiving positively about the reproductive rights of women in Kishenganj have been substantially lower than the other districts. Overall, it was found that more men in the selected districts are recognizing the reproductive rights of women and the situation is better compared to the respective state level perception of the men. In Bellary and Guntur, 92–96 per cent of men believed that women have the right to decide about the contraceptive method to be used which was higher than the other districts. As low as 63 per cent men in Bellary perceived that a woman has the right to decide about termination of pregnancy.

Perception of Women about Control over their Own Sexuality

The perception of the women of India about the control over their own sexuality under different circumstances has been discussed below.

Perception of Women about Control Over their Own Sexuality in India and Selected States

From Table 4 it was found that four-fifths women in India do not justify 'wife beating' by husband, when she refuses sex. The figure is also high for Uttar Pradesh (88%) and Bihar (85%), but strikingly it is low in the southern states of Andhra Pradesh (63%) and Karnataka (68%).

Table 4

Women's perception about the Sexual and Reproductive rights of women in India and selected states, 2005–2006

States	*Percentage of women not justifying wife beating if she refuses sex*	*Percentage of women perceiving that wives are justified in refusing sex when husband is having STD*	*Percentage of women perceiving that wives are justified in refusing sex when husband has sex with other woman*	*Percentage of women perceiving that wives are justified in refusing sex when she is tired or not in mood*
Bihar (9492)	67.9	78.4	75.6	74.2
Uttar Pradesh (18953)	84.9	86.3	83.6	75.7
Karnataka (7412)	88.3	80.2	84.1	84.5
Andhra Pradesh (9545)	63.4	69.9	68.2	66.7
India (124385)	81.7	77.9	79.3	77.4

Figures in brackets indicate Number (n)

The percentage of women justifying that wife can refuse sex under the circumstances of husband having STD, husband being adulterous and when she is tired/not in mood, is high in the states of Uttar Pradesh and Bihar (more than 80%) and it is even better than the national average. Andhra Pradesh and Karnataka again lag behind with relatively low percentage of women perceiving positively about their own sexual rights. It was also found that ever married adolescent females in India and the states are less aware about the sexual and reproductive rights and their sexual autonomy.

Wealth quintile is inversely associated with women's perception of justifying wife beating and not justifying wife's refusal to sex. More women from the poorest wealth quintile supported wife beating than their counterparts in the richest wealth quintile. With increasing education, more women are perceiving positively and less women tend to justify wife beating and use of force for sex by husbands. In most of the states, women having more than 3 sexual partners are of better opinion than women having less sexual partners. Proportion of women justifying wife beating when she is unwilling to have sex, is markedly increasing when the perception about intensity of gender role is decreasing, thus when they agree to all wife beating variables.

It was found that women who are currently married, exposed to mass media, living in urban areas, who heard about STIs and AIDS are more aware about their bodily rights and have assenting view towards their sexual autonomy. Similar to the results of the present study, another research by Oyediran and Isiygo Abanihe (2005) found that rural residents in Nigeria and those who did not have formal education tended to agree more than their urban counterparts that a husband is justified in beating his wife. Their study also found that married women who listened to radio daily were less likely to justify wife beating compared to those who have never listened to radio.

Perception of Women about Control Over their Own Sexuality in the Selected Districts

CHARCA dataset (2007–08) used little different indicators for the perception of women about their sexual and reproductive rights. Women were asked about whether they can say no to sex, and whether women has the right to decide about contraception, spacing of children, number of children, sex composition of children and right to terminate pregnancy. Results from Table 5 indicate that almost 98–99 per cent of women in Kanpur and Guntur have opined that women can say no to sex when not wanted. Percentage of women in Bellary perceiving positively about the right of women to decide about the spacing, number, sex composition of children, contraceptive method to be used and termination of pregnancy, is far less than the other selected districts. More than 90 per cent of women in Guntur and Kishenganj perceived that they have the right to terminate their pregnancy when not wanted as against 49 per cent and 79 per cent women of Bellary and Kanpur respectively.

Table 5

Women's Perception about Sexual and Reproductive Rights of women in some selected districts of India, 2007–08

Districts	*Sexual*	*Reproductive*				
	Women can say no to sex when not wanted	*Women has the right to decide about*				
		Spacing of children	*Number of children*	*Sex composition of children*	*Contraceptive method to be used*	*Termination of pregnancy*
Kishenganj (465)	90.3	96.5	95.9	92.5	92.3	96.4
Kanpur (632)	97.4	95.1	94.1	89.9	83.7	79.6
Bellary (556)	82.9	64.2	72.1	68.5	71.9	49.2
Guntur (417)	99.5	99.1	98.6	96.9	92.6	91.4

Figures in brackets indicate Number (n)

Gender Gap in Perception about the Sexual and Reproductive Rights of Women

One of the objectives of the present study is to assess whether there exists a gender gap in India while perceiving sexual and reproductive rights of women or not. Surprisingly, it was found that women perceive less positively about their sexual rights, reproductive freedom and sexual autonomy as compared to the men in India. It was observed that, when the same questions were asked and same circumstances were given to both men and women, then women tend to answer less positively and more women justified wife beating and use of force by husband for sex, as compared to their male counterparts.

Table 6

Gender Gap in Perception (States)

Sexual Rights	*India*	*AP*	*Karnataka*	*Bihar*	*UP*
Wife has the right to refuse sex when					
Husband is having STD	3	18	2	4	2
Husband is having sex with other women	no gap	2	8 (W)	11	6
When wife is tired/not in mood	7	16	6(W)	10	15
Wife beating is justified if she refuses sex	8	24	no gap	23	7

Gender Gap in Perception (Districts)

Sexual and Rep. Rights	*Guntur*	*Bellary*	*Kishenganj*	*Kanpur*
Wife has the right to decide about				
Spacing of Children	8 (W)	22	8 (W)	2
No. of children	10 (W)	5	11 (W)	No gap
Termination of Pregnancy	4 (W)	13	23 (W)	2
Can say no to sex	2 (W)	1	5	1

'W' indicates that women perceive more positively than the men. All the numbers indicate percentages.

Women in India and states, on an average, are ten per cent less likely to justify that wives can refuse sex to husband when husband is having STD. The gender gap is found to be the highest in Andhra Pradesh (Table 6).

Figure 3

Gender Gap in Perception that Wife can Refuse Sex when she is Tired/not in Mood

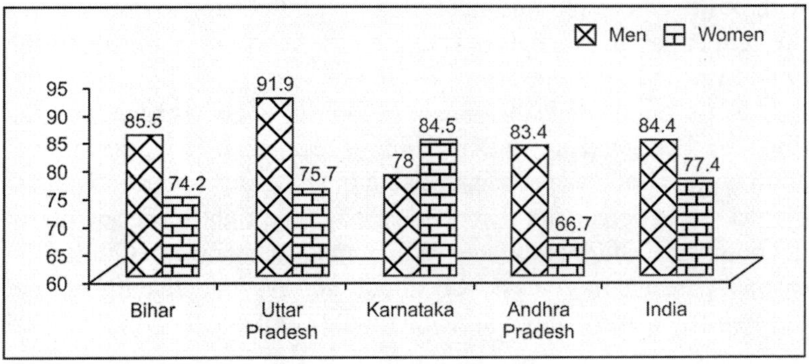

Figure 3 shows that on an average 70 per cent of women perceived that women can refuse to sex when she is tired or not in mood. On the other hand, close to 90 per cent of men believed and opined that women can refuse sex when she is tired or not in mood, thus making a gender gap of about 20 per cent. Only in Karnataka the women perceived more positively than the men. The gender gap is found to be the highest in Andhra Pradesh and Uttar Pradesh.

In India, more than 80 per cent women do not justify wife beating by husband if she refuses sex. On the other hand, around 90 per cent of men feel that wife beating is not justified when their wives refuse for sex. The gap is highest in Andhra Pradesh and Bihar.

Figure 4

Gender Gap in not Justifying Wife Beating if she Refuses Sex

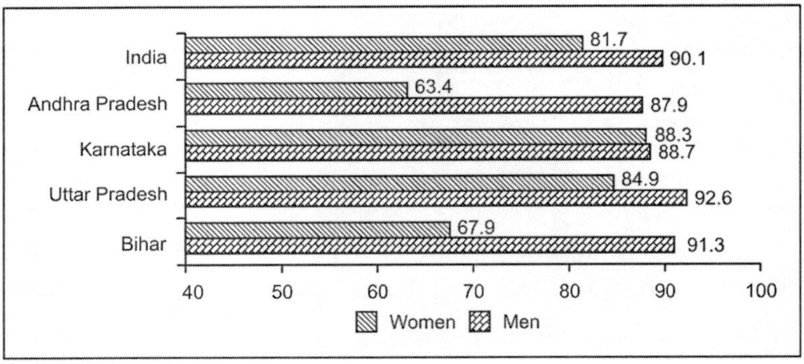

When wealth quintile is considered, it has been found that with increasing wealth quintile, the percentage of both males and females with positive perception is increasing. It is interesting to find out that the gender gap in perception is highest in the richest wealth quintile and lowest in the poorest wealth quintile.

The scenario of gender gap in perception slightly changes for the districts. The gender gap is becoming less when the district level analysis was done as present in Table 6. No gap is found in Kanpur district while perceiving that women have the right to decide about the number of children to have. While, in Kishenganj and Guntur the women perceive more positively about their reproductive rights than the men when asked about decision on the number of children to have or about the spacing of the children. This also shows a gap but in a different direction. Only in Bellary, the men perceive more positively than the women and this gap is almost 22 per cent while perceiving that women have the right to decide about the spacing of her children.

Figure 5

Gender Gap in Perception that Women have the Right to decide about the Spacing of Children (Districts)

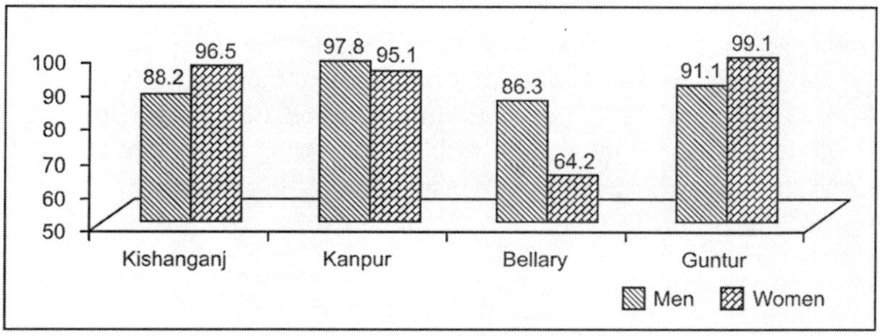

With regard to religion, it could be seen that the gender gap while perceiving that it is not justified to beat wife if she refuses sex, was almost same in all the religious groups of India. This gap was little lesser among the Hindus and little more among the Muslims and 'Other' religious groups. The gender gap is more in the rural areas of India while perceiving that wife can refuse sex if she is tired/not in mood.

Summary of Findings and Conclusion

Indian men do have a positive perception and attitude about the bodily rights of their women, though lesser percentage of men perceived positively about the reproductive rights of women. The women on the other hand feel that they have less control over their own sexuality. This makes a gender gap prevalent in India while perceiving the sexual and reproductive rights of women. This may be due to submissive role of women in the family, traditional norms of sexuality and the gender roles attributed to both the sexes in the family and society. The underlying factors influencing the perception of sexual and reproductive rights among both the males and females were age, wealth quintile, educational attainment, alcoholism, and exposure to mass media. Lesser percentage of people who are poor, uneducated, drink alcohol, who are not currently married and unexposed to mass media, perceive positively about the sexual and reproductive rights of women. Adolescent youths may be less aware about bodily rights of women and that is why they tend to perceive less positively about these rights. Jejeebhoy (1998) also found that knowledge about sex, reproduction, contraception as well as awareness of STIs, HIV/AIDS is limited and vague among adolescents. This ignorance is compounded by reluctance among teachers and parents. On the whole, it was found that the perception of men about reproductive rights in the selected districts are far better than the state and national level.

Despite universal positive perception among men about sexual and reproductive rights of women, it can be deduced that mere positivity in perception is not enough unless it is reflected in positive action of respecting women. The nub of the issue of gender gap recommends that women's awareness should be enhanced by positioning programmes like 'Me and My Body ... My Body and My Rights'.

References

Felson, R. and S.F. Messner. 2000. 'The Control Motive in Intimate Partner Violence', *Social Psychology Quarterly*, 63(1): 86–94.

Gartner, R. and R. Macmillan. 1999. 'When She Brings the Bacon: Labour Force Participation and the Risk of Spousal Violence against Women', *Journal of Marriage and Family*, 61(4): 947–958.

George, A. 1998. 'Differential Perspectives of Men and Women in Mumbai, India on Sexual Relations and Negotiations within Marriage', *Reproductive Health Matters*, 6(12): 87–96.

Goode, W.J. 1971. 'Force and Violence in the Family', *Journal of Marriage and the Family*, 33, November: 624–635.

Grady, W.R., K. Tanfer, O.G. Billy and L. Hansen. 1996. 'Men's Perceptions of Their Roles and Responsibilities Regarding Sex, Contraception and Childrearing', *Family Planning Perspectives*, 28(5): 221–226.

Hunt, Paul. 2004. *Report of the Special Rapporteur on the Right to Health*. Office of the High Commissioner for Human Rights, New York, United Nations.

Ilika, A.L., P.I. Okonkwo and P. Adogu. 2002. 'Intimate Partner Violence among Women of Childbearing Age in a Primary Health Care Centre in Nigeria', *African Journal of Reproductive Health*, 69(3): 77–88.

International Council on Human Rights Policy. 2009. *Sexuality and Human Rights*. Geneva, Switzerland: ICHRP.

International Institute for Population Sciences (IIPS) and Macro International. 2005-06. *National Family and Health Survey (NFHS-3), India 2005-06*. Mumbai: IIPS.

International Institute for Population Sciences (IIPS). 2007-08. *CHARCA End Line Survey Report*. Mumbai: IIPS.

Jejeebhoy, S. 1998. 'Adolescent Sexual and Reproductive Behavior: A Review of the Evidence from India', *Social Science Medicine*, 46(10): 1275–1290.

Mogollon, C.V. and A.B. Haver. 2003. Sexual and Reproductive Rights and Health: Perceptions, Problems, and Priorities Identified by Asháninka Women of Peru's Río Ene Region, International Women's Health Coalition.

Ogunlayi, M.A. 2005. 'An Assessment of the Awareness of Sexual and Reproductive Rights among Adolescents in South Western Nigeria', *African Journal of Reproductive Health*, 9(1): 99–112.

Oyediran, K.A. and U. Isiugo-Abanihe. 2005. 'Perceptions of Nigerian Women on Domestic Violence: Evidence from 2003 Nigeria Demographic and Health Survey', *African Journal of Reproductive Health*, 9(2): 38–53.

Pradhan, M. 2008. Gender, Sexuality and Reproductive Health of Rural Youth: A Study of Puri District (PhD Thesis). Mumbai: International Institute for Population Sciences.

Programme of Action of the International Conference on Population and Development, Cairo, Egypt, September 5-13, 1994 (1995). Para 7.3, U.N. Doc. A/CONF.171/13/Rev.1. Retrieved from https://www.unfpa.org/sites/default/files/event-pdf/icpd_eng_2.pdf

Santhya, K.G. and S. Jejeebhoy. 2005. 'Young Women's Experiences of Forced Sex Within Marriage: Evidence from India', in S. Jejeebhoy, I. Shah and S. Thapa (eds), *Sex Without Consent*. London: Zed Books, 9–45.

Shabana, K.A., M.E. Shiek and N. Samir. 2003. 'Women's Perception and Practices Regarding their Rights to Reproductive Health', *Eastern Mediterranean Journal*, 9(3): 296–308.

Singh, S.K. and V.L. Singh. 2008. Perceived Sexual Rights and Sexual Violence among Adolescent Females in India: A Longitudinal Cross Cultural Analysis. Conference Paper, Mumbai: International Institute for population Sciences.

UNFPA. 2000. State of World Population, Chapter 4: Men, Reproductive Rights and Gender Equality.

United Nations Report of the International Conference on Population and Development, Cairo, September 5–13, 1994. Available at: http://www.un.org/popin/icpd/conference/offeng/poa.html.

Wahed, T. and A. Bhuiya. 2007. 'Battered Bodies and Shattered Minds: Violence against Women in Bangladesh', *Indian Journal of Medical Research*, 126: 341–354.

List of Contributors

Editors

Harihar Sahoo, Assistant Professor, Department of Development Studies, International Institute for Population Sciences (IIPS), Mumbai.

F. Ram, Director and Senior Professor, International Institute for Population Sciences (IIPS), Mumbai.

B. Paswan, Professor, Department of Population Policies and Programmes, International Institute for Population Sciences (IIPS), Mumbai.

H. Lhungdim, Professor, Department of Public Health and Mortality Studies, International Institute for Population Sciences (IIPS), Mumbai.

Dipti Govil, Assistant Professor, Department of Population Policies and Programmes, International Institute for Population Sciences (IIPS), Mumbai.

Contributors

P.M. Kulkarni, former Professor, Centre for the Study of Regional Development, School of Social Sciences, Jawaharlal Nehru University, New Delhi.

D.A. Nagdeve, Professor and Head, Department of Fertility Studies, International Institute for Population Sciences (IIPS), Mumbai.

Ravi B.P. Verma, Consultant and Researcher, Ravi Verma Associates, Ottawa, Ontario, Canada.

Priya Bhakat, Research Scholar, Centre for the Study of Regional Development, School of Social Sciences, Jawaharlal Nehru University, New Delhi.

Shewli Shabnam, Assistant Professor in Geography, Bidhannagar College, Kolkata.

Rati Parihar, Research Scholar, International Institute for Population Sciences, Mumbai.

B. Paswan, Professor, Department of Population Policies and Programmes, International Institute for Population Sciences (IIPS), Mumbai.

Akash Wankhede, Project Co-ordinator, ICDS, Bihar UNICEF, Patna.

Pravat Kumar Sarangi, Associate Professor and Head, P.G. Department of Statistics, Ravenshaw University, Cuttack, Odisha.

Rajesh Raushan, Associate Professor, Indian Institute of Dalit Studies, New Delhi.

Mukesh Ravi Raushan, Research Scholar, International Institute for Population Sciences, Mumbai.

Shanti Bhushan Kumari, Research Scholar, Department of Geography, Patna University, Patna.

H. Lhungdim, Professor, Department of Public Health and Mortality Studies, International Institute for Population Sciences (IIPS), Mumbai.

N. Jayenta Meitei, Research Scholars, Centre for the Study of Regional Development (CSRD), School of Social Sciences, Jawaharlal Nehru University, New Delhi.

Ruchi Singh, Research Scholar, School of Economics, Central University of Hyderabad, Hyderabad.

D.P. Singh, Professor, Centre for Research Methodology, Tata Institute of Social Sciences, Mumbai.

Vijay Vir Singh, Director, NITI Aayog Chair, Department of Economics, University of Rajasthan, Jaipur.

Shalini I. Meshram, Research Scholar, International Institute for Population Sciences, Mumbai.

Abdul Jaleel CP, Research Scholar, International Institute for Population Sciences, Mumbai.

M.R. Singariya, Lecturer in Economics, Government College Jaitaran, Rajasthan.

Ankita Siddhanta, Research Scholar, International Institute for Population Sciences, Mumbai.

S.K. Singh, Professor, Department of Mathematical Demography and Statistics, International Institute for Population Sciences (IIPS), Mumbai.